The Wo

D1150842

Supei

The World of Superservice

CREATING PROFIT THROUGH A PASSION FOR CUSTOMER SERVICE

 Ken Irons

Addison-Wesley

Harlow, England • Reading, Massachusetts
Menlo Park, California • New York
Don Mills, Ontario • Amsterdam • Bonn
Sydney • Singapore • Tokyo • Madrid • San Juan
Milan • Mexico City • Seoul • Taipei

Addison Wesley Longman Limited
Edinburgh Gate, Harlow,
Essex CM20 2JE, England
and Associated Companies throughout the world.

Published in the United States of America
by Addison Wesley Longman Inc., New York

First published 1997

ISBN 0201 40384 6   PPR

British Library Cataloguing-in-Publication Data

A catalogue record for this book is
available from the British Library

Library of Congress Cataloging-in-Publication Data

Set in Garamond by 30
Produced by Longman Asia Limited, Hong Kong
NPCC/01

*To Thorstein Øverland, who has
given so much help and inspiration
over the years.*

*"The only way to survive the new world of twenty-first century business will be through **Superservice**. It has to be a passion or your brand courage could be damaged.*

This book will be a good starting point for those who want to move to a customer orientated culture."

Richard Branson

Contents

Preface

We are usually aware when we have received 'good service', but find it much harder to define 'why' it is good. Even more, to say how or why some organizations are able to consistently deliver good service, while others never seem to at all. This book aims to fill that gap. To provide insights and practical help to any manager, indeed anyone, in a service environment who is seriously interested in a deeper understanding of what makes a service successful – consistently, over time.

'Success' in this context is achieving your goals – whether these be in money terms or something deeper – by meeting the needs of the people who are your customers. If you believe that the only measure of success and reward is profit, rather than seeing profit as the result of achievement with the customer, then it is doubtful that you will find much here to attract you. It is probably better that you concentrate on that task and do not allow yourself to be diverted.

But you would be wrong to see such a fixation as the true embodiment of free enterprise, the only logical reflection of capitalism. It certainly would not have met with the approval of Adam Smith, the first person to codify the principles of modern capitalism and free markets, who saw that the 'Interest of the producer ought to be attended to only so far as it may be necessary to promoting that of the customer'.*

Nor would the evidence of late twentieth-century experience be on your side. For the message from those service organizations which have achieved success, not just in one year or two but consistently over 5 years or 10, or even 20, is that you have to prize achievement with the customer above all else – and have a single-minded focus on this achievement, which grips the imagination of all of those involved.

Hopefully, this book not only recreates some of that excitement but also gives a feel for the often gruelling hard work that has to go into recreating the service offer, day after day. Hopefully, too, it shows convincingly that the manager who wants to achieve such excitement and success will have to recognize that the aim of the ideas – the vision – is interwoven with the implementation in a service and does not allow for the simplicities of old-time, purely directive management.

Such changes mean, too, that we have to see management as 'stewardship' – or maybe that we have to see management as reverting to stewardship, a return of the age-old concept of a manager as being someone who has been entrusted with an estate which he or she should exploit but must also leave improved.

The manager's estate is pre-eminently economic resources (principally money and property) and people (customers and staff). In recent years, arguably too much emphasis has been given to the economic. Yet if a manager is to leave the estate in a better condition than when he or she received it, then there is a need to bequeath not only more money but also more satisfied customers – who cherish their supplier – and staff – who cherish the opportunity and the challenge of their work and take responsibility for their work and for the future.

It is surely this – demonstrating that you have used the shareholders assets wisely and well and are able to deliver back more value across all of these assets than you were given – which is pertinent, rather than vague notions of stakeholder value. Too often this can lead to conflict between what seem to be opposing aims, profit and people, when in truth they are but two sides of the same coin – and of equal worth in valuing the assets – the worth of the shareholders' investment.

This book is a start in the direction of achieving such a balance but above all it is a song of praise for those service leaders who have already pioneered the way, often with few or no guiding lights, and frequently little understanding or support from others in the wider business community. To them a thank you, for their help and for their legacy for the future.

*Adam Smith (1770) *The Wealth of Nations.*

What makes superservice?

To get the whole world out of bed

And washed, and dressed, and warmed, and fed,

To work, and back to bed again,

Believe me, Saul, costs worlds of pain.

John Masefield, *The Everlasting Mercy*

Colouring outside the lines

Glenn Woods has reason to feel pleased. They call it 'Black Wednesday', the Wednesday before Thanksgiving, when all America seems to be on the move and when every one of the 18,000 seats available on Southwest Airlines from Love Field Airport in Dallas has been booked. It is nearly the end of the day and so far it has all gone according to plan, thanks to the efforts of everyone – not only the normal staff of groundcrew and customer service, but the willing helpers from many office staff and management, who have rallied round.

While 'Black Wednesday' is an exceptional day, what Glenn Woods and his colleagues do that day is only possible because every other day of the year is, in a sense, a rehearsal. 2,000 departures, 2,000 arrivals, 200,000 passengers throughout the Southwest network, standard turnaround times for a 137-seat Boeing 737 of 15 minutes – and if need be 10 minutes – and a constant pressure from customer queries, the weather, technical hitches and all the other factors that make running an airline, or any other service business, more an art form than a science.

How is it that Southwest Airlines manages to do this? Not just physically, but in total safety; with consistent profit, for 25 years, when other airlines have been posting bigger losses than they have ever earned in the whole of the existence of air travel; a fare basis massively below that of competitors (often 50 per cent or even more), and a customer rating of excellence that other airlines can, for the most part, only dream about?

What is it that persuades Arja Toivanen in Finland to get up very, very early every morning, winters included, when the temperature can frequently be –35° C, and cheerfully go to work cleaning the offices of Finnair at Helsinki's Vantaa Airport, with her colleagues but without any supervisor or immediate management help, and so make SOL Cleaning not only extremely profitable but a byword for effective service in Finland – and be seen as a model company for the future?

Why does David Starkie, a driver at Lane Group's Normanton depot in Yorkshire, start the day believing that whatever the weather or traffic throws at him, it is his personal responsibility to deliver all the drops he has on his vehicle? To do this cheerfully and with a level of service and helpfulness to the customer that is very rare in the distribution industry? And what is more, actively 'sell' Lane Group to prospective customers, giving out brochures and reporting back on events.

The precise answers are different in every case, but running through all of these illustrations, and many more examples that could be related, are some common threads.

▶ A management who believe passionately in what they are doing and share this passion with those who have to make it happen.
▶ A vision for the business which sees profit as the outcome of achieving something worthwhile for the customer, in the customer's own terms.
▶ A conviction throughout the business that they will only achieve their goals through the willing contribution of everyone to give that bit extra – to take risks and 'colour outside the lines'.

Superservice is no secret

Dig down to find the secret of success of any 'superservice' business – and a lot of 'manufacturing' businesses, too – and you will find that in any truly competitive situation, it is no secret but a passion, a vision and people, an understanding of the nature and importance to customers of service, which has made that success possible.

To leave it at that would be superficial. Creating an organization in which service truly gives a competitive distinction takes a deep understanding of both the market opportunity that exists and the dedication to the unremitting hard work needed to convert that opportunity into a solution through the efforts of the team. What this book sets out to do is to help the practising manager to understand both how others have found it possible to bring in the passion, clarify the vision and release the potential of the people *and* apply the thinking – not just copy the ideas – in his or her organization.

Like actors in a play, the organizations which provide the illustrations for the key points move in and out of the book, highlighting an issue here, supporting a point there. Some play large parts – they have much to teach – others small. Throughout, though, it is the story rather than the players which is important, creating long-term value by making service more than just an afterthought and good enough to make lasting success, superservice in fact.

So what's the barrier?

The world which service, or 'would be service', organizations seek to serve has changed, and in ways which make it vital that the lessons from such examples are understood and put into everyday practice.

Despite the successes of Southwest, SOL and Lane Group, and the many other service organizations like them around the world, such achievement remains rare. Excellent service, the sort of service that is remarked on and creates distinctiveness for an organization, still has to be sought.

There is no one barrier to this being more commonplace but possibly the most pervasive is the misunderstanding of the relationship between price and service, seeing them as if they were opposite ends of one continuum.

Regularly you hear the management of service companies repeating the mantras, 'customers are no longer prepared to pay for service', or 'all customers are interested in is price'. Although customers are interested in price, as they should be if they have any discrimination at all, the superficiality of such views on the part of anyone seeing services as key to their future is highly dangerous and damaging to their cause.

It is true, customers have become more aware, less prepared to simply accept what is offered without question. But they do want service! They do want to be treated as an individual and not just another sales target. Service, true service, provides that!

In fact, today's 'discriminating and aware customers' want both keen prices and service. Their experience increasingly tells them they can get both. They are very aware of price but they also want to be seen as individuals. They want to feel they have some control over events, even if their decisions are to hand over responsibility. For this is what service is – creating individuality and showing that the person you are dealing with truly matters.

The transformation that has torn through British Airways, another organization where service has become core to its strategy, changing it from a bureaucratic, nationalized airline, which many people avoided, into a world leader, which many seek out for preference, has been achieved not by simply adding services. Those have been a part of the mix, but the real thrust has been through refocusing the airline around its passengers, not its planes.

Service is not the same as services

'Service' should never be confused with 'services'. Services are really a form of product, and as with products, customers may or may not be prepared to pay for them. That is a question of understanding the customers' needs. But whatever the price, they are looking for service, to be treated as someone who matters to you.

Unlike services, for which there should always be a price, you may never be able to charge directly for service but it will be service that will give you the edge in price competition and it is service which will bring the customer back, time and again. Service has become the key to creating good business because it has the power to transform a mere transaction into an event, to make the commonplace both special and different. In a world in which products are more and more alike and freely available, wherever you are, it is service which remains distinctive and gives distinction. Service shows you care!

Southwest Airlines is a world-class example in this respect

Like many other world-class service winners, Southwest Airlines are the lowest cost operator in their field. Their success is due to their having stripped out 'unnecessary' (and largely unwanted) services, concentrating instead on those things their customers do want – reliability, low fares and the recognition that *they* matter, regardless of the price they have paid (Box 1.1). They only provide what the customer wants and is prepared to pay for. They are a success because they never forget that the purpose of the business is to create satisfied customers and to earn profits through that. Southwest staff 'colour outside the lines', do what they believe is right rather than just follow a manual, and make sure that that satisfaction is real and felt.

SOL Cleaning, too, have brought colour to the drab world of cleaning

They provide better service for their customers and more profits for themselves, and work to much the same principles as Southwest. Chairman, Liisa Joronen says,

> *Our customers don't benefit by our having big offices and cars or having lots of managers interfering in the work, so we don't have them! We concentrate on providing what they (customers) want, and sometimes advise them on how they can reduce their costs by cutting out unnecessary work – but we never compromise on service. It's not enough anymore that the customer is simply satisfied. They have to be truly happy with what we do – 'sunny customers', as we call them.*

Lane Group have invested heavily in developing their values

They have created a basis for the business which will allow them to build not only long-term and profitable relationships with customers but do this with a staff who, through their own relationships within

The World of Superservice

BOX 1.1 *It's service that counts*

At first glance, Southwest Airlines and Four Seasons Hotels couldn't seem more different. Southwest is typically described, rightly, as 'a no frills carrier' or, wrongly, as 'having rudimentary service' (*Financial Times*, 8 December 1993). Four Seasons is unblushingly expensive but has performed the unique feat of creating a worldwide luxury brand in hotels, under one name. A stay at a Four Seasons is a delightful succession of services, tailored to make your stay comfortable – and a pleasure.

But that is where the difference stops. Both organizations are not only dedicated to service but stress that it is this service which creates the difference.

Low-fare airlines have come and gone – and mostly gone – because they have been unable to deliver consistently to the customer. Southwest have stayed the course for 25 years. All that time they have been profitable, winning recognition for excellence in service. Four Seasons have deliberately set out to be a top-quality international hotel company, though unlike many rivals they are never condescending, and to create an atmosphere where people really matter and are made welcome whoever they are. Four Seasons, too, have collected outstanding awards.

Listen to the management of these two organizations and you will quickly spot the common thread that underpins their success.

Herbert Kelleher, Chief Executive Officer, Southwest Airlines:
'From the day we travelled our first route, we have believed that air travel should be inexpensive, hassle-free and fun. We have never believed that consumers have to give up service to get low fares.

(Service businesses) call for individuals who can work against the industrial ideals of hierarchy, management power and bureaucracy that are the hallmark of most organizations. They also need to manage efficiency and engage in leadership relationships.

When you get into (a) systematic approach to your company, the quantitative aspect of it, you lose an awful lot of what should be true about an excellent service company, which is not quantitative, it's qualitative. It's not objective, it's subjective. There's a chemistry and magic to a service business. You can't measure charisma.

It's like this labour lawyer who came around to saying: "What I've finally learned about you is that you don't need systems to take care of (staff relations) because you do it on a person-to-person basis, every day".'

John Sharpe, President, Four Seasons Hotels & Resorts:
'Although we will often be the most expensive hotel in town, we must not be condescending or formal but must be perceived as being there for the convenience of our guests.

In a service business like ours, you can't control the outputs, just the inputs – have you given that member of staff enthusiasm, made them feel welcome, too? Customers being comfortable in their environment can only come from staff being comfortable in theirs.

As managers, we have to act as part of the team. When we stay at our hotels, we don't demand the best accommodation. We don't block phone calls in the office – by machines or secretaries – and no one uses an answering machine during the day.

In service, consistency is more important than excellence. Anyone can have excellence for a day, whereas we have to deliver service consistently, every day.'

the organization and support for each other, give that extra that creates superservice. '*You need to recruit the right people – and that includes the aptitude to get on with everyone, not just be a chauffeur*', says Tania Webb, an operator at the Normanton depot.

Nor are these examples of organizations which 'colour outside the lines' to be found only in the spheres of 'physical' work, such as air-lines, trucks and cleaning. Svenska Handelsbanken, the biggest Swedish bank and without any doubt the most successful both with customers and in terms of profit, have built the whole organization around service and putting it where it matters most to the customer, at the branch. They also have the lowest cost ratios of any European bank according to independent research by a rival, Swiss-based UBS.

For all these companies, and many more you will meet in the pages of this book, the key to the world of superservice is to capture the organization to a vision in which it is the customer who matters and that superservice can only be delivered through people who want to deliver it and are prepared to take on that responsibility.

The customer is more than a target

This requires a consistency of approach, a dedication to believing in the customer as more than a sales target, being driven by them and their needs. Delivering against expectations each and every day, and being prepared to go that bit extra. It requires a willingness to become engaged, to enter into a relationship, whether that relationship is fleet-ing, a single transaction, or is over the long haul. That is what a service is, a relationship – and good service is a good relationship.

In true service companies, the customer is integral to the business, not a target to be sold to. Barbara Ferrell at Canadian Pacific Hotels, another hotel company dedicated to superservice, describes it as: '*Service is getting inside the mind of the customer*', a comment echoed by Gordon Bell, Customer Service Manager at their Chateau Whistler Resort: '. . . *Pleasing customers, going beyond their expecta-tions is my forte – it becomes a challenge to change unhappy guests to happy ones*'.

It is the development of this relationship which lies at the very heart of success, but to achieve it, consistently, needs more than wanting. It has to be integral to what the organization is doing and has to be a part of everyone's work.

If staff are to play their role in this, they have to have the confi-dence and conviction to carry out their role. They have to believe in what they are doing, not in some abstract way but as a living, real part of their lives. They are dedicated to the customer because that is what they feel is right not because that is written in the mission statement or a set of standards. Such a relationship implies that the communication has become two-way, that there is a dialogue. Furthermore:

► it cannot be subject to functional disputes – it must be 'seamless',
► it must be driven by a desire to make the customer genuinely satisfied with the outcome.

These elements are at the centre of any drive to make service a central issue in an organization's development – putting staff in the focus, building seamless solutions around the customer, free of functional 'warfare' and being driven by the customer. Each of these points will be developed in the later chapters.

Eight key areas

Talking of the changes brought about in the (Dutch) PTT Telecom, as they prepared for a deregulated market, Wim Dik, the Chief Executive said: 'When we started to change our business, I said it would take five to seven years to achieve our ambitions. Now, five years on, I am amazed at what we have achieved in such a little time, but I also realize that it is going to take a lot longer than I first thought. In fact, it will never be finished'.

Creating a service culture where there has never been one or, even more difficult, changing a poor service culture to a consistent and excellent one, takes time and patience. The process that has to be gone through is as varied as the organizations that have to do it but there are eight key areas that can be commonly identified.

1. Clarify precisely what it is that matters to the customer

Most service businesses provide a mishmash of services that have grown up over a period of time and either never did offer any coherence, or have lost whatever they did have. What is provided should be driven by the customers, their priorities and, from this, an understanding of their preparedness to pay.

Southwest saw that the customer had a clear set of priorities – reliability, low fares, personal treatment – and set about rigorously building the airline around meeting these needs and cutting out those other things the customer either did not want, such as changing planes at a 'hub', or was not really prepared to pay for.

It is people who will make it happen. The people in the business and, even more importantly, the management and *you*, are the 'raw material' of service. Only those who are passionate about success are worth taking on the voyage.

This is often missed out entirely in plans for achieving service consistency and excellence. Key questions are not asked such as: 'Do we have or could we have the people that can carry out these tasks, regularly and not just on some odd days?', and 'Are we as a management team able to give the leadership required?'. Yet they must be. Leading a service relationship-based organization is wildly different from most managers' notion of their task, as shown by the remarks from Kelleher and Sharpe in Box 1.1.

Recruitment and redeployment are key issues in this. Identify the characteristics, not just the technical skills, that make for successful people in your business, and in the different types of jobs. Put round pegs in round holes!

The importance of this is, that you will only ever achieve externally what you are capable of delivering internally. In the final analysis, it is better to modify the plans and set a target that can be achieved than to go on pretending that you will achieve some nirvana that is always beyond reach!

3. Develop a clear 'vision' of what this means

Most service organizations that have achieved consistent success tell of the need to be crystal clear about what they stand for and where they aspire to go. It is doubtful whether any organization has achieved superservice without such a guiding light.

This vision should be for the customer, for the staff and for the owners. Set clear and measurable objectives and equally clear and measurable 'values' – the way it is intended that these objectives should be achieved, 'the way we are going to work around here'.

4. Communicate, communicate and communicate

Rebecca Jenkins, Managing Director of Lane Group, talks about the need to '*Not only communicate but to communicate why you are communicating*'. Ensure that everyone not only knows what is to be achieved but why, and give him or her a chance to contribute to *your* understanding, and participate, too.

Make sure that the vision, the passion infects every corner, every action, from answering the telephone to dealing with the inevitable hiccups that affect any service enterprise.

5. Learn from experience

Experience is one of the most potent sources of learning but the learning organization not only collects information from its own experience, and that of others, but then uses it to risk a future which may be radically different.

In this context, learning is more than problem solving or correcting errors. It is getting insight, as much or more about oneself as about events and others, and using it to effect.

Novotel, the three-star range of hotels owned by the French Accor group, have built their hotels around a rigorous delivery of those things the customer is really interested in and cutting out those things that are unimportant. They have kept pace with change by using their experience and insights into themselves to know what they had to keep and what they had to change.

6. Lead, don't just manage

Embracing service as the central part of creating distinction can be a frightening process. So many of the past certainties ebb away, such as the comforting certainty that it is the 'product', like a meal or an insurance policy, that is being sold. Instead, we have to come to grips with relatively chaotic problems such as behaviour. This often as not is 'our behaviour' (or mine!) and this has to be treated as central, not marginal, to achievement.

In superservice organizations, managers care about service and they realize to make it happen that they have to lead from within, not just preside as managers over implementation.

7. Recognize that value arises at the point of interaction with the market

If you were to attempt to summarize the differences between manufacturing-based situations and service-based situations in one illustration, it would be that in the service situation value has meaning to the customer at just one key point, the interaction between the organization and its market – its customers. It is this which should be the focus of everything you do.

In this, it is no longer the creation of value for a passive customer but the creation of value with the customer in dialogue. Quality control is no longer an internal affair but is about that balance between what happens internally and what you need to achieve externally. It is not a question of simple operational effectiveness but of gaining strategic distinction in the market.

8. See the delivery as integral

Services are a series of dynamic forces which come together at delivery, at this point of interaction. Staff are a part of the 'product' they create, as are the customers, who influence and shape what is delivered.

Delivery is not, therefore, something that happens after the plans have been laid but is integral to those plans. It shapes and moulds them and the result needs to be linked back into the strategic process, so that reality of events can modify and change the future.

A map for guidance

These eight points serve to act as a quick checklist of what needs to be done if service is to become superservice, a positive feature of an organization's competitive difference and success. They will each be looked at in turn and in more depth in Chapters 3 to 10, providing a map for guidance through the key issues involved. Inevitably, there will be some overlap and necessary reiteration since service issues are holistic and cannot easily be compartmentalized. Chapters 11 and 12 will look at how in practice it can all be made to happen and the momentum be maintained, once the initial fervour has passed, so that the initial enthusiasm keeps up and service remains superservice.

First though, Chapter 2 will look at the background to change and understand why 'service' is not just an operational issue, a passing fad, but a reaction to a significant shift in society as a whole.

Successes and failures

There are many stories throughout of success and failure but two will serve to illustrate the difference between service in its true sense and the practices that are all too frequently served up as service.

Saga, the travel-to-insurance-to-publishing group dedicated to 'older' people, is an excellent example of the modern service company.

So, for Saga it has been important that:

▶ Despite the diversity of their range of services – all built around their target markets perceived view of their strengths, an understanding of older people – customer service staff can call up information on other sections. This allows Saga to have a natural dialogue with the customer – who may want to say how much he or she has enjoyed a particular hotel on their last holiday, even though the customer may have called about their insurance policy.

▶ When they had a spate of complaints about a particular hotel they had used for some of their customers, Saga decided to send a cheque to compensate everyone who had stayed there that year, regardless as to whether the customer had complained or not, because the company felt it was likely that dissatisfaction had been widespread.

This is service – knowing your customers, respecting them and going to great lengths to give them satisfaction.

In contrast to this, Continental Lite, which was Continental Airlines' answer to the competitive threat of 'no frills' airlines, such as Southwest, has died a death after just three years of unhappy and unprofitable operation.

Seeing the threat of cheap fares as simply being about passengers saying, 'Strap me in that metal tube and get me there as cheap and as fast as possible', avoided having to come to terms with the fact that Southwest were offering a totally different concept, not just cheap fares but cheap fares plus a more direct way to go than flying via a hub – and the recognition that you, and the people you met in the airline, were still human!

Southwest had broken away from the existing frameworks and changed the rules of the game for low fare airlines. Continental either could not see this or could but did not understand the importance of it. Wedded to their existing investment, and past experience, they tried to retain features such as seat allocation or connections to other airlines which *they* not the customer saw as important. They used check-in and other staff that were common to other Continental operations, so were not able to create that buzz which gives Southwest such a special feel. They saved money by not serving meals but because they used common aircraft continued to lift the galleys into the air, not extra passengers.

For Saga, it is the needs of their very specific target customers who decide what is provided; for Continental Lite it was still the seat that was in the focus. This contrast between seeing the problem from the customers' side – being customer driven and not systems or purely cost driven – is starkly shown by the different approaches taken by the following:

▶ Dixons Group and their Mastercare service arm (Case Study 2.1), where they have closed the central repair depot and returned 'service' to the shops, and a large number of in-shop service centres visibly scattered throughout the country, and

▶ the retail banks in the UK, who have moved almost all the specialized functions away from the branch to various central points, distant from the branch and the customer. 'It is cheaper', but it ignores the point that for the customers it creates a gulf, between them and the banks and, as importantly, within the banks.

Although Dixons acknowledge that the direct costs are higher, they see a major return in the form of both direct service to the customer and in the build up of confidence between repair staff and shop staff.

By contrast, the banks have seen service levels slip to a point where a recent survey showed that they had become the most disliked organizations in the country – not, it must be stressed, because of this one action taken with regard to centralizing services, but because of the mind-set that this betrays. The customer is secondary to the system and to operational efficiency, even though, paradoxically, it leads to more discontent and, eventually, to defecting customers. As Svenska Handelsbanken shows (Case Study 5.1), good local service need not result in higher costs, relative to the returns.

In conclusion

Superservice is the result of a mind-set – a mind-set that sees people as individuals who want to be treated as individuals, whether they are a customer or an employee, a member of staff or an executive. It results in organizations which use this as a basis for a vision which is driven by the imperative to bring value to the customer and to reward employees and owners (shareholders) for doing this superlatively.

There is no one route. Organizations in the same sector of the service industries, such as British Airways and Southwest Airlines, have found different ways of achieving a customer focus which are only in part due to their different market positions. Like people, they both have a character and it is the release of the potential of that – by the individuals as a team – which makes service into superservice.

Acknowledgements and further reading

page 1   The quote from John Masefield is with acknowledgement to the Society of Authors, who administer his literary estate.

The following companies all gave generously of their time and material, providing insights for this and subsequent chapters.

British Airways, Heathrow Airport, London.
Canadian Pacific Hotels & Resorts, Toronto, Ontario.
Four Seasons Hotels & Resorts, Toronto, Ontario.
Groupe Accor, Evry, Paris.
Lane Group, Bristol.
SOL Cleaning, Helsinki.
Southwest Airlines, Dallas, Texas.

There are many books available on service and these are just a few which will help to provide some deeper insight into the issues involved.

Collins, J. C. and Porras, J. I. (1994) *Built to Last: Successful Habits of Visionary Companies*, Harper Business.
Grönroos, C. (1982) *Strategic Management and Marketing in the Service Sector*, Helsinki: Svenska Handelshagsskolan.
Irons, K. (1993) *Managing Service Companies: Strategies for Success*, Wokingham: Addison-Wesley.
Normann, R. (1984) *Service Management*, John Wiley & Sons.
Vandermerwe, S. (1993) *From Tin Soldiers to Russian Dolls*, Oxford: Butterworth Heinemann.

Why service is here to stay

The challenge in the present age is to move from the principles of accumulation to those of utilization. The new frontier in economics is one of functionality – value is associated not with production but in terms of what the customer gets.

Joel Bonamy and André Barcet, *Revue d'Economie Industrielle*

About this chapter

The American management guru, Tom Peters, talks about '*Crazy times call for crazy organizations*'. This is misleading in two ways – it suggests that today's situation is 'crazy', and implies that it is simply a phase. It sounds like an invitation for some 'sixties' style, anything goes solution.

The times may be difficult – and for someone brought up in the strict conditions of manufacturing-based American business even 'crazy' – but the changes are largely a reflection of permanent changes in the pattern of society. The solutions need to be seriously thought through as a response, though that need not stop them from being fun. The next ten chapters will review 'how', but the final recipe for your success cannot be just a copy of what others have done, or crazy.

Service is not a management fashion but part of a profound change in society. These changes impact deeply on customers' demands and expectations, and with equal force on the demands and expectations of employees. Those organizations which have grasped service as a core issue, and not an add-on, have been able to create not only a better and closer relationship with their customers, and staff, but have improved profit.

This chapter will look at the background to change and the forces at work which make service so key.

▶ The shifts in society and the service revolution.

▶ The exit culture we increasingly serve.

▶ The underlying changes in customer demands.

▶ The issue of global markets versus local delivery.

▶ The place of technology in this change.

▶ Service as a strategic issue.

The shift in society

The growth and importance of service is not primarily business driven as much as a response to the wider forces which are creating change in society as a whole. In this sense it is unlike the largely internally driven changes such as total quality or process re-engineering. The distinction is important since such operationally-driven initiatives more often fail than succeed.

For example, in a report published as part of the Economist Intelligence Unit (EIU) series, the authors concluded that Total Quality Improvement programmes had at best delivered incremental improvements and at worst made it more difficult to increase organizational competitiveness. Various other studies, from both sides of the Atlantic, have suggested that up to three out of four, or even four out of five, 'customer improvement programmes' of this kind have failed to deliver tangible results.

Though not the intention, in practice they ignore the need for a deeper understanding and consideration of the changes that are affecting the world we seek to serve; not only customers but managers and employees, too.

Most people are faced with an opportunity for choice that was undreamt of by all but an elite until 40 or 50 years ago. That they do not always exercise it wisely, either as customers or employees, should be no surprise, because neither did that elite. They just happened to be few in number and to exercise enough power to ensure that their will prevailed.

It is also true that the focus of society as a whole has shifted from the acquisition of 'product' to the usage of that product. From simple 'need', or the pleasures of possession, to a concern for function and use, where delivery becomes as important as the product itself.

Manufactured goods are increasingly the same, increasingly offering only a temporary competitive advantage, and produced under different names in the same factories, wherever unit costs are lowest. Technology offers people untold advantages in terms of accessibility, whether through travel or ordering by telephone, to take but two examples. It also changes perceptions of what is both possible and reasonable and, so, expectations.

For the manager facing pressing, immediate problems, today, it is important to recognize that service is not just another passing fashion in management, but the reflection of a deep and abiding change in society. A change which is arguably as big a watershed as was the Industrial Revolution in the eighteenth and nineteenth centuries.

In this situation, service is a necessary component of meeting the changed, and still changing, expectations of people. It is also an antidote to the sameness and loss of identity that can be a result of globalization.

What is more, such change is not confined to our customers but is a part of the change experienced in ourselves and in our staff. These are the very people who have to perform service – and transform the way we all work if service is to truly become part of our activity. Any successful outcome to meet the needs of customers will only result from recognizing that it depends crucially on meeting the aspirations of those who perform the service too.

The service revolution

This is the service revolution, a paradigm shift in both society and the way we have to work. Driven by deep and profound changes in people's beliefs and attitudes (Box 2.2), customers have become increasingly aware that they are in the driving seat and can exercise the right to decide.

Bob Tyrell's view of service as a 'bridge' (Box 2.1) is a very real reflection of the role that service has to play, as a bridge from 'our world', that internal world of the business itself, and 'their world' – what it is the customer is looking to gain from the transaction, making that transient meeting into something distinctive for 'me'.

BOX 2.1 *A background to change*

The Henley Centre has specialized for 23 years in forecasting social change and helping business to understand what it means for them. Bob Tyrell, Managing Director of the Centre, describes our current society as,

'An exit culture, the choice is wide and we can do anything. As a result business is much more transaction based and if it does not work we have no loyalty to stay – we simply exit'. He goes on to say: 'It is not a cosy world but service should be the bridge to create positive reasons to stay. This needs to have integrity if it is to work;

it has to mean something real to me as an individual. Most loyalty schemes, for example create negative barriers to exit, I am "trapped". What is needed are positive barriers, that encourage me to feel that I can have what I want, my favourite seat on a plane, for example. In this new world, traditional sources of advice are increasingly seen as either unreliable or out of touch, whereas people you know and can trust are increasingly important. The views of family and peers carry more weight than bosses or the establishment. Word of mouth becomes a more telling method of giving information'.

It is particularly important to re-emphasize the distinction made in Chapter 1, between 'service' and 'services'.

▶ Services are closely analogous to products and their cost has to be justified against real demand.
▶ Providing service, however, is a basic necessity for competing in the new world.

Again, as we saw in Chapter 1, there is no continuum, with at one end 'low cost/low service' and at the other, 'high cost/high service'. Customers demand, and increasingly get both and, significantly, most long-term successful service operators are low cost too. They only spend money on what the customer wants, not on internally driven beliefs or industry norms.

It is a consumer's world, not simply for the conspicuous consumption of goods but as a part of life. Shopping has become more of a leisure function, to be enjoyed for itself and not simply for what it brings. People talk more about products or services, and the experiences they share are more widely drawn and compared from across a range of situations.

When the pizza delivery comes to a customer's house in 30 minutes with a complete, tasty meal and no hassle, it is doing more than delivering food. It is giving an object lesson in what *is* possible. It is made possible by the credit card, issued very likely by a bank. Tomorrow, that customer will apply that lesson to other service areas and have higher expectations of what to expect. Paradoxically, if it is a bank they will probably be very disappointed. The bank has helped to create an expectation of service they, themselves, cannot – or will not – achieve.

When that same customer flies on his next holiday and is given a constant update on timings and what is happening, the experience will be applied the next time he or she travels by train or ferry, and again, the chances are it will be found wanting.

More and more the customer wants to feel that he or she can exert influence. He or she has a desire to be involved, to be recognized as someone who is an individual, and not to be the unheeded target for a sale. It means that as a supplier, it is even more vital that you 'buy' attention, not primarily through spending money but through demonstrating that you recognize the person, that individual, at the other end.

It is also a world where the definition of what a service organization is stretches way beyond that traditionally applied. So, for example, Jack Welch, Chairman and Chief Executive Officer of what is one of the great success stories among manufacturing companies,

BOX 2.2 *The new world*

The changes we see in society around us are driven by a number of deep, underlying currents.

▶ **An increasing demand to be treated as an individual**
Sometimes self-centred, but more often an expression of a recognition that I am allowed to be who I am, and to demand that others recognize this, too.

▶ **An increasing ability to be able to exercise economic choice**
Not simply or even most importantly, quantitatively but qualitatively. John Maynard Keynes recognized this as an inevitable outcome of the changes he saw coming, when he wrote in 1928 that, '*Man will be faced with his real . . . problem – how to use his freedom from pressing economic causes*'. He saw this as taking 100 years but today you can see that this plays a key part in the 'exit culture', as customers move their 'favours' around in pursuit of '*Their brand name quest for instant gratification*' to quote Kenichi Ohmae, the Japanese business guru and writer, or as employees ponder whether they should accept that promotion when it means interference in their lifestyle or undue disturbance to their family.

▶ **An increasing acceptance that 'soft' issues are important**
Care and concern for the environment, or balancing the conflicts of personal life and work, are of equal importance with the 'hard' issues, such as winning. These soft issues are sometimes called confusingly 'feminine characteristics', hard issues being 'male'. Such a distinction is becoming increasingly irrelevant, and the psychologist's terminology also hides the fact that men and women have elements of both, though the traditionally feminine characteristics have been seen as both more 'womanly' and of lesser importance. Of particular significance in the context of the subject of this book, is that the 'service ideal' is a feminine characteristic.

▶ **An increasingly ageing population**
In society today, older people, particularly the middle-aged, are holding the reins of commercial power. Such a change has profound consequences for business because it means that life experience and stability will become issues of greater importance.

Such changes are not part of a steady flow from one era to another but rather a confused and confusing tumbling of cross-currents, with back-eddies, whirlpools and sudden, alarming changes of direction and force. They are producing a society in which:

▶ loyalty to others or to organizations is less highly thought of yet, paradoxically, seeks to come to more socially acceptable answers or embrace environmental issues;

▶ individuals seek to be seen as 'me' but, paradoxically, also want to express themselves through 'belonging' to a 'group', in which stability is important to give balance to uncertainty.

It is not always a 'brave new world' but it is what we have and is likely to go on being changing and confusing for some time to come.

and a long-time bastion of manufacturing values, General Electric (GE) in the USA, says *'GE can no longer prosper on manufactured goods alone. Our job is to sell more than the box. We are in the service business – to expand our pie'*.

Welch has always stressed the need to get into service but until recently this had largely meant developing service companies, such as GE Capital, which now provides nearly one-third of the operating profits of the group. Now, to fuel continued revenue growth the focus is more on making service the critical element of all GE operations. It is epitomized by deals such as the 10-year contract with British Airways not only to supply their aircraft engines but to service them and the existing engines in use from rivals Rolls-Royce and Pratt & Whitney.

Global market/local delivery

Service offers another bridge, that between the need to be 'global' and the need to be 'close' to the customer. In a world in which manufactured goods are increasingly the same and are available readily anywhere (and are less of a focus than before) it is service which can offer the distinction. It is service which can engender confidence, create a dialogue, establish that you know and appreciate the buyer.

In a world in which technology can bring the gift of seemingly limitless information and choice, it is service which can provide a path through complexity. It is the key plank in combating 'the exit society'; in building barriers to exit and reinforcing the beliefs about rightness of choice and minimising the uncertainties of change.

In the past, loyalty was often able to be taken for granted because there was a less discriminating customer and fewer alternatives. As a result, the problem of 'negative restraint' was not an issue. Now it is. Ties that bind a customer unwillingly, such as frequent-flyer schemes or loyalty cards which offer no deeper benefits in the service itself, are likely to build up a deep resentment, even while the customer is enjoying the benefits.

The effect of negative restraint through unavailability, at a reasonable price or convenience, is even greater. So I may not shift my bank account because I do not believe anyone else is better but that does not mean that I am not building up a resentment at my 'enforced' stay – and in time, given the chance, I will take my revenge.

Being 'local' does not necessarily need a local presence. Modern technology has made that unnecessary or even on occasions irrelevant. It does mean that you have to be local in spirit and in response

CASE STUDY 2.1 THE BENEFITS OF BEING LOCAL

The Dixons Group is one of the most successful retailers of electrical goods in the world. Through their Dixons, Currys and PC World chains in the UK, they sell a wide range of goods and, in particular, televisions, hi-fi and other so-called 'brown goods'.

Their reputation has been built on price but as the market began to change, management recognized that price was no longer enough; it merely provided the entry to the market. This led them to see that service was not a cost at the edge of the business but was a '*Central marketing device, crucial to our positioning in the marketplace*', says David Hamid, Managing Director of Dixons Group Commercial Services. He continues:

> The world outside had changed and if we wanted to maintain our growth and carry our customers with us we had to respond to this new climate. In this new climate, with customers who are not only aware of their rights but are also more vocal with it, even maintaining a stable complaint rate was progress. Our customers today are still attracted by price and location but they also want to be treated differently, to get service. We decided that we had to provide tangible evidence that we cared and although a key part of what we did was to decentralise, the inspiration was to change our relationship with the customer.

Dixons provide service through a separate subsidiary, Mastercare, which they 'inherited' when they bought the Currys chain. At this time, it was seen as peripheral to the real business, selling, and of dubious value to the business as a whole. Mastercare, an effective organization for all the comparative neglect, provided service through a network of local offices and home-call engineers. Where possible, repairs were carried out in the home mostly in working hours, but the more difficult or complex repairs were dealt with at a large and efficient repair depot at Doncaster.

In a less demanding age, and as a peripheral service, it worked, especially if customers could be home during the day to meet the engineer. Despite the quality of the individual work, however, it added little to the value of the sale and was seen as distant and impersonal to the shop staff, who tended to merely hear the bad stories, when an unhappy customer hit at the one target he or she could, the shop.

But it wouldn't do today, and change was required of a radical nature. The answer was built around sound marketing principles and service. Get closer to the customers and show them that Dixons cared more about them than simply selling them a piece of equipment. There were two main parts to this:

▶ closing down the central repair facility at Doncaster and moving repairs to the shop itself, and

▶ changing the orientation of the home service engineers from being time based to being job based, thus giving them more flexibility to adjust their own working days but working to times that suited the customer.

More specifically:

▶ Repair Shops were introduced into Currys Superstores. These were designed to be user-friendly in layout and to become a feature of the store. They had clear price-lists for repairs, so that there was no feeling of hidden surprises; the working area was on view, so that there was an air of immediacy and tangible reassurance; there was a turntable on the counter so that the engineers could look at the problem more freely *with* the customers; the engineers themselves all had to undergo a test for customer-mindedness before they could take up a position in the new jobs.

▶ The contracts for the home-service engineers were renegotiated to be based, not on hours per week but on jobs per week (effectively as long as it took to get the jobs done) and including evening and weekend work, if needed. If the TV breaks down on Friday, you want it repaired for the weekend not the next week.

▶ The 'day' would run from 10 o'clock – any repair reported by then would be dealt with that day – no exceptions. Clocks in the offices were marked up with a red mark at '10' to emphasize this point.

▶ Failure to honour their commitment would result in the customer receiving a £20 voucher for goods – rare and therefore not expensive.

▶ In addition, there was 'Finishing Touches', a way of working where there were a number of small touches emphasizing that Dixons cared – for example, a 'cable tidy' whenever they had to make a home call; 'packaging training' so that a customer's equipment came back looking as if they cared about the customer.

The whole of this concept was based around delivery and recognizing that people are involved. It is not the cheapest way, but it is one which takes Dixons closer to the customer and the benefits are to be felt across the business as a whole. So, for example, a prospective purchaser will often go to a Currys' Repair Shop and seek a view about the reliability of a piece of equipment; the engineer is seen as being more objective and not out to sell just anything. Staff in the stores are much more ready to recommend service contracts, because they can see the result – and so can the customer. David Hamid says:

We were particularly keen on this type of approach to give us a competitive edge because we were sure that our competitors would find it difficult to follow. It wasn't just a question of doing it, though. It had to be worked on over a long period and we had to get everyone onside. There was quite a lot of resistance initially, especially to the changes in the home service engineers' working, but we carried out some pilot work. For this we took one of the more doubting managers, known for his scepticism. He became totally converted and his conversion helped carry the day. We also decided not to use a standard, such as BS 5750, because we felt it was an inhibitor to change, though admittedly without that as a focus it did make things more difficult – but the outcome is the better for it.

to those subtle cultural differences that make the difference between service and good service. In fact, it makes them even more important, because what may previously have gone unnoticed or unremarked has become obvious and a barrier.

In setting up their new hotel in Milan, Four Seasons Hotels were anxious to make it an 'Italian hotel', not a North American import – to bring to it their skills and experience, but to translate that into a local vernacular. So they insisted on finding an Italian manager, even though that meant a very considerable investment of top management time and money to both select the right individual and provide extra senior expertise at the opening period to help bridge the gap in Four Seasons' experience. Such attention to recruitment in service is a key factor (pp. 62 and 230).

An even more illustrative story is that of Dixons (Case Study 2.1). It demonstrates clearly that if you want to be competitive in the market-place today you cannot rely on product and price alone. Service near to the customer can bring sufficient reward to offset the costs involved and provide a 'difficult to match' competitive lead.

Technology – good fairy? evil genie?

Technology has the capacity to make service superlative or to make nonsense of all of the ideals. It all depends on whether it is built around shortening the distance to the customer, creating that bridge, or erecting barriers. Typically, though, technology becomes its own master, creating technology-driven 'supply' even where there is no demand, making obscure what might have been clear, developing functional and tactical variations which strangle the very purpose of a strategy. The exercise of linking investment in technology with any return in value to the customer is lost, if it was ever given consideration!

The service organizations we tend to admire usually avoid that. Marks & Spencer's ability to be a world leader in pre-prepared fresh foods, using technology to match supply and demand, would be as nothing, or worse, if they did not understand that technology has to be the servant, not the master. The investment that Federal Express has made in technology would have done no more than make them a more efficient parcel delivery company were it not for the fact that this has been developed around their customers. They also provide an information source for their customers on just where their package is via the internet.

Collapsing time-scales apply to technology more than anywhere else, so much so that we simply cannot absorb all the potential or avoid all the pitfalls. For many of those directly involved, the sheer wizardry of their technology is an end in itself, and the rest of us know too little to stop them. So the power that technology has to shorten distance and bring customers into a mutually shared relationship, instead becomes a barrier. It blocks dialogue and reduces customers to numbers.

The success for those who can grab this tiger by the tail – and tame it to their needs – is great, but it requires more than technicians to realize. Such developments need to be an integral part of what is being done for the customer, not some separate set of activities.

These reducing time-scales also mean that the lead time to exploit new developments has become increasingly short. So much so that it becomes less and less important or worthwhile to seek traditional patent cover. Rather it is easier to create added value through the use of copyright and trade marks. This again, adds pressure for the creation of service.

Profit from service

The focus on service is not soft. Paradoxically, the development of power close to the customer has to be linked with a consistently strong approach to management. In an organization which depends on its operatives to deliver the promise, there has to be both a high expectation of performance and a clearly defined set of measures of that performance. Consistent delivery to the customer requires equally consistent leadership and appraisal of that effort.

It is, perhaps, for these reasons that service organizations which have experienced the greatest success with the customer also tend to be among the most profitable operators in their sector. In addition to Southwest Airlines already mentioned in Chapter 1, notable examples are as follows.

▶ British Airways, which almost alone among the major intercontinental carriers, has remained profitable since being privatized in 1983.
▶ Svenska Handelsbanken which, in addition to winning the award for best customer service in the annual independent survey conducted by the Stockholm School of Economics, has been not only profitable since 1973 but has been above the average profitability for all Swedish banks over that period with the lowest cost base.
▶ Marriott Hotels who have been able to increase profitability by three times by stabilizing their workforce around a service ethic.

In contrast, few organizations which have focused on internal initiatives have achieved much lasting success. The American

Management Association reported, for example, that the most common outcome of downsizing has been a slump in morale rather than an increase in profits.

The strategic issue

It must be clear that service is not a tactical issue, to be sorted out once the plans have been laid, but is the very core of those plans. If an organization is to be customer-focused in this new world, it is necessary to plan for service right from the start and to build the organization around this as a key issue.

Where service is left as an operational issue, then like technology, it most likely will become overloaded with functional detail, for that is what operational managers are good at and have to offer. The original guiding idea will become lost along the way, as immediate pressures and personal priorities gain the day. For this reason, strategy in a service can never be dissociated from its implementation, but must form part of a complex interweaving of planning, testing, revision and rethinking.

Strategy must be much more a method of guidance, allowing for creative input but always towards an agreed 'vision' – a destination everyone understands and has bought into. This 'strategic management' approach to strategy and its implementation is a crucial element in creating long-term success in a service situation (see also Chapter 5). At the core it must be driven by the customer and the next chapter will look at what is involved in being driven by, and not just focused on, the customer.

Acknowledgements and further reading

page 15   Bonamy, J. and Barcet, A. (1988) 'Services et Transformations des Modes de la Production', *Revue d'Economie Industrielle*, Numero Special 43. Quoted in translation from '*From Tin Soldiers to Russian Dolls*' (p. 14).

page 17   Binney, G. (1992) *Making Quality Work*, Economist Intelligence Unit Management Guides, No. P 655.

page 20   John Maynard Keynes, 1928, in the valedictory article by Norman McRae, in *The Economist*, 12 August, 1989.

page 20   Ohmae, K. (1990) *The Borderless World*, Collins.

page 21   *Letter to Shareholders*, Jack Welch with Paolo Fresco and John D. Opie, from Annual Report, 1995 of General Electric Corporation.

The following companies all gave generously of their time and material in providing insights for the background to this and other chapters.

Dixons Group, Hemel Hempstead.
General Electric Corporation, Fairfield, Connecticut.
The Henley Centre for Forecasting, London.

For the manager keen to keep abreast of events on the wider scale of change, *The Economist* provides an excellent base, as do most issues of the OECD annual reviews (and see especially *Structural Shifts in Major OECD Countries'* in the Annual Review, 1992). The studies and forecasts, both general and company specific, of The Henley Centre for Forecasting, 9 Brideswell Place, London, EC4, provide excellent, and more directed, insights into change and its potential impact on business.

Additionally, the originals of the books and articles acknowledged above are worth seeking out and other possible reading includes:

Gribbin, J. (1986) *In Search of the Big Bang – Quantum Physics and Cosmology*, Heinemann.
Handy, C. (1994) *The Empty Raincoat – Making Sense of the Future*, Hutchinson.
Leshan, L. and Marganeau, H. (1983) *Einstein's Space and Van Gogh's Sky*, The Harvester Press.
Roach, S. S. (1996) 'The hollow ring of the productive revival', *Harvard Business Review*, Nov/Dec.
Thurow, L. (1996) *The Future of Capitalism*, Nicholas Brealey.

Being customer driven

... she (the flight attendant) looked after other passengers, of course ... but we felt we were her most important clients at the time

Letter from a passenger, Southwest Airlines

About this chapter

The passion that sets superservice apart comes from the deep inner conviction that value to the customer is what matters – and the motivation to create that value, time after time. To see this as 'customer focus', however is not enough. There has to be a more deep-seated *drive* to meet a customer's needs.

Such a drive has to be built around the interaction, a seamless response bringing into play – and into balance – the dynamic forces behind service. Functional splits can often cause fragmentation of effort at this point. In effective service environments, function is subordinate to the needs of the customer at the point of interaction. In turn, these are a relationship over time, not a series of static events. The 'product' will be as good as the weakest point in this process.

This chapter will look at what is involved in being customer driven.

▶ The need for passion.

▶ Putting the customer in the driving seat.

▶ Understanding what drives the customer.

▶ Defining the 'product' in the service context.

▶ The need for a 'service mix', rather than a 'marketing mix'.

▶ The service task and the implications for functional activities.

▶ Why small details make superservice.

▶ The need to accept responsibility for taking the initiative.

A passion for the customer

Julian Metcalfe would not be most people's idea of a chief executive. For a start, he does not find work '*A naturally enticing environment*', describing himself as 'lazy' and work as a 'pain'. Like many such people, he, in truth, works very hard but what drives him is a natural ambition to succeed, fuelled by a deep inner conviction that the customer who wants fast food deserves better than they have traditionally received and a passion for Pret A Manger to provide instead, natural, healthy food at affordable prices.

He describes Pret, as the business is more fondly known, as 'Really just a sandwich shop', but goes on:

> *We are manic about quality. Every sandwich is made on-site, in the branch, that very day it is to be sold – not in some factory a 100 miles away. That can mean 1,500 to 2,000 sandwiches – and the preparation of those fillings – being produced in a branch to a rigorous standard – for example, 'Is there butter right up to the edges of the bread?' – but, and this is the key, by people who care as I do about the customer's experience of that sandwich.*

Such a passion for the customer experience may not be common but it is behind the examples given in Chapter 1 of Southwest Airlines, SOL Cleaning and the Lane Group, and is a characteristic of all service organizations which are successful over the long term.

Customer focus is not enough

This passion is vital because in a service customers must feel that it is 'me' who is important, 'me' who is the centre of that effort. That is more than the conventional 'customer focus' of so many organizations, looking merely to solve their own problems. This is often no more than a superficial reworking of what has always been done, with a few new words to make it appear as if the customer is at the centre. Rather, it has to be a creative drive to succeed through understanding the true needs of customers – and the balance between their needs and their willingness or ability to pay – and then meeting, even exceeding, their expectations.

Most people have become profoundly cynical of organizations which just talk about them as being the centre of attention. They can see only too clearly that they are simply a sales target, someone to be sold to. Where a customer expresses satisfaction with a service, invariably you will find at the heart lies a feeling that they have been seen as someone, as an individual. That they have felt that in some way, however small, that they were at the centre of all that has been done.

Many organizations – and banks and insurance companies are particularly guilty in this respect – have made promises about their service which they have then not delivered. Compare, for example, the approach taken by Dixons/Mastercare in the case study in Chapter 2 with the general approach of most banks.

Dixons have moved service close to the customer. An outworn and inappropriate industrial model has been replaced by a true service concept, driven by the market and not solely by internal cost parameters. The pay-off has been seen to come from both a deeper relationship with the customer – Dixons are accessible – and a more effective working relationship between the sales and service staff.

Banks, on the other hand, have been moving service away from the customer, to meet industrial concepts of efficiency. The argument that 'banking is different' and that the customer is unwilling to pay the price for service is not only questionable, given the need for service that today's market calls for, but is also emphatically given the lie by the most successful full-service bank of them all – Svenska Handelsbanken.

▶ **Handelsbanken have not simply kept their branch network largely intact but have made it the very centre of their business.**

'We don't see our branches as a distribution channel because they are the bank'. As a result they have been not only consistently profitable, but have been seen by their customers as providing a superior service for 'me'.

▶ **Novotel, too, have designed their whole offer around specific customers.**

They carefully ensure that they provide exactly the services that these specific customers want, equally carefully ensuring that they do not provide services that the customers may want but are not prepared to pay for.

▶ **Canadian Pacific Hotels have invested as heavily in the development of staff as they have in the development of the hotels themselves.**

For virtually every dollar spent on refurbishment over the past years, they have spent similarly on the development of their people. The company believes that an investment in buildings will be wasted if the increased expectations of the customers are not matched by an increased level of service as perceived by those customers.

▶ **American Express have shifted the focus from the card to the benefits of the card.**

They have responded to what they see as more knowledgeable customers by shifting the focus of their business from the prestige of the card – a product-driven strategy with a customer focus – to the added value and usefulness (the utility, to flash back to the comments on change in Chapter 2) of the service and opportunity the card can bring – a strategy driven by the customer.

The new wave of convenient everyday restaurants that are sweeping across London and into the country, such as Pret A Manger and Café Rouge, are tapping into the increasing sophistication and demands of their customers by providing freshly prepared foods made in the branch. It is more costly to do it that way, but they see their long-term future growth and profitability as dependent on responding to those things that drive the customer – a more personal approach to eating – linked to a commitment by everyone involved to provide quality from the heart, not simply to a standard.

Being customer driven as opposed to being merely customer focused, means designing or rebuilding the business around the customer:

▶ not simply relabelling 'passengers' as 'customers',
▶ or calling the sales clerk a 'customer service manager',
▶ or creating a customer service team who have, in reality, no power to transform the service the customer can expect.

What drives the customer?

Customers are essentially selfish – they want to be at the centre. Meeting this drive is what service is about. Increasingly, customers are the experts in this process – or at least, increasingly their experience leads them to feel able to evaluate and criticize service. In making a choice, however, the customer faces a problem which is significantly different to simple 'product' situations – the difficulty of evaluating a service, since they all seem alike.

The 'core products' of a service are frequently indistinguishable from competition and, indeed, may often be so similar as to make no difference. The attempt at creating distinctiveness through the product is either met with disbelief – think of buying petrol or insurance – or an unwillingness to invest the time and effort involved in making distinctions.

Rather, the customer, or prospective customer, is driven to turning the problem around. He or she ceases to evaluate the *intrinsic* value of the offer – the inherent good or bad properties, the specifications – and instead concentrates on the *extrinsic* – 'what does it do, or mean, for me?'

The result is, the customer draws conclusions about 'rightness' from the clues that he or she gets from the organization at the many points where they meet. Expectations and experiences mingle here and a successful outcome to the customer's drive to realize his or her own desires will be largely a reflection of the personality and behaviour of the person or persons they meet at these interactions.

The service triangle

This decision-making process by the customer is critical to managing a service. The service offer has none of the direct simplicity of the conventional product.

Most people will quickly form a word image of a product if it is mentioned. For example, most will be able to express a clear image in words of a solid object such as a Ford car or a Mars bar. But a service is usually much more difficult to capture so clearly. Any firm view will usually be associated with a personal experience with that organization or, very likely, a person within it.

Such experiences cannot be seen in isolation, however. Success at this point can only be a reflection of success in creating an internal culture which supports the external aspirations, a point which will be examined in more depth in Chapter 4. So, in turn, these interactions are dependent on what happens internally. This can be seen as a triangle, where the aim is to provide a balance between the three arms as shown in Figure 3.1.

Conventional thinking sees the main thrust of an organization's activity with its market as being along the top axis. Most attempts to correct this for service, through customer focus, will generally be about either trying to improve this link or about the bottom axis, creating – or attempting to create – a relationship with the customer at this external point.

Customer-driven companies, on the other hand, will look at the whole relationship inherent in the triangle and will make sure that it is the whole organization which is geared to the meeting of the customers needs.

For Novotel or for SOL Cleaning, to take two of the examples already discussed, that external drive is matched by an inner drive which mobilizes the organization. They cut out effort that is wasteful

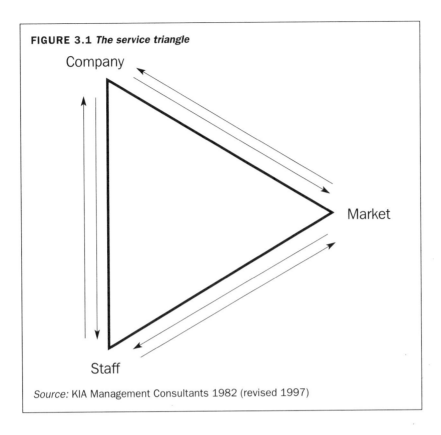

FIGURE 3.1 *The service triangle*

Company

Market

Staff

Source: KIA Management Consultants 1982 (revised 1997)

or not needed, even though it may be dear to the heart of those who have grown up in such businesses over the years. The effect of this is that the customer is not buying a product in any conventional sense, but is buying a solution to the drive to be seen as an individual with individual needs. The product has become:

▶ **a definite set of solutions**
▶ **to a definite set of problems**
▶ **for a definite set of people**
▶ **at a particular point in time.**

The service mix

This reinforces the point already made – service is the outcome of a series of dynamic forces which come together at the interaction. This is the product. A service organization is not selling 'plane seats or meals or an insurance policy but millions and millions of interactions, every year and even every day. These are the moments of truth when the ideas that have been behind the strategy and the thinking and the plans are turned to success or to dust.

It is this which lies behind the concept of the Service Star (Figure 3.2) where the interaction is the *outcome* of the bringing together, and in balance, the 'dynamic forces' exerted by the five elements that make up the service product, the offer to the customer. These five factors together create a service. They are the 'service mix'. Unlike a lot of attempts at creating a variant of the 'marketing mix', it

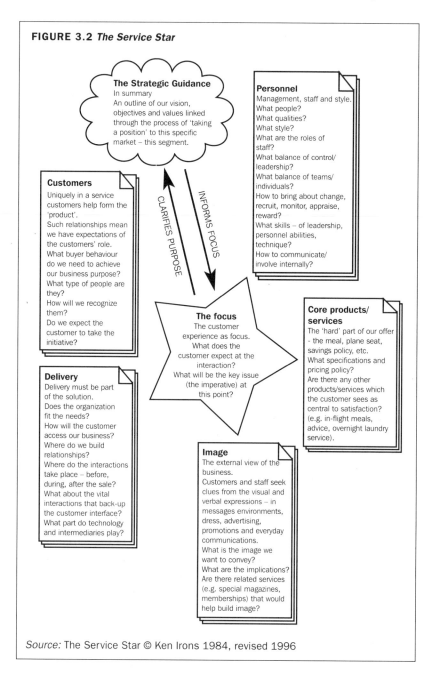

FIGURE 3.2 *The Service Star*

The Strategic Guidance
In summary
An outline of our vision, objectives and values linked through the process of 'taking a position' to this specific market – this segment.

Personnel
Management, staff and style.
What people?
What qualities?
What style?
What are the roles of staff?
What balance of control/ leadership?
What balance of teams/ individuals?
How to bring about change, recruit, monitor, appraise, reward?
What skills – of leadership, personnel abilities, technique?
How to communicate/ involve internally?

CLARIFIES PURPOSE   INFORMS FOCUS

Customers
Uniquely in a service customers help form the 'product'.
Such relationships mean we have expectations of the customers' role.
What buyer behaviour do we need to achieve our business purpose?
What type of people are they?
How will we recognize them?
Do we expect the customer to take the initiative?

The focus
The customer experience as focus.
What does the customer expect at the interaction?
What will be the key issue (the imperative) at this point?

Core products/ services
The 'hard' part of our offer - the meal, plane seat, savings policy, etc.
What specifications and pricing policy?
Are there any other products/services which the customer sees as central to satisfaction? (e.g. in-flight meals, advice, overnight laundry service).

Delivery
Delivery must be part of the solution.
Does the organization fit the needs?
How will the customer access our business?
Where do we build relationships?
Where do the interactions take place – before, during, after the sale?
What about the vital interactions that back-up the customer interface?
What part do technology and intermediaries play?

Image
The external view of the business.
Customers and staff seek clues from the visual and verbal expressions – in messages environments, dress, advertising, promotions and everyday communications.
What is the image we want to convey?
What are the implications?
Are there related services (e.g. special magazines, memberships) that would help build image?

Source: The Service Star © Ken Irons 1984, revised 1996

is not just a list but a set of forces which come together dynamically at the 'moment of truth', the interaction.

What is more, it can be seen that customers themselves are a key element of this, not simply an external target. A vital concept in any service is that the customer is a participant, helping to form and shape the offer. The customer may even be more experienced than the operative. In building its business, Four Seasons have always considered that the type of customer attracted to their hotels is going to be one who brings a rich experience of travel and of using services in many different situations.

As thinking about service progresses, it becomes possible to see how each of the forces generated by the elements of the service mix come together – or should come together – to provide a solution at the interaction, the 'product'. A glance forward (Figures 10.2 and 10.3), will illustrate more clearly what is involved in creating a balance to achieve different solutions. The impact of the dynamics is in the meantime explained in more depth in Box 3.1.

The service task

Service has to be a complete concept – a seamless solution to the customer's problem. It is the drive by the customer which is central and which, in turn, should drive the organization. It is a more complex concept than just the creation of, say, a meal or the sale of a holiday.

With manufactured products, efforts are largely aimed at non-reactive targets, the 'product'. It is possible to exert a rigorous control at the factory gate. In a service they are aimed at reactive targets, people. Customers and staff are directly involved, shaping and forming the eventual 'product'.

Such contact is widespread, across many people and before, during and after the sale. Nor does the customer see these interactions as separate from the purchase – so much so that the person he or she is dealing with is integral to the purchase itself.

As a result, if service is to truly reflect that drive on the part of the customer, everyone involved in the management of a service will be faced with a fundamentally different task to a counterpart in manufacturing.

▶ Operational roles cannot be organized free of customer interference.
▶ The tasks of personnel and marketing overlap and may even be at odds, fighting for the attention and commitment of the very same people.
▶ Finance is much more concerned with hard-to-measure variables. and 'soft', quality issues may be more important to measure than hard finance.

BOX 3.1 *Service dynamics*

Conventional approaches to marketing – even when customer oriented – rely heavily on 'product' as a means of defining 'market'. This is because the product itself is the focus. Research to establish consumer preferences and reactions is centred around the product; changes to meet such expressed wishes will rarely be radical and more often confined to minor changes of specification, maybe just the packaging! But service is about all of the elements in the service mix and about the balance they produce at the interaction.

For example, as a result of product orientation, most business-to-business providers see 'small business' as a single target group or segment. This is based on their requirement for similar levels of product complexity and technical service. It ignores the wider issues in the service mix and the particular nature of the interaction, where the dynamics of the elements meet and create service.

The difference these forces can exert with different types of customers is illustrated in Figure 3.3. Using a technique called Service Dynamics

Profiling, a 'map' of the overall relationship is created. In this illustration, relationships between one retail bank and two groups of small business customers, 'professionals' and 'artisans', is described. For simplicity, the number of 'criteria' involved in the relationship have been reduced to the 12 most important. Those criteria are then weighted, according to importance in the customer/bank relationship. Those that have the greater importance are towards the outside of the circle; those with a low importance are towards the centre.

While both are small businesses, they can be seen to be driven by a quite different set of dynamics. Most significantly, the professionals are happy to be at a distance; the artisans want to deal directly with people. A quick glance at criteria 5 and 6 will show why most banks don't realize this – the 'product/technical' needs are very similar. Product focus obscures the service dynamics.

The value and usage of Service Dynamic Profiles are discussed in Chapter 7.

Achieving the shifts needed is not simple. There is a natural tendency to focus on the product or the services, rather than the outcome, the service. Service is seen to be 'additional', to be a surround to the core, rather than integral.

As a result, many of the functional splits in organization which are taken for granted in manufacturing are often used in a service without regard to the different circumstances. They obscure the customer focus. This is positively dangerous. Robert Townsend caught the feel of this in his book *Up the Organization*, which recounts his

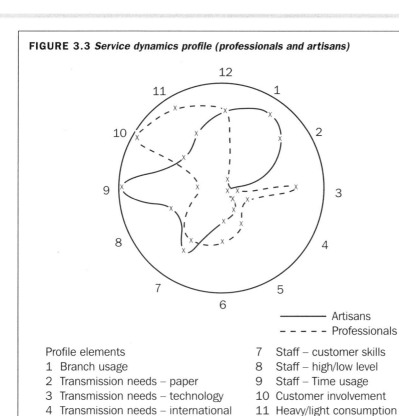

FIGURE 3.3 *Service dynamics profile (professionals and artisans)*

——— Artisans
- - - - - Professionals

Profile elements
1 Branch usage
2 Transmission needs – paper
3 Transmission needs – technology
4 Transmission needs – international
5 Product complexity
6 Staff – technical skills
7 Staff – customer skills
8 Staff – high/low level
9 Staff – Time usage
10 Customer involvement
11 Heavy/light consumption
12 Price strategy – high/low
High/frequent to outside

Source: KIA Management Consultants 1984, Service Dynamic Profiling © 1996

experiences in bringing Avis back from the brink of extinction when he wrote:

> *'Marketing' departments – like planning departments, personnel departments, management development departments, advertising departments, and public relations departments – are usually camouflage designed to cover up for lazy or worn-out chief executives. Marketing, in the fullest sense of the word, is the name of the game. So it had better be handled by the boss and his line, not by staff hecklers.*

It is doubtful that Robert Townsend truly realized the full significance of this, since it is not specifically 'marketing', 'planning' or 'personnel', but all non-operational roles which must be subordinate to the real purpose of the organization. Refer back to Figure 3.2. The figure shows that there is very little that is not part of the service mix. As a result:

▶ Typically 70 to 90 per cent of a service organization's staff, and not uncommonly 100 per cent, are in roles which impact directly on to the market and customers.

▶ This is a marked contrast to the average 10 per cent in a typical manufacturing business, where this 10 per cent acts as a 'bridge' to the market and so creates a distinctive role for marketing, related to this bridge.

In a service operation, dealing with the customers is the task. Everything else is of value only inasmuch as it adds value to this activity.

▶ For marketing, it means that it simply cannot be the closed circuit operation found in the traditional manufacturing/product environment. A fair definition of marketing would be:

Those aspects of management activity whose objective is to relate the organization, and its unique abilities and competence, to the specific market place most suited to the optimization of its resources, whether existing or reasonably available.

In a service, marketing is the business, so the role of any specifically 'marketing' function must be primarily strategic, ensuring that the market, in particular the interaction, is the focus at all times and that activity supports this. The role has to be to connect, to help management guide the organization through the maze of change in the market to a future based on being customer driven. Handelsbanken, for example, has eliminated its marketing department, keeping just two people to provide a central coordination and information activity.

▶ For human resources, it means not only that managers have to accept more responsibility but that many areas of traditional 'human resource' activity, such as behavioural change, become central to the manager's task.

▶ For finance, it is necessary to be overtly involved in ensuring that financial measures not only reflect the ambitions of the organization, relative to its market, but that purely money or short-term measures are not allowed to override the long-term and non-financial.

▶ For technology, it means being sure that the technical support increases the value at the interaction – shortening distance not creating barriers – and can be used effectively by those involved.

These changes are simply headlines of what is involved. The example of SOL over the next few pages gives a better feel for the change involved in real service.

When Liisa Joronen proposed that the head office of her family's laundry firm, Lindströms, one of Finland's most respected and well-established companies, should have a non-territorial office as part of the construction of: '*The cleanest and most beautiful laundry in the world, with a fountain in the middle and art all around*', it was simply too much. Her ideas on flexible-working arrangements – putting immense trust in employees and giving them great freedom of personal choice in working hours, for example – had already created tension but this went too far. Clearly, Liisa had lost touch with the reality of the business! Four years later, Liisa is Chairman of SOL, one of Finland's most successful companies – and the former cleaning and waste division of Lindströms – which Liisa took over at the parting of the ways.

The SOL name was chosen as just one of the (more visible) breaks with the past. It is not only intended to convey happy feelings, but to underpin the vision. This was to create a company that was based on uncompromising views that a service business could only prosper in the long run if it worked single-mindedly for customers. In turn, it would only be able to achieve this through employees who had been given the chance to perform at their best and be happy. Liisa recounts:

> '*I was fortunate that at the time of the breakaway, a number of the best people at Lindströms took a personal risk and followed me. We had 2,200 people and 2,500 customers but we had an extremely bad economic situation in Finland at the time and we had to move fast. But I was equally convinced that if we were to succeed it would not be by being conventional or taking fright because of this.*'

Liisa and her team realized they not only had to do the cleaning well but had to go further – and they have built the business around the sun and a smile. Marketing cleaning is very dull but they have tried to do it in a very different way, to build a business which is 'sunny'. The cleaners get a lot of flexibility but they are expected to 'sell' and to be a part of the marketing of SOL – '*We expect our cleaners to think*'.

Liisa continues,

> *You have to have low prices but you have to deliver quality if you are to retain the business. Often a customer will move for price but return after experience elsewhere. We try to meet this head on by not only discussing price but helping our customers to find ways of reducing costs, by reducing frequency in little used spaces or changing the patterns to a more economical way of working. We have been very successful at reducing costs for our customers, so*

Continued

much so that if we still had the same customer base we had five years ago, working the same contracts, we would have forty per cent less revenue today than then! So, we have had to work hard to get increases in revenue and profitability.

Above all, I had formed a view that service companies which are successful, achieve this because they are built around their customers. Yet I observed that most managers want to build the business around themselves. They will do things for themselves at home but as soon as they get to the office they can't even pour a cup of coffee! At weekends they will involve themselves in mammoth physical tasks but not at the office. They think that at work only managers can think and workers can't, so that is what happens. They build up defensive mechanisms around them to protect this way of life and to make the divisions even more clear. But my customer does not benefit from my having a big office or a secretary. The customer pays for everything, so unless we can justify it for the customer, we don't do it.

Nor can you simply stop there or become complacent, thinking that by making some changes you have achieved everything. Once you start down this road, it is one of permanent rediscovery of better and simpler ways to do things, not least because as people get used to exercising their common sense and responsibility, so they see it could be done better or without so much cost.

One key outcome has been that we have virtually dispensed with managers, because our staff, both cleaners and those in head office, have queried their value. In some contracts, we have even been able to dispense with supervisors and the cleaners have created a self-directing team, which not only sees itself as responsible for the successful meeting of the contract but for getting a renewal too.

At head office, the office people do not have managers 'disturbing' them, as they describe it. They don't work to specific hours either. They simply have individual goals and they can work when, where and how they choose, so long as they achieve them. If they want advice they can ask anyone, usually our Managing Director Any Aronen, the only other 'manager', besides me.

It is the individuals who set themselves the deadlines and are responsible for carrying the work out, accurately and to time. Seventy per cent of their salary is a base salary, which they are paid whatever; the balance is only paid if they meet their deadlines with accurate work – and there are no excuses. If the computer *breaks down and they are late, they don't get the bonus – that's life. In fact, we rarely get a computer breakdown that interferes with the deadlines because it affects the computer person, too, and we have peer pressure, not management imposition. The 1995 results were available by 3.27 on the morning of the 2 January. I know that because they were sent to me at home by fax, and I could see the time!*

We have tried to integrate the sales more effectively with the contracts themselves. So, when we get a new contract, the salesperson involved has to work on the contract for the first week. Further, he or she does not get all the commission until after six months when we have a review with the customer. Only then, if the customer feels we are fulfilling the contract, do we pay.

Their offices, SOL Studio, formerly a large hanger-like film studio, reflects their philosophy and challenges the conventional. Why should an office look like an office? Why should people work set hours, have rooms, have 'office' furniture?

So there are no personal spaces or personal desks. Instead, there are lots of different types of workstations, often using distinctly domestic furniture and fittings, where employees – including the management and supervisors – will work where it suits them best or the fancy takes them. There are also lots of meeting places, some of them designed for 'stand-up' meetings, '*So that we don't feel that if we have a meeting that it has to go on for a long time*'. Only the Union representative has retained a desk but relations with the Union are amicable – '*They respect us and realize that the way we work is the way the staff want it.*'

People like bank managers say, 'you are lucky, you have such good staff' but they don't recognize they have the staff they have because they cling to all their status. They talk about new values but the values have to be in your soul. Because people in SOL do believe what they say, they can do so much more. It used to take a month to get a new customer up and running but now it can be done next day or next week. We had a recent case, where we got an offer in by midday on the day we were asked to quote, had it accepted by 19.00, informed the cleaners later that evening and were on site and working at six the next morning. It gave everyone involved an immense sense of achievement.

Five years on, SOL is thriving. In a difficult market, where most cleaning companies are making losses, SOL is making record profits.

BOX 3.2 *Service as a process*

An example of understanding this process (see below and next page) and the nature and importance of discontinuities is quoted by Thorstein Øverland, now Group Executive President of the Norwegian bank Kredtikassen, and reflecting on his early days in the financial service sector.

*'When I joined the insurance industry in 1979, from the field of fast-moving consumer goods, I started out having a traditional product marketing model in mind. Our product was an insurance contract, which was delivered in the form of a policy and conditions printed on paper. For many people, both the need for and the contents of such a contract is quite difficult to under-*stand *and, therefore, I knew that the staff of an insurance company played a more important role in delivering the product than in a manufacturing company. However, I mainly looked upon the staff as a necessity to help deliver and explain the product, and not as part of the product itself.*

As a consequence of this view, most of our marketing activities in those days were directed at explaining the benefits or price advantage of a particular product or coverage. We supported this with various promotional activities which were inspired by fast-moving consumer goods marketing thinking. All of this had very little effect on our sales results.

Small details make superservice

A further key issue is that the 'product', the interactions at the centre of the Service Star, are not static but dynamic. They are not individual events but are a series, which go on over time. Sometimes this is a period which is transient, as with a one-off sale in a shop; others may be over a long period, as with an insurance contract.

In this process there are a number of discontinuities where the customer draws clues about what he or she might expect, or about the 'rightness' of that service for him or her. This process is, in effect, the map of the relationship with the customer. The discontinuities are the key experiences that go to make up this relationship, re-inforcing good vibrations or confirming bad ones. Because of this, the greatest service idea is dependent on the smallest detail.

▶ A superlative meal can be spoiled by sloppy or inappropriate service; great service on board a ferry can be battling against the already formed impressions gained on the dockside.

▶ The customer may never take you very seriously again after the treatment received at reception or on the telephone.

▶ All the good work that has gone into making a flight a successful experience may be ruined by poor baggage handling at the airport, or simply the lack of someone sympathetic to deal with it.

I remember that we blamed this on the fact that any product improvement or good promotional idea was immediately copied by our competitors. But we did not have to be very brilliant to see the truth, which was that our sales results were directly related to the quality and motivation of our sales people. Good people steadily produced good results, irrespective of changes in products or price levels. When we have bad results, more often than not the reason could be tracked to the people working in the area in question.

The consumer-goods marketing model evidently did not apply, and had to be changed. Our reasoning went like this:

▶ *the customer is not buying a policy, but financial security;*

▶ *security is a matter of both being and feeling secure;*

▶ *the feeling of security is not something that can be delivered as a commodity, but is a matter of trust between the customer and the insurance company;*

▶ *the level of trust is formed by each single contact the customer has with the company;*

▶ *the decisive factor influencing the outcome of each contact is the way our personnel handle the situation, and not the wording in our policies, conditions, etc.*

Therefore, our products are not delivered at one particular moment ("here is your security") but through a process. The main ingredient in this process are our personnel and not the papers'.

Understanding that it is a process that is being sold, a process that is made up of all those 'moments of truth', and that it has to be in balance throughout is important. This is never easy to achieve and may often be extremely difficult since, as it is so often true with the baggage example above, you may not have a direct control over the 'discontinuity' – though you still 'own' it!

Other such examples can be poor weather or immigration playing a part in an airline passenger's beliefs about the service. These events are certainly difficult to 'control' but recognizing them for what they are may lead you to provide a kind of reassurance in some cases. To 'buttress' potential bad experiences either side with good service and recognition.

Taking the initiative

A crucial feature of the service process, is that it is never entirely predictable. The customer is driving; you have to react. 'Colouring outside the lines', getting people to go that little bit extra to meet the customer, can only come from the heart.

The manager in a service is like the manager of a football team. Events are largely out of control, once the game has started. The skill is to prepare the players – as a team and as individuals – to recognize and understand the situations as they arise and to accept personal responsibility for taking action, at that precise point. That

BOX 3.3 *The ancient art of digging holes*

The origins of this story are uncertain. In 1995 it was published in one British national newspaper as an authentic, recent happening. Others say the origin is a Shelley Berman sketch from the 1950s. It can also be found on the internet. Whatever its origin, it is not only humorous but illustrative of a common situation, when staff know that the only safe course is to play by the rules.

Dear Maid,

Please do not leave any more of those little bars of soap in my bathroom since I have brought my own bath-sized Dial. Please remove the six unopened little bars from the shelf under the medicine chest and another three in the shower soap dish. They are in my way. Thank you,

S. Berman

Dear Room 635,

I am not your regular maid. She will be back tomorrow, Thursday, from her day off. I took the three hotel soaps out of the shower soap dish as you requested. The six bars on your shelf I took out of your way and put on top of your Kleenex dispenser in case you should change your mind. This leaves only the three bars I left today which my instructions from the management is to leave three soaps daily. I hope this is satisfactory.

Kathy, Relief Maid

Dear Maid,

I hope you are my regular maid. Apparently Kathy did not tell you about my note to her concerning the little bars of soap. When I got back to my room this evening I found you had added three little Camays to the shelf under my medicine cabinet.

I am going to be here in the hotel for two weeks and have brought my own bath-size Dial so I won't need those six little Camays which are on the shelf. They are in my way when shaving, brushing teeth, etc. Please remove them.

S. Berman

Dear Mr Berman,

My day off was last Wed. So the relief maid left three hotel soaps which we are instructed by the management. I took the six soaps which were in your way on the shelf and put them in the soap dish where your Dial was. I put the Dial in the medicine cabinet for your convenience. I didn't remove the three complimentary soaps which are always placed inside the medicine cabinet for all new check-ins and which you did not object to when you checked in last Monday. Please let me know if I can be of further assistance.

Your regular maid, Dotty

Dear Mr Berman,

The assistant manager, Mr Kensedder, informed me this a.m. that you called him last evening and said you were unhappy with your maid service. I have assigned a new girl to your room. I hope you will accept my apologies for any past inconvenience. If you have any future complaints please contact me so I can give it my personal attention. Call extension 1108 between 8 a.m. and 5 p.m.

Thank you.

Elaine Carmen,

Housekeeper

Dear Miss Carmen,

It is impossible to contact you by phone since I leave the hotel for business at 7.45 am and don't get back before 5.30 or 6 p.m. That's the reason I called Mr. Kensedder last night. You were already off duty.

I only asked Mr Kensedder if he could do anything about those little bars of soap. The new maid you assigned me must have thought I was a new check-in today, since she left another three bars of hotel soap in my medicine cabinet along with her regular delivery of three bars on the bathroom shelf.

In just five days here I have accumulated 24 little bars of soap. Why are you doing this to me?
S. Berman

Dear Mr Berman,
Your maid, Kathy, has been instructed to stop delivering soap to your room and remove the extra soaps. If I can be of further assistance, please call extension 1108 between 8 a.m. and 5 p.m.
Thank you,
Elaine Carmen,
Housekeeper

Dear Mr. Kensedder,
My bath-size Dial is missing. Every bar of soap was taken from my room including my own bath-size Dial. I came in late last night and had to call the bellhop to bring me four little Cashmere Bouquets.
S. Berman

Dear Mr Berman,
I have informed our housekeeper, Elaine Carmen, of your soap problem. I cannot understand why there was no soap in your room since our maids are instructed to leave three bars of soap each time they service a room. The situation will be rectified immediately. Please accept my apologies for the inconvenience.
Martin L. Kensedder,
Assistant Manager

Dear Mrs Carmen,
Who the hell left 54 little bars of Camay in my room? I came in last night and found 54 little bars of soap. I don't want 54 little bars of Camay. I want my one damn bar of bath-size Dial. Do you realize I have 54 bars of soap in here. All I want is my bath-size Dial. Please give me back my bath-size Dial.
S. Berman

Dear Mr Berman,
You complained of too much soap in your room so I had them removed. Then you complained to Mr Kensedder that all your soap was missing so I personally returned them. The 24 Camays which had been taken and the 3 Camays you are supposed to receive daily (sic). I don't know anything about the four Cashmere Bouquets. Obviously your maid, Kathy, did not know I had returned your soaps so she also brought 24 Camays plus the 3 daily Camays. I don't know where you got the idea this hotel issues bath-size Dial. I was able to locate some bath-size Ivory which I left in your room.
Elaine Carmen,
Housekeeper

Dear Mrs Carmen,
Just a short note to bring you up-to-date on my latest soap inventory.
As of today I possess:
On shelf under medicine cabinet – 18 Camay in four stacks of 4 and one stack of 2.
On Kleenex dispenser – 11 Camay in two stacks of 4 and one stack of 3.
On bedroom dresser – One stack of three Cashmere Bouquet, one stack of four hotel-size Ivory, and eight Camay in two stacks of 4.
Inside medicine cabinet – Fourteen Camay in three stacks of 4 and one stack of 2.
In shower soap dish – Six Camay, very moist.
On north-east corner of tub – One Cashmere Bouquet, slightly used.
On north-west corner of tub – Six Camays in two stacks of 3.
Please ask Kathy when she services my room to make sure the stacks are neatly piled and dusted. Also, please advise her that stacks of more than four have a tendency to tip. May I suggest that my bedroom window sill is not in use and will make an excellent spot for future soap deliveries.
One more item, I have purchased another bar of bath-size Dial which I am keeping in the hotel vault in order to avoid further misunderstandings.
S. Berman

responsibility must include deciding whether an event calls for sharing or 'going it alone'. The player must be prepared to live by the outcome; the manager to encourage the individual to 'risk' and accept the result.

That outcome will usually be negative if every time a risk is taken the result is merely criticism or blame. While the inadequate manager or member of staff, no less than the underperforming player, must expect to be judged by success or fortune in the long run, few people will even attempt to contribute if they work in a culture which does not support them and 'raise their game'.

That not everyone finds this easy is illustrated by the story in Box 3.3. It illustrates too what can happen when the approach to the customer is not driven by the customer, but is seen in 'industrial' terms – applying rigid standards.

Acknowledgements and further reading

page 39   Townsend, R. (1971) *Up the Organization*, Hodder Fawcett.

page 40   Irons, K. (1996) *The Marketing of Services*, McGraw-Hill.

The following companies all gave generously of their time and material in providing insights for the background to this and other chapters:

Pret A Manger, London.
Svenska Handelbanken, Stockholm.

Not only are the books listed above about the need for service organizations to be driven by the customer but so, too, is most of the reading listed under other chapters. Some further titles are:

Albrecht, K. and Zamke, R. (1986) *Service America: Doing Business in the New Economy*, Dow Jones Irwin.
Glen, P. (1990) *It's Not My Department*, William Morrow.
Heller, R. (1994) *The Quality Makers – the leaders and shapers of Europe's quality revolution*, Norden Publishing.

Getting everyone onside

Organizations do not simply react to their environment as a ship might to waves. They actively select, interpret, choose and create their environment.

Fons Trompenaars, *Riding the Waves of Culture*

About this chapter

Successful service organizations rely on their people taking the initiative, colouring outside the lines to achieve that little bit extra – with the customer or with a colleague. This is impossible to achieve unless everyone is onside to the ideas that guide the organization – believes in them, as if they were theirs. To achieve this requires that the passion be shared, that there is a 'strategic cohesion' which has everyone pointed in the same direction.

For the customer to appreciate it, the delivery also needs to be consistent. This is not a matter of laying down a mass of rules and standards, but of providing a clear pathway toward a common aim – a vision – with a clear guidance on 'how we get there'. Such a 'guiding light' is also the statement of the 'brand'. It is the way an organization behaves which is the crucial factor. Such behaviour must be for everyone – management and staff alike, as an individual and as a member of the team if the 'brand' is to be more than a wish.

This chapter will look at what it takes to get everyone onside.

▶ Sharing the passion and what it takes to achieve this.

▶ The need to have everyone aligned toward the same aim and, further, for this to be seen by everyone as *their* aim.

▶ The need for the delivery of this to be consistent.

▶ What is a 'brand' in a service and the implications of this.

▶ The vital importance of recruitment, getting the right 'raw material'.

▶ Equally, the vital importance of a guidance document, a 'guiding light'.

Sharing the passion

Café Rouge is one of the new wave of restaurants that is helping to transform the everyday eating experiences of the British. Although over the past 30 years the scene has changed dramatically, it has been largely due to the great increase of Chinese and Indian restaurants – for many people, giving them their first experience of eating out, other than on special occasions – and a few, more upmarket restaurants. Attempts at inexpensive French-style bistros or brasseries rarely achieved lasting success and were often wildly inconsistent.

Karen Jones, the founder of Café Rouge, had a different ambition – to launch a network of restaurants that were open throughout the day and welcomed everyone, whether for a meal or to read a newspaper over a cup of coffee. They would serve good fresh food that, while consistent in its quality, would be prepared on the premises as in an individually-owned restaurant. Finally, Café Rouge wanted to be local, to bring the same customers back, again and again, which meant having highly-motivated staff who wanted to work in a restaurant and wanted to please customers and create the right atmosphere. Seven years on and Café Rouge is a feature of most London neighbourhoods and its 100+ branches are to be found as far afield as Edinburgh and Dublin.

For Jo Cumming, who started in the first Café Rouge in 1989 and is now Managing Director, the importance of preparing food freshly – even the sauces are made daily from fresh ingredients, no bought-in bases – goes beyond the customer experience.

> We are not simply selling people food but a complete experience. For this to work consistently, we need to have people who can believe in what they are doing and are proud of what they serve, not in some inward way but because they feel they are being honest with the customer. So, we take great care not only with the menus – which we change every three months – but with their introduction to the staff. Our development chefs work with each branch chef individually, ironing out problems and getting close to perfection; then we close the branch for an afternoon and invite all the staff to taste and learn about the new menu.

Development Chef, Peter O'Sullivan echoes this:

> Not only do the staff get to understand the menu more thoroughly, and so can advise customers, but they can offer us good advice. They are in touch with the customer all the day. As a result they feel a very real sense of ownership. I am not sure that all the customers recognize the differences our approach (to preparing food,

fresh locally) makes but I know that it creates a difference to what I and the branch chefs and the other staff believe. The customer benefits directly from that. We share our passion together with the customer and are genuinely concerned to see that he or she gets a good experience.

Café Rouge is not an exception in the world of superservice. Sharing the passion underpins all superservice and getting everyone onside to the core idea and ideals is key to their success.

It needs more than hope!

While few would dispute the value of sharing the passion, the achievement of this is not widespread. 'Why?' is a key question. World-class service can only be achieved at the point where the organization meets the market-place. Whatever the passion – or originality – of the idea, it is as nothing if there is no passion – or originality – in the delivery.

The commonest problems centre around the lapse of the passion into merely wordy enthusiasm – 'the customer is king' and other, usually empty, slogans. Too little time, often none at all, is spent on seeing how the 'passion' relates to the realities of delivery and what are the barriers presented by the bureaucracy of the organization. Indeed, is a strong 'bureaucracy' compatible with passion, as in 'we are passionate about on-time departures', or incompatible, as in 'during your stay/conference at our hotel, we will tailor our services to your precise needs'? In the one case there is a match; in the other not.

The factors involved are well illustrated by some important research carried out in the USA among bank staff and customers. The research was based on the view that all service organizations are a blend of bureaucracy and enthusiasm because:

▶ without some bureaucracy things don't happen, and
▶ without some enthusiasm for the customer the bureaucracy would take over.

Passion for the customers' experience has to be a blend. Total bureaucracy would exclude the customers – 'the trains run better without any passengers'; total enthusiasm would lead to chaos.

The research took the form of a survey of attitudes toward the two extremes and involved 23 branches – so there were 23 models to compare. The results showed that there was a positive correlation between customer experiences and a balance of bureaucracy and enthusiasm, but not in the form you might have expected.

▶ Enthusiasm was no more likely to be linked to positive feelings by the customers than bureaucracy.

▶ What made the difference was a consistency across the results in a branch, with regard to both management and staff.

▶ Where there was agreement between branch management and their staff about the issues involved in these two aspects – and the balance between them – customers reported positive service experiences.

▶ Where customers reported bad experiences was, for example, where management shouted the odds about the importance of customers (enthusiasm), but staff reported an overriding emphasis in reality, to get things right, filling in forms correctly and not making mistakes (bureaucracy) – 'Our management talk about customers but all they are really interested in is our achieving sales or not causing problems'.

In other words, when a team has a common aim in what it is they are providing and in the way they are to work to achieve it, a mutual purpose, then they are consistent in their delivery, in word and deed, and the outcome is recognized and appreciated by the customer.

Because 'bureaucratic' sounds pejorative, it can be difficult to accept these findings at first. But stop and think about organizations like McDonald's or Swiss railways. Both are very highly thought of by their customers – for consistency! Both of these organizations are essentially bureaucratic, in the non-pejorative sense of the word – *they deliver a certainty which the customer values.*

Strategic cohesion

This is strategic cohesion, an harmonious or cohesive internal culture, with low levels of role ambiguity or role conflict around a clear and worthwhile external focus. In such a cohesive culture, the passion gets through. More of what goes in at the top comes out with the customer.

An understanding of the significance of culture is crucial to understanding how this is achieved. Involving customers and being more responsive to their needs is a part of the social change that affects and shapes attitudes and expectations of staff, too. Such changes make it increasingly difficult to get the best staff to work in 'bureaucratic' situations. Richard Smith, an Operations Manager at Pret A Manger, talking of his time at McDonald's says: '*It was marvellous training but I couldn't stand the lack of opportunity to be individual, to be creative*'.

Changing an organization to meet such market demands requires a wholesale change of behaviour if it is not to be stillborn, an idea never to achieve reality. The critical ingredient in this is the culture –

that is, the set of inherited ideas, beliefs, values and knowledge which together make for a shared basis for action. Without such a framework it is difficult, if not impossible, for people to collaborate; with it, it is possible to give direction, at least to some extent, towards common goals.

Such a concern with culture is not simply an indulgence. For example, one unpublished study of 22 firms showed that over an 11-year period those with a cohesive culture in word and deed outperformed the others by a huge margin:

▶ they increased revenues by 682 per cent versus 166 per cent;
▶ they expanded work forces by 282 per cent versus 36 per cent;
▶ they improved their share prices by 901 per cent versus 74 per cent;
▶ they improved their net incomes by 756 per cent versus 1 per cent.

Mapping cultures

The distinctiveness, the competitive edge of a service, is largely – and in some cases entirely – a reflection of culture. In a service, this culture also needs to be orientated externally. In other words, the external impact of the internal values is critical, as with Café Rouge.

To understand what makes for a 'strategically cohesive' culture, it is necessary to go beyond the simple model of 'bureaucracy versus enthusiasm', already outlined. While such a model is simple, and compellingly illustrative of the factors involved, organizations and their cultures are more than two dimensional.

Some later (European) research built on this and identified a number of other aspects that required mapping, if the true nature of a culture and its relationship to market performance was to be understood. Figures 4.1 and 4.2 show what is involved.

▶ Figure 4.1 shows that bureaucracy and enthusiasm have four basic dimensions – in one map, 'routines' are cross-linked with 'implementation' (of the routines), while in the other map, 'style of management' is cross-linked with the 'level of confidence' people feel in their work.
▶ Figure 4.2 shows the degree of identification with the key objectives and values of the organization.

The influence of 'management style/confidence' is dealt with in Chapter 8, but the lessons that can be drawn from the other aspects of this type of research are well illustrated in the results from research carried out in two airlines. In this study, the views of management, at two broadly identified levels, and staff have been

FIGURE 4.1 *Culture mapping – outline 1*

AMBIGUITY

How clearly do staff agree on the purpose of structure and style of the organization?

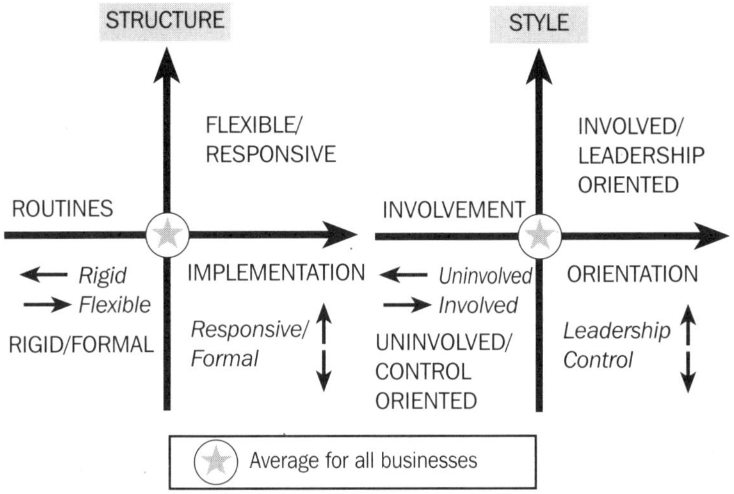

STRUCTURE

STYLE

FLEXIBLE/
RESPONSIVE

INVOLVED/
LEADERSHIP
ORIENTED

ROUTINES

INVOLVEMENT

← Rigid   IMPLEMENTATION
→ Flexible

← Uninvolved   ORIENTATION
→ Involved

RIGID/FORMAL   Responsive/
Formal

UNINVOLVED/
CONTROL
ORIENTED

Leadership
Control

⭐ Average for all businesses

Source: Service Matrix Analysis © KIA Ltd 1991

FIGURE 4.2 *Culture mapping – outline 2*

How closely are the same objectives and values shared in the organization? How much are these 'mine' as well as 'theirs'?

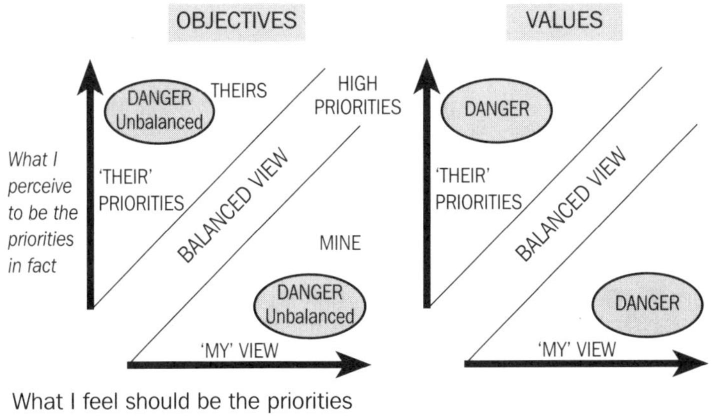

OBJECTIVES

VALUES

DANGER
Unbalanced   THEIRS   HIGH
PRIORITIES

DANGER

What I
perceive
to be the
priorities
in fact

'THEIR'
PRIORITIES   BALANCED VIEW

'THEIR'
PRIORITIES   BALANCED VIEW

MINE

DANGER
Unbalanced

DANGER

'MY' VIEW

'MY' VIEW

What I feel should be the priorities

Source: Service Matrix Analysis © KIA Ltd 1991

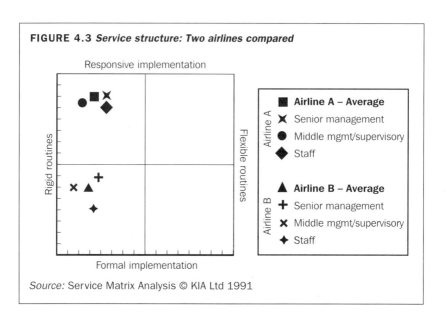

FIGURE 4.3 *Service structure: Two airlines compared*

Responsive implementation

Rigid routines

Flexible routines

Formal implementation

Airline A

■ **Airline A – Average**
✕ Senior management
● Middle mgmt/supervisory
◆ Staff

Airline B

▲ **Airline B – Average**
✚ Senior management
✖ Middle mgmt/supervisory
✦ Staff

Source: Service Matrix Analysis © KIA Ltd 1991

recorded from answers to a specialized questionnaire. In Figure 4.3, ('Service Structure' as in Figure 4.1), both airlines can be seen to be towards the left-hand side of the horizontal axis, a not surprising result, since airlines do depend on routines to a high degree to function effectively.

What differentiates them is their respective positions on the vertical axis, marked 'implementation' – the willingness to respond to the customer within the confines that these routines create.

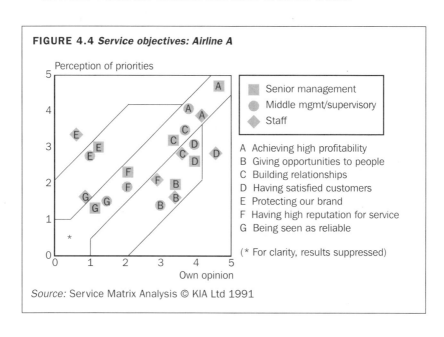

FIGURE 4.4 *Service objectives: Airline A*

Perception of priorities

Own opinion

■ Senior management
● Middle mgmt/supervisory
◆ Staff

A Achieving high profitability
B Giving opportunities to people
C Building relationships
D Having satisfied customers
E Protecting our brand
F Having high reputation for service
G Being seen as reliable

(* For clarity, results suppressed)

Source: Service Matrix Analysis © KIA Ltd 1991

While both are consistent in routines, Airline A is more responsive than Airline B in the way in which it handles those routines. Further, it has a much greater *cohesion* across management and staff than Airline B. Although both airlines report good customer responses, those for 'A' are more often truly positive – that is, are seen by customers as excellent; the results for 'B', are muted, that is, 'averagely all right'.

A provides superservice; B just provides service

A clue to the reason for this can be taken from a look at the results of another battery of questions in the same research concerning beliefs about the objectives in Figures 4.4 and 4.5 (as in Figure 4.2). The respondents within the two airlines have been asked to rank a set of objectives. Some of these have been drawn from the published strategic documents, such as a vision, others from the everyday priorities people within the organizations express. There are also some additions as 'tests', to see if other common views within such organizations are held, despite not being articulated openly.

First, respondents are asked to rank the 'objectives' in the order they believe should be the priorities; then to rank them again, but this time in the order they perceive to be the reality. These are then mathematically calculated and transferred to the 'maps', with 'own beliefs' on the bottom (horizontal) axis and 'perceptions of reality' on the left-hand (vertical) axis. Airline A is shown in Figure 4.4; Airline B in Figure 4.5. The visual discrepancy between the two is striking – and explains much about the differences in performance.

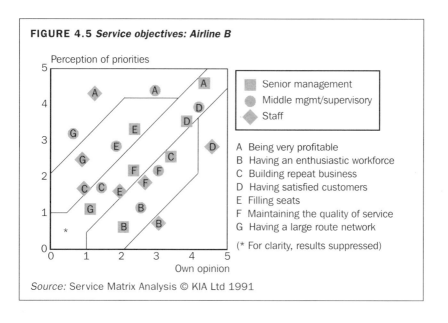

FIGURE 4.5 *Service objectives: Airline B*

Senior management
Middle mgmt/supervisory
Staff

A Being very profitable
B Having an enthusiastic workforce
C Building repeat business
D Having satisfied customers
E Filling seats
F Maintaining the quality of service
G Having a large route network

(* For clarity, results suppressed)

Source: Service Matrix Analysis © KIA Ltd 1991

In Airline A there is a substantial agreement – between different groups and between 'my beliefs' and 'their priorities'; Airline B has no such cohesion.

The need for consistency

A review of over 40 such studies in service sectors across Europe, shows that, overwhelmingly, it is consistency which matters; that a 'bureaucratic' organization can be as acceptable and popular with customers as an 'enthusiastic' one – if it is sustained. It cannot be for 'sometimes'. Managers who want to talk about 'surprising and delighting' customers need to understand that surprise and delight cannot be now and then. It must be delivered all of the time, through all of the interactions that make up the service offer – that process the customer buys.

Customer expectations are a complex outcome of hope, experience and, generally, a pragmatic recognition of the possible. Such expectations can be stretched far by past experience and are being modified all the time by the efforts of others, as in the pizza delivery example (see p. 19). Expectations will also be modified by other pressures. So someone desperate to get to a destination by a certain time or in need of, say, some medication at an odd hour of the day – or night – will have raised their expectations. In such an environment customers value consistency – the certainty that the experience they are going to go through, or rely on, will be as they expect.

John Sharpe at Four Seasons makes this point strongly when explaining the success of their hotels and resorts:

> *I am very attached to the belief that consistency is at the root of our success. At any given moment, almost any good hotel can be the best hotel in the world – for that moment. We aim to be consistent across different hotels but more importantly across the, say, two or three days of someone's stay. That means we have to be consistent in our management, too. Obviously, though what we have to aim to deliver in any individual hotel will vary in response to the environment. The guest may have a different expectation in New York or London to, say, Austin, Texas.*

Unless such talk is to be an empty set of phrases – to customers and to staff – it has to be a genuine and realizable promise for both. Staff are not only 'delivering' the offer but are an integral part of it. What is more in a service environment, virtually everyone has a role with the customer. Even those who don't, are going to be close to and interdependent with customer contact staff.

Many staff are going to be primarily 'technicians'. For them, it is highly possible that they will see customer contact as incidental to their work. The bank foreign exchange expert or the hotel electrician are examples. Yet they, too, impact on the customer. Their behaviour is a part of the experience.

This calls for a consistency of effort across both people and time. It underscores the need to get people in the organization to see that it is their personal contribution at those moments that is critical – to colour outside the lines, and find a way around the problem, rather than erect barriers or abdicate responsibility.

Service brands

The delivery of that promise to the customer is going to be in the hands of a great number of people and the consistent delivery of that promise is going to take consistency of effort, every day at every interaction – no 'ifs' and 'buts'. In a service, it is this delivery – the service – which is the 'brand'. The promise of this brand may be dashed by an ordinary delivery.

So, what is a brand? More particularly, what is a service brand? The essential point about a true brand is that it is a guarantee to the customer. It cannot just be a 'badge'. What, for example, is the consistency to be associated with 'Forte' or 'Sealink'? They were simply badges of marketing convenience and have suffered decline and death respectively, as a result.

Branding is an extremely old concept. It has been a feature since commodities or products from specific locations became recognized as having superior qualities, as in 'Brussels lace' or 'Burton beer'. In the nineteenth century, specific product brands became widely used to reassure customers that the product was safe, as in the advertisements for Horniman's Tea: 'Horniman's Tea has no injurious facings or fillings'. More recently, branding has become as much associated with a lifestyle – as with Swatch watches – as it has with the specific properties of the product itself.

Brands are a guarantee, something to be relied on, that is consistent. A true brand cannot have 'sometimes' elements. This creates a problem. It is easy enough to quality control a product, if necessary by draconian inspections at the 'factory gate'. It is not so easy to quality control the delivery of service.

Indeed, by definition, service brands are going to be delivered away from much supervision, and very probably no immediate supervision at all – at the interaction. Any attempt to quality control at that point will change the event. Further, many attempts at service branding, say a 'five star' insurance policy or a 'business class' seat, may have to share delivery systems with 'lesser' brands.

Brands will work most effectively in the service environment where there is a possibility of coordinating all of the elements. It is doubtful, therefore, whether brands have much value when the delivery is mixed with the delivery of other brands which have different demands. Staff, in particular, will find it difficult to switch quickly from one demand mode to another and customers may feel slighted if they see premium delivery to others.

Service as the brand, as the guarantee to the customer, is more likely to realize its promise if delivery is by someone who has a clear view of the key objectives and values which govern the brand. Someone who sees them as their own, not just something 'they', that is management, have decided on.

Further, the values required to achieve the promise externally need to be a reflection of the reality internally. It follows that the way an organization behaves internally is a part of the brand. A service brand cannot, for example, have integrity if the management don't have integrity. The way in which a service organization behaves is the key part of a service brand.

Few organizations have followed the logic of this through, but an exception is Woolworths. Woolworths have created a set of links

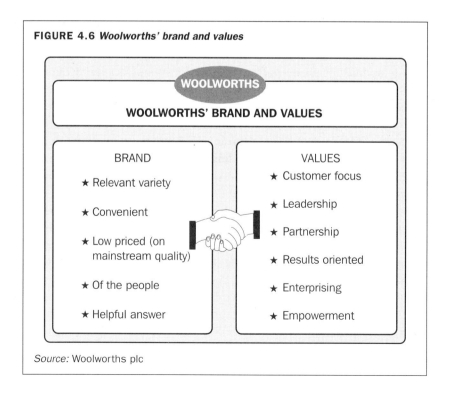

FIGURE 4.6 *Woolworths' brand and values*

WOOLWORTHS

WOOLWORTHS' BRAND AND VALUES

BRAND	VALUES
★ Relevant variety	★ Customer focus
★ Convenient	★ Leadership
★ Low priced (on mainstream quality)	★ Partnership
	★ Results oriented
★ Of the people	★ Enterprising
★ Helpful answer	★ Empowerment

Source: Woolworths plc

between their brand values and the internal values that they, as a business, must have to achieve success. They have then gone on to link these values with the behaviours that are necessary to deliver these values. Figures 4.6 and 4.7 show this.

This has been an important part of Woolworths' transformation from a 'no hoper' into a retail chain with a solid view of itself internally, relative to its chosen market, and a very real story of success. Figure 4.6 illustrates how the internal values that are needed to deliver the external expression of the brand are related, one to the other. Figure 4.7 shows how these values are then translated into the behaviours required, from management at all levels as well as staff. In other words, behaviours underpin or undermine the brand.

Two further examples of organizations which have made a success from service, seeing their 'brand' as the consistent delivery of superservice from their people, are Southwest Airlines and Svenska Handelsbanken (Box 4.1).

FIGURE 4.7 *The Woolworths way*

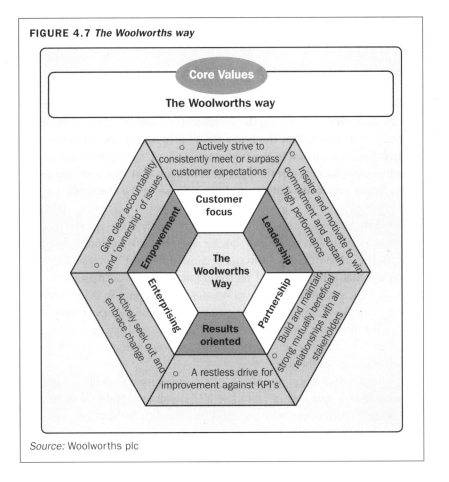

Source: Woolworths plc

Such considerations are of increasing importance. While some observers have suggested that 'brands' are a declining feature, in reality we see:

▶ a more discriminating and aware customer becoming both more challenging of past assumptions of superiority;

▶ similarly, more comfort with change, so greater preparedness to move around;

▶ and in parallel, a massive switch away from the material product to delivery, from product brands to 'delivery' (i.e. service) brands.

This is a reflection of the move from a focus on accumulation to utilization (Chapter 2) and of the growing power of service as a way of creating distinctiveness. It is also an indicator of the importance that brands are going to play in the future in the service arena as part of the task of providing incentives not to 'exit' when things don't go exactly right (see p. 18 and the reference to the 'exit culture' that we live in). The grass in the other field may look greener, but is it as certain as the 'brand' we already know and – give or take a hiccup or two – trust?

Getting the right people

The raw material of a service brand is, therefore, the people who provide that service, who are the brand at the point of interaction. A key factor in ensuring that the brand lives up to its promise is getting the right people on board in the first place. In fact, having the right people is the only guarantee of the right behaviours – that vital underpinning of the brand values and fulfilment of the promise to the customer.

This has an importance which goes way beyond the question of the direct costs involved. These can be high but are nothing compared with the hidden costs of management time and benefits lost. The impact that a high level of recruiting activity has on management is almost incalculable in its diversionary effect. Time which should be spent on developing staff and customer relations is spent instead on chasing new staff and on low-level induction training. Colleagues are diverted from their work by the constant need to give support and training on the job.

Getting the right people is not a question of skills – or even behaviours – but one of attitudes. It is possible to train for skills and, through leadership and example to modify behaviour, but you cannot train attitudes – and 'road to Damascus conversions' are too rare to be relied on.

BOX 4.1 *Culture and success*

Two of the great success stories of modern service development are Southwest Airlines, based in Dallas, and Svenska Handelsbanken, based in Stockholm. They are both sizeable operations: Southwest have around 20,000 employees and Handelsbanken 7,000; Southwest have over 200 aircraft; Handelsbanken over 500 branches. Both have brought about radical change not only within themselves but have set markers for their industry sector. The significant features of this are that each has done the following:

▶ Sustained success for over a quarter of a century.
▶ Operated in a field of activity which has not generally produced outstanding service *and* profit performances (no other airline has been so consistently profitable as Southwest; no Swedish bank has been so consistently profitable as Handelsbanken).
▶ Linked consistent profitability to the highest standards of customer service – in both cases by reference to independent research, from the Department of Transport and the Stockholm School of Economics respectively.
▶ Maintained the lowest costs in their sector.
▶ Has the reputation for being among the best employers, with an extremely stable workforce.
▶ Involved staff in sharing the outcome with generous staff share schemes, and

▶ Achieved all this with absolute safety (Southwest has never lost an aircraft or had a major accident, Handelsbanken alone among leading Swedish banks – and most Scandinavian banks for that matter – has not had to seek Government support in the recent banking crisis).

Their 'secret' is that they have both seen such success in a service based on people and have put their people, all of their people, into the driving seat to achieve change and their objectives. Further, they have treated change and the maintenance of what they achieved as holistic, combining all of the elements of service, good service, into a balanced whole. The culture has been a key ingredient of their success.

So, for example:

▶ Svenska Handelsbanken could have simply promoted themselves as 'the bank where branches count', or some such empty phrase. But without the accompanying total cultural transformation needed to put the customer and branch in focus, it is doubtful if they would have enjoyed such outstanding success for 25 years;
▶ Southwest Airlines could have simply gone for low, low fares but would have probably gone out of business long ago. They would most certainly not have been the sole US airline to enjoy uninterrupted profitability and have been consistently 'the best' without developing their culture as a key factor.

BOX 4.2 *Antarctic adventure*

Getting the right people does not necessarily mean hiding the drawbacks. The 'right' people will usually respond to a challenge.

The advertisement below appeared in *The Times* in 1910 and produced a massive response for Ernest Shackleton to choose from for his last expedition to the South Pole.

'People to undertake Hazardous Journey: small wages; bitter cold; long months of complete darkness; constant danger; safe return doubtful; honour and recognition in case of success.'

Four Seasons lay great store by both recruitment and management of the demanding staff they have recruited. Everyone working in a Four Seasons hotel – even part timers – goes through a process of several interviews, the final one meeting the General Manager of the hotel. This is to ensure that they are right for the culture of Four Seasons. In turn, managers are expected to apply themselves consistently to the task of managing people. '*A bad manager is one who is capricious in his actions, who thinks he can indulge his own moods. You have to be consistent*', says John Sharpe.

Recruitment as key is true whether or not it is a new organization. Canadian Pacific Hotels, for example, were not 'new' when they started their transformation project in 1987 but they have gradually changed their people in line with their vision. They have achieved this both through new recruitment and using the skills they have applied to recruitment to moving existing people into jobs for which they are better suited (Case Study 4.1 and also Case Study 12.1 on 'recruitment').

Canadian Pacific Hotels have been an object lesson in recognizing the need for a totally integrated approach to change. Refurbishment of the hotels has been directly linked to an external vision for success. This has included changing the culture – and crucially management behaviours within that culture – with a deeper understanding of the markets they wished to serve, reward and recognition based on the demands of the new culture and, crucially, getting and developing the right people.

A guiding light

Getting people onside, welding the organization into a consistent brand, also requires that there be a focus to activity. The composer Igor Stravinsky said that he found it impossible to compose without a 'simple idea' to provide a focus for his thoughts and to guide his efforts. It is this concept, of a simple idea to provide a central theme, which lies behind the concept of a 'guiding light'.

These form an important part of strategy (see also Chapter 5), but are also a key part of culture. A guiding light is more than the general overview provided by a vision or mission statement. Visions and mission statements can all too easily simply become empty phrases. A guiding light is more an aid to achievement. It should combine the simplicity of the vision with a clear idea of what is involved in achieving that vision – the few key objectives and the key values, which will determine 'how we work' to get there.

As with culture, a lot of managers have rejected visions, mission statements and the like as of little or no value – 'simply words on the wall, saying what everyone knows', to quote the chief executive of one major UK company. Unfortunately, that is a reflection of the true experience of many managers. After a lot of deliberation, the 'vision' *has* finished up on the wall and no-one has taken any notice of it.

If that is all the vision is, then it is no vision at all. It has clearly failed to be seen as that simple and robust guide which, properly constructed and used, ensures that what happens with the customer is what was originally intended. Probably, it has left out the key values that in truth govern everyday life – or gives any real sense of purpose to daily activity.

If there is nothing to work beyond the selfish or the remote, dealing with the everyday problems is bound to become, at best, routinized and, at worst, a chore to be got through with the minimum pain. Seeing the value that is being brought to others is a critical part of long-term success – and makes the difference between superservice and service.

The precise usage of visions within a service context – and how to avoid them becoming simply 'words' – is described more fully in

CASE STUDY 4.1 – CANADIAN PACIFIC HOTELS

Cross northwards out of Vancouver, over the beautiful Lions Gate Bridge, and follow the spectacular Sea to Sky Highway into the Coastal Mountains, and you will come to Whistler, perhaps one of the best modern ski resorts in the world, a real village with humanity. The Canadian Pacific hotel, Chateau Whistler Resort, reflects this in style but, even more importantly, in the atmosphere of relaxed friendliness.

Simply typically Canadian? To an extent, yes, but not all Canadian hotels are like that. Chateau Whistler Resort is more than just another hotel. Behind it lies a story of service development which few other organizations have equalled.

Canadian Pacific Hotels have been around a long time and grew up alongside the westward push of the railways. They are a proud 'brand', with a long tradition of service through all forms of travel but the hotels are one of the most visible symbols, occupying some of the most attractive sites in key cities and resort areas – often with buildings which are themselves landmarks, both physically and as a part of Canadian history.

Yet, when Canadian Pacific Hotels, made the decision to instigate a major relaunch of their business in 1987 they realised that spending money on the fabric of the hotels and new marketing approaches were not nearly enough. Their plans to spend significant sums on refurbishment and to open up their marketing to new markets – such as visitors from Europe – would have little effect if the service wasn't upgraded to match. They had to deliver the new vision, not only by making a stay comfortable but by making it a special experience because the people one met, both understood and shared your expectations – whether you were European, American or Japanese.

Seeing the hotels as being essentially the delivery to the customer, not as buildings, seeing the success at that point – the moment of truth – as being the outcome of not just careful design but an integration of all of the elements at this focus – just as in the Service Star in Figure 3.2 – that is what makes a hotel like Chateau Whistler Resort different.

David Roberts, Manager of the hotel and himself an Englishman, talks about 'Navigating change' and the enormous differences that have had to be made by managers such as himself in order to make such a venture a success.

> We are beyond the first stage now and are concentrating much less on training in the conventional sense, but more on experiential learning – getting teams together and working through experiences where we can really come to terms with each other. It hasn't been easy. For a fairly traditional manager, such as myself, it can be very hard to be made to live up to your ambitions. I thought I had come a long way but at our

most recent event, at the rather aptly named Blood River, I was forced to recognize that I still tended to retreat into my old style defensiveness when I was put under pressure or when it suited me. I wasn't as open and easy going a leader as I had thought I was. But the team pulled together and helped me through this. We have a much better understanding of what we have to do to achieve our ambitions.

Lori Mitchell, Human Resources Director at the hotel supports this.

It was more of a surprise for David than anyone else, but we saw no problem because we saw all of us as working towards the same goals for Chateau Whistler Resort, to be one team working towards the guests. We have a lot of staff who pass through this hotel but it is essential that they all feel that it is 'their Chateau Whistler' and that the guests are 'their guests'.

Behind this development lies an enormous amount of work. Carolyn Clark, Vice-President of Human Resources, was involved right from the beginning.

I think our success with people has been because we looked at the solutions over a much wider range of activities and did not see them as isolated aspects. We started by spending six months identifying the sort of people we had to have, analysing what makes a successful employee and turning that into 'key themes' for each type of job.

But this is just one aspect. We have also developed three other aspects in conjunction with this.

▶ *A series of custom-designed programmes on, for example, 'what makes a good co-worker' and 'what makes a good manager?' These are based around 30 or so 'vignettes', moments of truth, when participants can join in and identify the correct action or why there is a problem.*

▶ *Our 'Service Plus' employee-recognition programme, which has both immediate, local aspects – 'star employee', 'star leader' of the month, for example – and national aspects, including an annual meeting in Toronto for the very best and special marks of recognition throughout the year for outstanding service.*

▶ *A programme of development for management, to enable them to be able to use these new opportunities effectively. The management aspects are currently our greatest priority and we are introducing a number of new and different approaches, mainly experiential in nature rather than classroom based.*

There was a lot of scepticism at first, but the sceptics have seen the results and have realized that the investment was fully justified. Now they are the greatest champions. We have everyone onside.

Chapter 5, but the purpose is graphically summarized in Figure 4.8. Here the typical approach to planning – management by instruction – is compared with the service management approach – management by guidance.

Management by instruction seeks to create three-sided boxes, from which there is usually only one way to escape – work harder to sell more. Management by guidance seeks to encourage creativity toward an uplifting goal, 'The Guiding Light', allowing and harvesting a great deal more from freedom and creativity.

Guiding lights, and core visions, can be seen to be most successful when they tap into the desire of people to achieve something beyond the everyday. Something more than just earning money, for themselves or for shareholders. David Packard, for example, always emphasized that Hewlett Packard must see profits not as the goal but as a reward for 'making a contribution to society'. Such a focus is true of all of the superservice organizations referred to in this book.

Finally, an organization is also much more likely to keep people onside, be consistent even at a time of change, when the future

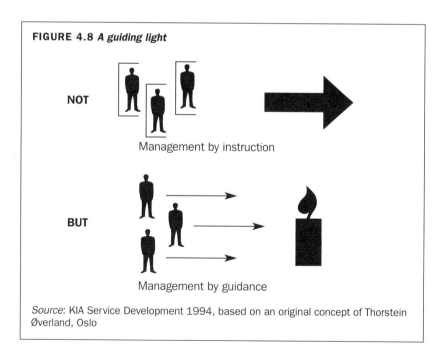

FIGURE 4.8 *A guiding light*

NOT

Management by instruction

BUT

Management by guidance

Source: KIA Service Development 1994, based on an original concept of Thorstein Øverland, Oslo

builds on existing strengths, tapping into the good things from the past, not rejecting them. How can people be positive about the new values and work as a team when they are being asked to reject all their past? It can only give rise to the 'East German syndrome' when a large part of those involved will be at best unwilling participants, even when they believe in the direction of events. They have lost too much self-esteem.

This is a difficult scenario for the group or for individuals to deal with. It will certainly weaken contributions in the early stages of transition. Better, by far, to build on what is there, to tap into, say, a value system which focuses on people and use that as a basis for creating a more effective and profitable organization.

Acknowledgements and further reading

page 49   Fons Trompenaars (1993) *Riding the Waves of Culture – Understanding Cultural Diversity in Business*, Nicholas Brealey.

page 52   Schneider, B. and Bowen, D. E. (1963) 'Employee and customer perceptions of service in banks, replication and extension', University of Maryland.

page 54   Unpublished research.

page 54   Irons, K. (1993) *Managing Service Companies: Strategies for Success*, Addison Wesley.

The following company gave generously of time and material in providing insights for the background to this and other chapters:

Café Rouge, London, part of the Pelican Group.

Woolworths plc, London.

For the manager interested in developing a wider understanding of culture and its value in business, the books of Charles Handy (see numerous references) and Chris Argyris (see also p. 118, 239) offer good insights, as do the original versions of the publications under 'acknowlededgments' – and the works of William Shakespeare, to mention but one of many classical writers who have shown an in-depth understanding of the human character and its reaction to events.

Other possible reading includes:

Bauman, Z. (1996) *Alone Again: Ethics after Certainty*, Demos.

Campbell, A. *et al.* (1990) *A Sense of Mission*, The Economist Books.

Handy, C. (1995) *Beyond Certainty – The Changing World of Organisation*, Hutchinson.

Majchzak, A. and Wang, Q. (1996) 'Breaking the functional mind-set in process organizations', *Harvard Business Review*, Sept/Oct.

Morgan, G. (1986) *Images of Organisation*, Sage Press.

Strategic management

The situation, that's the boss.

Ramrod, 'Roadie' for the Grateful Dead, to executive
frustrated by the band's methods of working

About this chapter

Successful planning for achievement in a service and the implementation of that plan are not separate operations but two interwoven threads, between the original idea and a successful outcome. The adoption of a strategic-management approach not only reflects this, concentrating on the possibilities and the achievement not just the figures, but also reflects the facts of life today – people want to be involved, to play a part, however small, in creating the future. The best people will only stay where this is a possibility.

This chapter will look at what is involved in strategic management.

▶ The principles of strategic management, a process as much as a plan, and one which is reflective of the demands of service organizations.

▶ What is involved in constructing a strategic guideline and a 'guiding light'.

▶ Some examples of strategic documents.

▶ Why budgets are a poor basis for development planning.

▶ The value and process of 'taking a position' – being exact about 'what precisely you mean to what market'.

The crucial link

Arne Mårtensson's office has a magnificent view over Stockholm's beautiful inner harbour and royal palace. But for Arne, it is just one of the places he works, for much of his time is spent visiting with branch managers and having discussions elsewhere in the bank. For Svenska Handelsbanken is managed by the principles of strategic management – not a word they use, and they were doing it long before the term was first coined, in any codified sense.

For them 'strategy' is a general guidance, interwoven with implementation into a seamless pattern. The ideas and ideals that lie behind the success of Handelsbanken are clear to see for all those who deal with the bank and they have created one of the most enduring twentieth century successes in banking. As much as any service can, the bank have ensured that what happens to the customer is what was originally planned.

In a service organization, this is the strategic skill – to ensure that what goes in the top, as the 'big idea' – is what consistently comes out at implementation. Strategy is the painstaking construction of a way of working which provides secure and lasting links between the vision of the organization and that vital interaction with the customer.

Strategic management

Old-style planning rarely comes near to achieving this. What is required is a more fluid and dynamic process, which allows for strategy to be open to the influences of implementation, and for management to be close to implementation. A system which provides simple links from the original idea and the direction of that idea to the coalface – with those who have to implement it out there with the customer – and with sensitive feedback.

This is strategic management, in which the creation of strategy and the daily management of the business are acts of constant recreation in response to events and experience. This is of particular significance. The 'product' cannot be manufactured to a precise specification before it is sold. Implementation will always be open to variability in interpretation and perception. This variability is an important part of providing individuality, the distinctive feature between one service and another. The crosscurrents and uncertainties that this can produce make it very difficult to make sure that the customer gets the experience that had been planned for.

To overcome the variability of implementation and perception requires that those responsible give from the heart not just the mind.

Those who are involved in implementation will give of their best when they feel they 'own' the strategy. Then, and only then, they will give from the heart.

In such situations, strategy is more likely to be effective when it is a guideline, not a rigid framework. The learning process that needs to be associated with this is an important feature of strategic management (see also Chapter 6). Rigorously applied, it has the effect of re-shaping and reforming strategy in the light of events. It goes too far to say, as some writers have, that as a result service strategy should be entirely 'bottom-up' or be 'the sum of its parts', as that would lead to total uncertainty about 'where?' the organization is going. It is this lead, a clear direction, which the guideline needs to give. The process is then dynamic; the further creation of thinking is interwoven with its implementation, both creating ownership and reflecting the realities of the interaction with the market.

Blurring the lines in this way may seem heresy to managers brought up in the belief that once delegated you stand back. The fact is that this was probably never a very realistic approach. It certainly does not fit with the situations which arise in developing service, or indeed the flatter, less hierarchical organizations generally in favour today. To succeed, strategic management needs:

▶ a dynamic system of developing plans which allows for intuition and insight;

▶ a hands-on feel for what is happening 'down there' and the opportunity for those at the coalface to communicate back what is happening – to colour, indeed alter, plans in the light of experience, and

▶ a relaxation of hierarchy.

It is doubtful whether any organization will be able to deliver consistent superservice without such an approach. Indeed, such an approach is already a reflection of most of the successful deliverers of superservice today. Arne Mårtensson at Svenska Handelsbanken, Herb Kelleher at Southwest, Liisa Joronen at SOL, Rebecca Jenkins at Lane Group, Julian Metcalfe at Pret A Manger, Jo Cumming at Café Rouge, all spend a great part of their time meeting with, and talking to, operational people at all levels in the business – Mårtensson assesses this at about 50 per cent of his time – and do so with no threat to their intermediate managers.

BOX 5.1 *Strategy in context*

Igor Ansoff, the originator of the term 'strategic management', wrote in his book, of the same title:

'A separation of decision and action leadership is somewhat artificial, because the two are opposite sides of the same coin, not separable in either time or place. Many studies of decision processes point to the fact that a separation of leadership into "planning" first and "implementation" afterwards does not represent the strategic reality in which decision and action are interwoven in a complex sequential-feedback situation'.

Over the years, strategy has, for the most part, become merely a way of describing 'superior plans'. It has also become weighted down with facts and figures. Not only does this create a situation in which it is difficult to develop dialogue – large quantities of figures have been shown to be a major barrier to questioning and the development of dialogue – but it usually results in the central purpose becoming lost. Further, while top management see a lot of meaning in highly quantified goals and measures, the individuals 'at the coal-face' find it easier to relate to qualitative issues that directly affect both what they do and is expected of them by the customer in the pursuit of 'satisfaction'.

The reaction to this situation, in which planning for the future seems to be more important than action, is often a complete rejection of planning in almost any form, except the easily quantified but generally stultifying budgets.

It was not always so. Strategy as we know it today, largely stems from the work of the military in the nineteenth century, and in particular the codifying of strategy by a Prussian colonel, Karl von Clausewitz in his classic book, *On War*. Strategy was the *guiding light* which gave general direction to the field generals and was meant to be *'taken with the army into the field in order to arrange particulars on the spot'*.

By the First World War, strategy had become sufficiently far from this ideal that it was being practised by distant generals who insisted on its slavish implementation, whatever the consequences. Those who were close to the 'action' knew it would not work but felt they had little alternative but to try.

Generally, strategy continued as remote planning exercises, and when it was adapted to business became increasingly centred on creating detailed forecasts for events that never transpired, at least in the form in which they were planned. Most people gave up and simply settled for short time scales and budgets.

The re-establishment of strategic thinking through strategic management is a revolution – in its original, true, sense as a return – seeing strategy as a source of inspiration and a guide, not as a straight-jacket that suppresses learning. The 'guiding light' (see Figure 4.8) can be seen as a direct part of this, providing everyone with a clear view of the aims and leaving considerable opportunity for interpretation, even improvisation, in the light of actual events and opportunities. It is the task of management to maintain the original concepts of the 'guiding light' and to drive out functional blocks and other barriers that impede its achievement.

BOX 5.2 *Some examples of vision*

Three examples, which while very different in their approach and content, share characteristics:

▶ they provide a short, but clear, over-view, and
▶ they tell you what the real purpose of the business is and what underpins it.

First, two interesting contrasts which reflect – and are reflected in – the cultures.

Southwest Airlines

The mission of Southwest Airlines is dedication to the highest quality of customer service delivered with a sense of warmth, friendliness, individual pride, and company spirit.

To our Employees

We are committed to providing our employees with a stable work environment with equal opportunity for learning and personal growth. Creativity and innovation are encouraged for improving the effectiveness of Southwest Airlines. Above all, employees will be provided with the same concern, respect and caring attitude within the organization that they are expected to share externally with every Southwest customer.

Pret A Manger

OUR MISSION is to create hand-made, natural food, avoiding the obscure chemicals, additives and preservatives common to so much of the 'prepared' and 'fast' food in the market today.

Southwest concentrate 100 per cent on people – Pret 100 per cent on the product.

Pret, a relatively new organization still establishing itself, has made a real breakthrough in providing food which is both fresh and interesting as well as wholesome.

Southwest are past that stage and are comfortable with the product – ongoing success is going to be sustained by people. For Pret, this will be the next challenge.

Another contrast is Mastercare. This reflects their (Mastercare's) need to support the Dixons Group's retail organization. It is somewhat internal, but clarifies what Mastercare have to do to be of value in the delivery.

Mastercare

It is our purpose to provide an after-sales service for Dixons and Currys, which is perceived by the customer as a positive factor in deciding where to shop.

In so doing we will seek to achieve this with maximum simplicity, economy and efficiency.

What all three share is a clear and unequivocal statement about who they are and what is seen as critical to their success. All give those who work for them the vision of building something greater than profit for a distant shareholder.

A strategic guideline

In strategic management, the creation of strategy is primarily concerned with the creation of a loose outline. This is more a direction toward an agreed aim than detailed plans. The starting point in this process is an overview of what the organization sees itself as being – the vision – then the key objectives and values. The whole forms the principle guideline, the 'guiding light'.

The first task in developing a 'guiding light' (Figure 4.8) is the vision or mission statement. This should provide a simple, robust overview, clear in direction yet flexible and dynamic enough to allow for and withstand the reality of implementation. For a vision to have a value it has to have real meaning in the business and to the people involved. It has to say something relevant about where that business is going in terms which create a feeling of 'going somewhere', of this being 'valuable and fulfilling'.

In fact, an explicit statement of this type is an important feature of almost every service which people generally admire, playing a crucial part in creating a guidance for activity and avoiding the quest for growth becoming merely a series of incremental steps, with little overall form or substance. Few have achieved a lasting success without a document of this kind. Some examples are shown in Box 5.2.

Visions can take many forms, from a few simple phrases to a booklet. Such booklets can be pictorial, as is the one for Virgin Atlantic. More often they will be words, but words worked in a way which steers the reader through the thinking rather than just setting out 'what'. A particularly good example is that of Svenska Handelsbanken. The style differs considerably from those shown Box 5.2, but as Arne Mårtensson says: *'We have a very strong framework and everybody has to believe in the way we are working. Instead of saying everyday what you have to do, we would rather set guidelines and within this it is up to you'.*

The book runs in total to 30 pages and is written by the Chief Executive himself. Entitled *Our Way*, it has a clear flow through from a 'personal' introduction, 'our objectives', to 'what we want to be', 'where we want to be' and 'how we want to do it'. It cannot be reproduced here because it is jealously guarded as one of the key strands in the Bank's strategy, but a flavour is given in Box 5.3.

BOX 5.3 *'Our way'*

Extracts from the Svenska Handelsbanken booklet

Preface

'An organization like ours cannot operate just on formal rules and regulations. We must share a common store of ideas and values about how to conduct our business. It is called a corporate culture. This culture must be kept alive in a continuous dialogue. This dialogue is also important to guarantee that our ideas change and develop in step with the times. If they do not, they will deteriorate to a bunch of assertions, withered and worthless. The constant will to change and improve our ways is the very lifeblood of our bank. It is not enough to be number one today. We should be number one in the year 2000 as well. This pamphlet is a contribution to that dialogue.'

Our objectives

'Our overall objective is to exceed average profitability for other Swedish listed banks. By profitability we mean return on equity after tax.

To retain our high profitability, we must ensure that our customers are more satisfied than those of other banks.

In the long run, above-average profitability can only be built on a cost advantage. We must make sure that our costs are lower than the other banks.

If we spend less money, but still make our customers more satisfied, we are more beneficial to society than other banks. We satisfy our customers' needs better, while consuming less resources. Our productivity is higher.

It must be fun to work for Svenska Handelsbanken. We try to hire the best people, and keep them until they retire. As far as possible, promotion shall be internal.

We must always keep inside the legal and ethical framework of banking.

We should be the best Nordic bank'.

A guiding light

To be a complete guiding light, however, it is necessary for it to be an aid to achievement. The vision needs underpinning with a set of specific aims – the objectives – and the way the organization intends to work to achieve those objectives – the values – if it is not to be mere hope.

Values are often underrated in their importance and confused with objectives. To clarify the difference, it may help to take another football analogy, this time as the owner of a football team. As the owner, you may decide to put money into the team with the intention of winning lots of titles, and you could be specific about these in terms of 'what' and 'time'. These are the objectives. But you might go further, and lay down some rules of conduct, such as not tolerating deliberate foul play, whatever the circumstances, or paying fancy prices or fees for star players. These are the values.

Both objectives and values need to be tangible and capable of measurement against achievement – and about the limits which management set on interpretation. So, for example, because of its strategic significance to the core idea, The Body Shop gives clear guidance on environmental issues; British Airways exercise control on the usage of their 'brand'; Canadian Pacific Hotels on the imperative to use their recruitment profiles.

Objectives and values should always be limited to a maximum of four of each, since that is all that can be borne in mind in the heat of battle, face-to-face with the customer. They should also be complete, that is they should cover all aspects of activity, such as finance, human resources, marketing and technology. Balance these out in the strategy, not as it goes along. Nothing destroys the value of a guiding light more surely than the introduction of key organizational objectives or values on top of and, often, unrelated, to this.

Perhaps the most persistent examples are those related to costs and cost saving. Few organizations are not concerned with minimizing costs and most have cost-cutting drives at some time. Since these are usually given considerable emphasis – and hard measures – they typically override, swamp even, all other considerations and leave everyone saying 'Well, at least we know the true priorities'. Paradoxically, because such efforts are detached, they often fail. The changes of effort and direction that would have made them achievable have not been touched. All that happens is that they destroy each other.

Some find it difficult to see how 'cost cutting' can be a value. It is not, but thrift is – a way we work to achieve our objectives as surely as any other value. If it is important, as it usually is, it should be stated as such. It can then be kept in balance with the other values and runs much less risk of becoming either diversionary or being seen as the 'flavour of the month'. It is not without reason that the best service organizations are usually the most thrifty, but as a value not as a stand-alone exercise.

Union Reinsurance Company (Union Re), a small Zurich-based reinsurer, is one company which believes its success was built from a clear guiding light. Their original 'Leitsatz' still reads well and is shown in Case Study 5.1.

The success of achieving a clear focus over the past few years has enabled Union Re to break away from just being a 'follower' in the reinsurance market, accepting percentages of risks, largely valued by others, to taking a lead in their own right. *'It's a major change and calls for a new Leitsatz'*, says Pierre Ozendo, the new Chief Executive. *'We have an excellent base from which to achieve our new vision, but excellence is not a place but a process. We have to continue to strive, and in our new role we want to become the preferred advisor and reinsurance partner to our clients'*.

CASE STUDY 5.1 – UNION REINSURANCE COMPANY

Union Reinsurance Company (Union Re) are a medium-sized reinsurance company based in Zurich. With just 200 staff in one control location, an international reputation and a traditionally entrepreneurial style, Union Re were well placed to offer an alternative to their more powerful parent, Swiss Re, both for the market (insurance companies) and for employees.

For employees, it could be an exciting prospect. In a country where traditional hierarchies and methods could make it irksome for young people it gave the promise of an opportunity to be involved and exercise independent thought, and at the same time offering Swiss reliability.

But things did not work out that way. Although there was a mission statement, it was insufficiently precise. Although there was an influx of bright new people, filled with enthusiasm and skill, there were no rules of engagement to allow them to develop ideas which challenged the status quo, at least without threat to others.

A key part of overcoming this was the creation of a new mission statement in the form of a guiding light, or Leitsatz, which not only clarified the 'mission' but said clearly what this meant in terms of key objectives and key values.

Looking back on it, Peter Colombo, who was Chief Executive in the crucial years from 1989 to 1996, says:

> We have come a long way since then and have more than doubled our net asset value, a crucial measure for a reinsurer. Now we are embarking on a new and extremely ambitious phase – and with the confident backing of our parent, who have agreed our plans and request for a substantial increase in capital. This has all been made possible by the transformation we went through in the first half of the nineties. The adoption of our Leitsatz was a crucial part of this, as it created a focus for everyone to rally round. It wasn't just a piece of paper but was used all the time. People often brought it out at meetings, to challenge or to clarify – 'why this proposal?'; 'what does it do for our strategy?'.

Union Re – Leitsatz

It is our aim to be a successful reinsurance company operating at world-market level and achieving our success through a reputation for providing solutions that make our customers successful.

We will provide this distinction for Union Re through personal contact, at all levels, with our customers. This will also ensure that they may have full confidence in our operations. To achieve this, wherever possible we aim to engage in a long-term partnership with our customers in a manner which is mutually beneficial, supporting our customers in the achievement of their objectives and meeting the needs of our staff and shareholders for a dynamic, secure and profitable organization.

Objectives

To fulfil our mission, we must achieve the following objectives:

▶ *Customer satisfaction.* In a changing world, the long-term viability and distinctiveness of Union Re will be best assured by ensuring that we understand our customers' requirements fully. Our services and solutions must actively help them to achieve their objectives. We will therefore build such relationships by demonstrating that we are an organization that understands them and is there to provide a valued and responsive service.

▶ *Security.* In order to guarantee security, we must maintain our financial strength through adequate capitalization and the continuation of that through profitable underwriting, information and the full backing of our shareholders.

▶ *Motivation of staff.* Staff are our major asset in any such achievement. We must motivate them through clear leadership and empowerment towards the fulfilment of our corporate goals. Our concern for the satisfaction and well-being of the staff must be evident.

▶ *Reliability.* Reliability means fulfilling our promises and our obligations to all of our partners (customers, staff, shareholders). It must be an integral part of our internal culture and of our dealings with our customers and our shareholders.

To achieve these objectives means we must adopt these key values.

▶ *Teamwork/cooperation.* We must all work together as a team, freely exchanging information and sharing concerns and problems, with respect, recognition and trust in and for each other's contribution.

▶ *Personal contact.* Through regular personal contacts, our partners will get to know the persons in our company to whom they may turn with all their queries. To this end, we will ensure a continuity of personal contact.

▶ *Technical excellence/professionalism.* We must ensure that we establish, maintain and practise a high level of professionalism. We must be seen as an insurer who uses these skills to help others to be successful.

▶ *Value.* For us quality stands for the optimal fulfilment of our services and while doing so we bear all the needs and requirements of our customers in mind.

The strategic process

But strategic management is more about a process than a document. Since service companies are characterized by large numbers of operationally-driven people – people who are happiest with 'doing something' and generally unhappy with lots of planning – this process, the interweaving of strategy and implementation, will be at its most effective where it taps into this bias.

The more it is a 'real' time exercise and not some generalized future plan, the more effective it will be. It must also be external, because the purpose of any enterprise must be to achieve on the outside. This applies not only to 'for profit' organizations. For a social club, the result should be happy and satisfied club members and their guests. For a school, the result should be students equipped with skills that can help them in later life.

It is also not budgets and, indeed, not primarily a financial task. Nor should it be seen as marketing, since that carries with it the thought that it is some specialized task which only affects some people, or requires some specialized training or knowledge.

Rather, it should be seen as being about:

▶ the development of the enterprise;
▶ linking the external with the internal;
▶ bringing into direct relationship the usage of internal resources against those activities most likely to lead to the achievement of the objectives, and
▶ being a bridge from 'our world' to 'their world' and considering the fact that these worlds are interwoven at that crucial point – the interaction, the moment of truth.

To achieve this, it cannot be simply incremental, a step-by-step plan which perpetuates the past. The differences involved are illustrated in the two models shown in Figures 5.1 and 5.2.

In Figure 5.1 the future is merely a set of incremental steps, where each step becomes progressively less and less in touch with the reality and less and less influenced by the drive of external events. It is simply a form of conventional operational planning most often based on budgets and characterized by a spurious exactitude, which often grows more exact the further it goes into the future.

In Figure 5.2, the guiding light has become the central point of 'our aim' – where we are going to. The strategic task is then to reach that

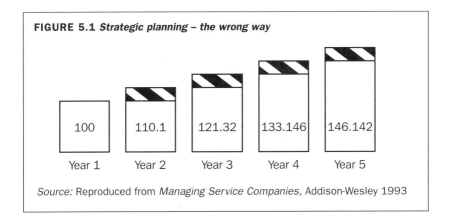

FIGURE 5.1 *Strategic planning – the wrong way*

100	110.1	121.32	133.146	146.142
Year 1	Year 2	Year 3	Year 4	Year 5

Source: Reproduced from *Managing Service Companies,* Addison-Wesley 1993

point, discarding activity which is not relevant to such achievement. It is at this point that the lines between strategy and implementation start to become blurred. Those closest to the action can see the most effective way of achieving the aim within the guideline, and their discovery, their actions may, and often will, lead to a modification of the way that strategy is realized, even to the very aim itself.

Using the principles in Figure 5.2, it is possible to:

▶ integrate the thinking about 'what' and 'how to get there';
▶ understand what has to be changed and what should never change because it is sacred to the whole reason behind the organization and its very existence;

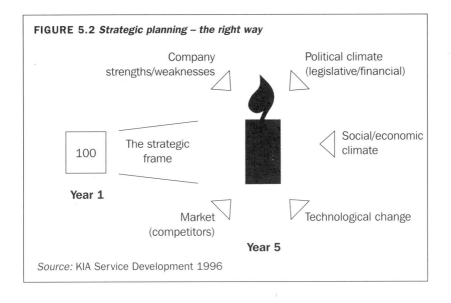

FIGURE 5.2 *Strategic planning – the right way*

Source: KIA Service Development 1996

▶ have the faith to be different because of a clear-sighted view of what the future may, or could, bring;

▶ give more objective consideration to matching internal and external efficiencies – that is, it is easier to stand back and look at what the organization is, or has, and what is needed for success;

FIGURE 5.3 *Guiding lights to service stars – a glossary of terms*

Some of these terms have not yet been mentioned in the main text but this short glossary will help to put the following sections into an overall context.

STRATEGIC MANAGEMENT

This is an overall approach to strategy which is more about the 'way we manage' than a plan. It sees strategy and its implementation as part of a dynamic, fluid process in which the process is as important as any documents which result. Documents are there for the record, to refresh and act as a guide in daily life and against which to judge action. There are two key parts.

1. The strategic guideline

The overall term for the 'guidance' documents such as:

▶ **A Guiding Light.** The broad guideline which would incorporate a vision (or mission statement if you prefer), which is an overview of the type of business you want to be and the benefits for those who have to invest their money or their careers together with a view of what has to be achieved to get there, and specifically.

▶ **Objectives/values.** The translation of the vision in terms of the key objectives that have to be achieved for the vision to become a reality and the way it is intended to work to get there (the values).

2. The business development plan

The main set of documents that take the strategic guideline forward and act as the basis for monitoring and correction. There are three core elements which can help to make this effective:

▶ **A destination.** The immediate tasks for the next 'n' years of:
 – what the organization will look like
 – what will be different
 – how it will feel different
 – what has to be done to get there.

▶ **Service Stars.** The translation of the destination into specifics for each market (segment).

▶ **Action plans.** The day-to-day control and monitoring documentation, providing a focus for feedback and review within a dialogue.

 The business development plan is discussed more fully in Chapter 11.

▶ from this, develop a sustainable competitive advantage, and

▶ provide guidelines – parameters – within which implementation may evolve to best meet the realities of events.

The important aspects of turning a guiding light into a business plan are covered in Chapter 11, 'Making it happen'. An overall outline of the elements in a typical strategic management process is shown in Figure 5.3. There are two aspects, though, that directly affect the process of planning at the early, guideline, level which require consideration. These are the need to be free of the constraints of a budgetary format and to be very specific about both the market it is intended to tackle and the value brought to that market.

Why not budgets?

The planning systems of an organization should be the framework that makes learning possible, providing an opportunity for experience to feedback. Unfortunately, it is often the planning system which is the barrier, cutting-off learning by focusing on a mechanistic system which extols correctness rather than creation, efficiency rather than effectiveness, short-term fixing rather than long-term remedy.

For a planning system to be a learning system, it should seek to:

inspire	**not**	**simply direct**
create	**not**	**just produce**
imagine	**not**	**just think**
be dynamic	**not**	**static**
be fun	**not**	**drudgery**
emphasize process	**not**	**content**

The conventional approach to budgets is rarely a good basis for a guideline. Whether at the organization level, as covered so far, or at action plan level, which will be touched on later, it is likely to create the wrong focus. From a business point of view budgets can be an important tool, but as a guideline they are more misleading than helpful. This is because they have a number of significant defects.

CASE STUDY 5.2 – SVENSKA HANDELSBANKEN

With their strongly-held beliefs about planning, Svenska Handels-banken have eliminated the budget process in its entirety and:

▶ control branches, the focus of all Bank activity, by simply relating costs to revenue. The ratio of 1:2.3 is the best in Europe, according to independent research by rival UBS of Switzerland;

▶ do not set targets for managers, but assume them to be doing their best to increase business within the potential of their area.

It works! Indeed, the Bank attributes its very successful track record of profit and customer acceptance to this very type of approach, encouraging managers to do what is right for the customer in the long term, or to quote *Our Way* again:

> *The foundation of our view of banking is that we focus on the customer, not on our products. How much we sell of each of our products is of no interest. Our mission is to fully satisfy the needs of each customer, while making a profit for the bank.*

Replacing budgets with a pure system of strategic management, Handelsbanken has:

▶ been crystal clear in its overall strategic objective of developing service relationships;

▶ insisted that the branch is the focus of all activity, even when the customer is a major company;

▶ based its report structure on being able to analyse branch prof-itability (the key 'building block' in the structure) by customer, and so by relationship;

▶ put considerable faith in the branch manager's ability to act in the best long-term interests of the bank, and given the support and encouragement necessary for this;

▶ been quick to take action when managers failed to measure up to the responsibilities;

▶ given branch management the help needed to create teamwork at the branch, and the reward system to match this (a generous company-wide profit-sharing scheme makes no distinctions of salary base);

▶ created a culture of leadership, where both regional and head office management see themselves as resources of the branches;

▶ kept open the channels of communication between levels of management, so that everyone may learn from one another and customers need never be more than two layers away from the top.

▶ Being money driven – and indeed largely cost driven – they tend to ignore the market potential, either overlooking opportunity or simply failing to take account of market pressures, especially local variances or competitive moves.

▶ Being short term, they most often accentuate the short-term return and so cloud the effort needed for long-term change, a key issue in services.

▶ Being numbers driven, they tend to be unattractive to anyone other than finance people and thus are seen as a chore to be completed quickly, not as an aid.

▶ With a focus on a 'point in time' and the current year they are likely to fail to emphasize the value of customers over time, and the need to link resource usage – particularly the key service resource of time – directly to the central tenet of service philosophy, the relationship.

While many organizations will feel that it is still necessary to underpin strategy with budgets, it may be better to think in terms of 'action plans'. Effective action plans relate resource usage directly to market aims. They combine both internal costs and external income in a form which brings them into direct relationship, one with the other (Chapter 11). Certainly few will have the nerve to carry out the radical approach adopted by Svenska Handelsbanken, where Arne Mårtensson's reaction to being asked 'Were they laid back about budgets?' was *'Laid back? We can't be, because we don't have them'* (see also Case Study 5.2). They have been applying the principles of strategic management since 1972. It is now embedded in the Bank as a way of life which everyone believes in and works by. To the outsider there are a number of features which seem surprising and – given the strong central control the Bank exercises – perhaps the most surprising of these is the lack of budgets and forecasts. They are simply seen as an unnecessary deflection from the real task of developing market-based activity, and to be more often wrong than right.

Taking a position

The purpose of this exercise, is to ensure what needs to be achieved, and with whom, has been clarified precisely. What you want the expectations of your customers to be of you and how you are going to meet those expectations consistently. It will expose as no other activity the strengths and shortcomings of the thinking. It will also ensure that not only are the plans strategically sound but that they are tactically possible.

There are four critical questions be answered.

1 Who are you competing against?
2 What are your strengths and weaknesses?
3 Which sources of business offer the most potential?
4 What are the buying incentives?

1. Who are you competing against?

This is not the simple question it may seem. An airline's main competition may be from alternative methods of transport rather than other airlines; a restaurant's from eating at home rather than other restaurants; an insurance company's from other methods of achieving savings or security rather than other insurance policies; an intermediary 'going direct' or from other advisers rather than other intermediaries in the same sector.

The thinking may start with the same core product – a hotel room, a hamburger, a life insurance policy – but then add value in a number of different ways to meet different consumer needs, as shown in Figure 5.4. Alternatively, it is possible – and in a pure sense, preferable – to start with 'need' and come back to the core product.

This particular question has a 'chicken and egg' aspect, since it will only be able to be fully answered once the process of taking a position is complete. However, unless there is at the start a broad analysis, later thinking will simply reflect a natural internal bias.

2. What are your strengths and weaknesses?

What are you good at? How does this relate to the strengths and weaknesses of the 'competition' you have defined?

It is important to consider this in relation to all of the various aspects of the 'offer' – the solution. Again, these are summarized in the service mix – core products and price, personnel, image, delivery and the customers themselves.

3. Which sources of business offer the most potential?

Not all potential markets offer the same possibilities of return on the resources employed. Retaining existing customers is a fundamentally different task from seeking out and capturing new customers. Dealing with customers who have time and want patient explanation is different to dealing with customers who want speed. Yet, to draw a parallel, many staff are spread across demand segments of such diversity that it is analogous to a McDonald's server doubling up as a

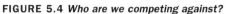

FIGURE 5.4 *Who are we competing against?*

Core product	Role	Consumer need	Substitutes/ Competition
Hamburger	1. A convenient meal	Speed	Not eating; other fast foods; snack foods
	2. An eating experience	Enjoyment	Other fast foods and restaurants; other social activities
Hotel room	1. A convenient stopping place	A roof; some-where to rest	Not stopping; other easily accessed hotels; bed and breakfast
	2. Prestige	To reflect one's position in life	Other grand hotels; apartments; villas; clubs
Life insurance	1. A form of pro-tection	Security	Taking a risk; personal saving; avoiding danger; reducing risk; other policies
	2. A form of saving	Income tomor-row/investment	Other forms of saving, both insurance and non-insurance

Source: KIA Management Consultants 1990

waiter in a stylish restaurant in the same shift! 'Attractive' segments may also be made unattractive by competition; the apparent large potential is, in reality, limited. Specifically:

▶ Is there a need for new customers? Or is there a need to extend the range of services used by existing customers, or increase usage of existing services?

▶ Is it necessary to take customers from competition? Or create entirely new customers?

▶ Is there a need to regain lost customers, or stem the flow of departing customers?

Simple questions, but without any sensible answers if the previous questions have not been fully analysed. Avoiding such a choice may easily destroy the chances of competing effectively because few people are equally good at both winning and retaining customers.

4. What are the buying incentives?

Think about the interaction, the focus of the Service Star, and be absolutely firm about what are the buying appeals which are most likely to motivate the chosen target in your favour, and against competition, at that point. What is it that is distinctive or unique about you?

The decision is crucial because it affects the basis on which value will be added. Is a plane seat a chance to sample glamour, a place to work or relax, or a prelude to a holiday or business trip? Or, for example, is an insurance investment value for money, peace of mind or the assurance of certainty, to mention but a few possibilities?

Once this analysis is complete, it is possible to review question one, competition. Has it changed the market position? Should it? In other words, is the positioning weaker or stronger in relation to competitors?

Carried through rigorously, this exercise will ensure that the finally-developed strategic guidelines are an effective response to the challenge of the future. Taking the guidelines through to implementation requires an equally effective communication, processes for learning from that implementation and leadership, not just management. These are the subjects of the next three chapters.

Acknowledgements and further reading

page 75   Ansoff, H.I. (1979) *Strategic Management*, Macmillan.
page 75   Karl von Clausewitz (1832) *On War*.
page 87   'Taking a position' is based on the work of Alvin Ackenbaum, 1973, then Executive Vice President of J. Walter Thompson, New York.

The following company gave generously of time and material in providing insights for the background to this and other chapters:

The Body Shop, Littlehampton, Sussex.
Union Reinsurance Company, Zurich.

Strategic Management and *On War* (see above) are both tough reading but worth the effort for someone deeply involved in developing strategy. Two other books which give a deeper insight into strategy as a process are:

Perry, L.T., Stott, R.G., Smallwood, W.N. (1993) *Real-Time Strategy*, John Wiley.

Trout, J. (1989) *Bottom-up Marketing*, McGraw-Hill.

Communications

I sure wish I had done a better job of communicating with GM people. I'd do it differently next time around and make sure they understood and shared my vision for the company.

Roger Smith, Former President, General Motors

About this chapter

Strategic management requires effective communication, internally as well as externally. Communication is the mortar that holds the service mix together; allows for its expression at the focus – the interaction with the customer.

The Service Star (Figure 3.2) is a reflection of this. Though it plays a more obvious role in 'image' and 'delivery', there is no one element of 'communication', rather it is a part of everything. To be effective, it has to be more than simply a relay of messages; it has to be dialogue, establishing common understanding and conviction.

This chapter will look at what is involved in communication.

▶ The need to create understanding through dialogue.

▶ Some of the common barriers to achieving dialogue.

▶ An appreciation of what is involved in listening.

▶ An understanding of why listening is such a key skill.

▶ The issues involved in both internal and external communications.

▶ The role of communication in establishing brand identity in a service.

Turning up the volume

The scene could be almost any organization, in any place. Those in the centre of things, who may have, and in fact probably have, spent the last few months in developing the thinking, reconciling their own opinions with those of colleagues and coming to terms with the implications, not least personally, are about to launch the 'big idea' or the 'great change'.

Great care has been taken to choose the right words. The possible objections have all been run through and unarguable answers refined. It is all being committed to slides or overheads, or perhaps computer-produced graphics. Rehearsal has been rigorous. Maybe expensive communicators have been hired to help get the message across with presentation, or even with celebrity acts.

The great day dawns, it all goes well – even that troublemaker Jenkins has been kept quiet – and the great mass have confirmed top management's view of them, that they are a good set of willing operators but have little to contribute to thinking.

Yet two years later, the 'big idea' or the 'great change' has sunk, without trace. Or it has been merely one of a number of 'even bigger ideas' or 'even greater changes', all now blending, expensively, one into the other, but with little discernible benefit to profits or the customer – nothing much has changed at the front line.

We are all inclined to think that improving communication means we have to say more, or say it better. We see it as telling someone, something. To use the phrase at the end of the second paragraph above, 'To get the message across'. If we find that people don't understand or, afterwards, don't know what is going on, we elaborate a little more or simply turn up the volume – or blame them for not listening.

But it rarely works, because unless those who must live the strategy feel that they 'own' it, that the ideas embodied in the plans are as much the expression of their own way of thinking, they can never give that bit extra that makes new ideas work, let alone be turned into superservice. Lost to the central idea, implementation will become prey to functional interpretations. There will be no strategic cohesion.

The need to create understanding

Such concerns are not 'soft'. They have real and tangible value. For Roger Smith (see quote at the beginning of this chapter) it was the chance he saw he had missed. He had failed, in his own view, to create that understanding – or even more that sharing – which, he clearly felt, would have transformed his tenure at General Motors.

If this was felt to be true even in a manufacturing company, where the objectives of people's work are largely passive goods such as cars, then in a service where the objectives of people's work are reactive targets – people – it is doubly so:

▶ **Externally, the purchase of a service can represent a high risk decision**

For the customer both because, in anticipation, it is so difficult to judge effectiveness and, once delivered, it can be difficult to 'undo' and usually impossible to exchange or take back!

For some services this risk factor is extremely high and so consequently is the need for understanding and dialogue. Hairdressing is a prime example but by no means the only one. British Airways reckon that if a customer has found someone to talk to after an event which has been the cause for a complaint, the customer is six times more likely to remain a customer than a person who has no one to listen to him or her.

▶ **Internally, those who perform the service must carry the message with conviction**

It is they who must lower the threshold of risk for the customers. They have to both believe and understand the problems and uncertainties of the buyer. An example of this is often to be found in the utilities and other privatized organizations. Changes to a more market-led approach coupled to the need to satisfy shareholders, leads to a concern 'that we don't care about our customers anymore'.

This paradoxical result is due to the fact that, historically, the organization has probably had a view of helping the customer, but in a paternalistic way: 'We know best' or, to quote an actual example, from a manager at British Telecom in its early days, 'Customers do not know enough about telephones to allow them to buy a cheap one – they will regret it later'. Too little time has been devoted to allowing those concerned to come to terms with the change, to understand the positive benefits to the customer and reconcile any reservations they may have.

This is further emphasized by the changes shown in Chapter 2, the shift in customers' perceptions of how they want to be treated, mirrored by the parallel shift on the part of employees. New methods of communication, for example E-mail, can increase the speed and accuracy of the communication but are essentially one-way. It is people – and in this context, particularly, middle managers – who must be more than relays in a cascade of directions or information.

In a service, 'communication' is not a separate element within a 'mix'. Rather it forms a part of everything that is going on. Within the service mix, 'image' may be partly 'advertising' but it is also the statement made by location, product range, pricing platforms and labelling, the behaviour and dress of the staff and incidentals such as background music and choice of colour. Similarly, communication is a part of the 'people', the method of 'delivery', the 'products' and 'price', and indeed the other 'customers' you meet or see. The impact of other customers can run very deep (see Club Med, p. 112).

Creating dialogue

For communication to play this role, there is a need to create the opportunity for others to go through the process of arriving at the 'big idea' – developing thinking, reconciling, coming to terms with the implications. Not monologue, all thought through with no chance to argue or wrestle with the worries, but dialogue, a two-way street for honest exchange.

Often when new and radical ideas are presented, those on the receiving end would very much like to open up a debate but feel inhibited because:

▶ they feel their concerns may be trivial;
▶ or more importantly, be thought of as trivial;
▶ or they may see it as a potentially dangerous exercise, which will be construed as a challenge by management.

So, despite their desire and their concerns, they keep quiet.

But it is worse than that. People usually want to believe that their bosses have got it right; they want it to succeed. In the face of such obviously well-thought through ideas, they don't want to appear negative. Unfortunately, the 'good' communication, far from bringing people in, has erected barriers to dialogue.

There are three common categories of barrier.

1. We don't want to be caught out

There is a fear that we may be seen as either lacking clout or not having thought of everything. We try to dot every 'i' and cross every 't', with the result that there is no room left for dialogue – 'They had obviously already made up their mind', is a typical reaction.

2. A variation of this – we 'over present'

Everything is put onto glossy slides – in some old-fashioned organizations even the dancing girls may be wheeled on! – and the audience are subjected to a monologue. The reasons may not always be defensive, sometimes it is simply an indulgent love of showmanship, a liking for technology or an attempt to 'please the boss'. Whatever the reason, the result is often predictable. It will either:

▶ get an enthusiastic response because it so good, with any doubts left to come up afterwards,

▶ or result in a feeling that there 'is nothing really to talk about – it's all been decided already.

3. We give insufficient time for assimilation

Time and again top management will deliberate over a new initiative over a period of many months, but will then expect everyone else to absorb it and reconcile their concerns in an hour or two, without the chance for a thorough debate. The result is that the action may be eroded by a lack of conviction by those very operatives who have to act on the ideas or the changes.

An imaginative example of how one company got round this problem is given in Case Study 6.1. Finding someone who the mass of people could identify with and who could challenge without personal threats, allowed for the creation of dialogue. It broke down the barriers.

The forgotten art

Communication in this sense, a two-way street, has become a largely forgotten art. Presentation is confused with communication, preparation for a meeting is built around 'What do we tell them?', rather than around 'What do we want them to hear?', advertising becomes 'telling people things', rather than lowering thresholds of concern.

Interestingly, the word 'communication' stems from the same root as 'community', that is *communis*, a bringing together. In a monologue we 'push' our ideas, rather than seek a community of thought. We have to learn to 'pull' ideas through, develop a two-way creation of understanding, not simply pass on information or instructions.

Good dialogue is mainly 'pull', helping people to come to sensible conclusions and understanding – 'why' that course of action, that necessity, that particular form of words. 'Push' communication – giving instruction, for example – will not disappear but managers will have to learn to vary their style to the needs of the situation, not just indulge their desire to take the shortest route, or what seems the shortest route but may, in truth, be no route at all.

The management of Hamburg Mannheimer, one of the largest and most successful life assurance companies in Germany, were aware of the pitfalls of communication when they introduced some major changes to the way their field force needed to operate. They knew there were some potentially negative aspects but were sure they could answer them – if only they had the chance! But if they started to list the negatives, it would erode the positive messages. Further, everyone would dismiss the 'answers' as 'They would say that, anyway'.

How could they get the field force to join in a debate?

At this point they realized they did have a 'member of the field force', who could ask all the questions everyone wanted to ask – but dare not! For years in their advertising the 'personification' of Hamburg Mannheimer had been an actor who played the part of a Hamburg Mannheimer representative, Herr Kaiser. He had a high customer awareness, was seen as someone the field force was happy to identify with – indeed had become almost 'one of them', participating regularly in internal meetings.

So they organized a conference and an apparently straightforward presentation of the plans. It all looked very conventional. The senior managers on a dais in a theatre; the salesforce as the 'attentive' audience. However, just as the Marketing Director was in full flow, Herr Kaiser walked on: 'What you say all sounds very plausible, but what about . . .' and he proceeded to voice all the fears and concerns that the field force had, but would probably not dared to have asked. At first the audience were stunned, 'Who was the intruder?', 'What would management think?' but as they realized who it was, and what was up, they cheered Herr Kaiser on.

Soon the debate extended. Herr Kaiser's 'example' changed the balance and the result was a huge success. 'Dialogue' had been created. Some further changes were agreed. The messages became not only accepted but understood and, in a very real way, 'mine'.

Such choosing of style, giving deeper thought as to how to get beneath the surface of message, is made all the more necessary by the vast amounts of information that are now available to customer and employee alike. This can be indirectly, through 'word of mouth' or reportage in the media, or directly through advertising, E-mail and the proliferation of contacts available today. The vastness of the information transmitted can effectively suppress all thought of dialogue or be an instrument – in some cases *the* instrument – of its achievement.

As Arne Mårtensson at Svenska Handelsbanken observes:

Deregulation means events move faster and we have to have more technology to be able to cope with this. But we have to take care that this vast investment, which can bring great benefits, does not in reality exceed the human capability to cope. We can see many banks putting in technical change of this nature yet failing to get the benefits. We have to use technology to simplify.

The creation of dialogue, communication as a two-way street, is the lifeblood of creating that vital strategic cohesion in the organization, getting everyone onside. It is as much about actions as words; as much about behaviour as the phrases used. What 'I hear' is a compound of 'everything you do' – not just what you say. Behaviour, posture, non-response, all these and many more aspects of non-verbal behaviour are quite as crucial.

The role of the individual

Communication is the way in which it is possible to forge cultures – teams with individuals, individuals in teams. Most service organizations rely on teamwork. All gain distinction from the individuality that the customer discerns in his or her treatment. Culture and team behaviour is not an alternative to individuals but rather the sum of the beliefs and behaviours of the people who comprise it.

Open cultures encourage individuality. In open cultures, the vision, a guiding light, provides guidelines but the culture encourages the use of them in a way which is constructive for the business and the customer – encourages colouring outside the lines, reacting to the events in a way which solves the customer problems, not adds to them.

To summarize, the development of the individual in a service organization can be seen to have a crucial significance for three reasons.

1 For the customer, the value of service is that it allows for 'me' to be treated as an individual and given that increasingly 'I' am concerned to be seen in this light, it is a key factor in my belief that I have been recognized.
2 For the organization, it allows for the 'idea', the strategic goal of the whole enterprise, to be implemented in a way which achieves this individualization.
3 For the individual employee concerned, it allows for an identification with those same drives in society, which are driving the customer to seek individuality.

The role of the individual in the organization can be seen, therefore, to be one of the most important factors in any service. Turning that final moment of truth – the key experiences of the customer – into success depends crucially on the development of individual responsibility.

The service provider can rarely be a loner. He or she must be part of a team and express this individuality through the team as well as personally. The moment of truth, when the individual is face to face with the customer – like the matador in the bullfight, to pick up the allusion in the term – may itself be lonesome, but it will usually be the result of teamwork and crucially depend on teamwork for its continuing delivery. How the waiter deals with the customer who has a complaint about the food may be a success or failure because he or she handles the situation well or badly at that precise point. Repeated success will be the result of confidence in the 'system' to provide backing.

As a leader, getting people onside as individuals within the team, is not just a matter of 'wishing' but a matter of creating a desire to become involved, even where the initial reactions are those of indifference. The experiences of Rebecca Jenkins at Lane Group (Case Study 8.1) illustrate this. Achieving it requires skills of interpersonal competence of a high level, the capacity to:

▶ receive and send information and feelings reliably;
▶ evoke the expression of feelings in others;
▶ process information and feelings reliably;
▶ take action on accurate perceptions, and
▶ learn from the experience.

Stop evaluating – listen

Achieving a high level of interpersonal competence needs the skills to listen, of taking heed and paying attention with all of the senses, not just hearing. Crucial to this are the 'breaks' in the cycle of communication, where sender and receiver 'filter' messages, as in Figure 6.1. Failure to recognize these filters usually leads to evaluation before there is understanding. As importantly, it can demonstrate how little interest there is in another point of view.

These filters are created by both the sender and receiver. Before there is time to sense the purpose and meaning of the message, it has been filtered through the personal or collective filters. Such filters can be due to many reasons: tiredness, emotion or fear, to name just three. Of deeper concern in the context of 'creating community', they are often preconceptions about the person delivering or receiving the message, rather than anything to do with the message itself. They may reflect prejudices about, say, workers or bosses, black people or white people, men or women.

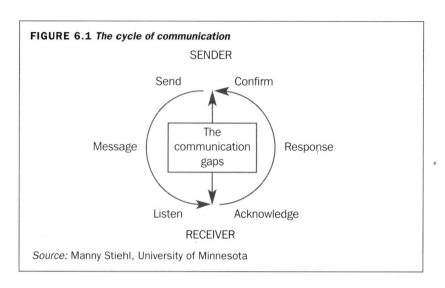

FIGURE 6.1 *The cycle of communication*

SENDER

Send   Confirm

Message | The communication gaps | Response

Listen   Acknowledge

RECEIVER

Source: Manny Stiehl, University of Minnesota

Such filters can never be entirely eliminated, but by concentrating on structure not just words, the effect can be reduced. It won't just happen, since the tendency to evaluate first and think afterwards is strong. It is necessary to take positive action. A useful model is shown in Figure 6.2, which gives a hierarchy of response.

Follow the hierarchy, building from the base. Think first, then ask questions and get understanding, before evaluating.

1. Sense the purpose of the message

Whether sending or receiving, try first of all to understand the 'purpose' behind the words or the reactions:

'Why has he/she come here to tell me this?'
'What are their reactions?'
'Why are they reacting like that'

The four levels of purpose of message (Box 6.1 and Figure 6.3) will be helpful in achieving this. Is the message part of an establishment of social contact, a need to bring into the open a concern or even a prejudice, simply a piece of information or is it persuasion, a call to action? Using such a structure has the great advantage of slowing down the dialogue at a crucial point – the formative stage – so allowing both a deeper assessment of the thinking being presented or of the reactions to it.

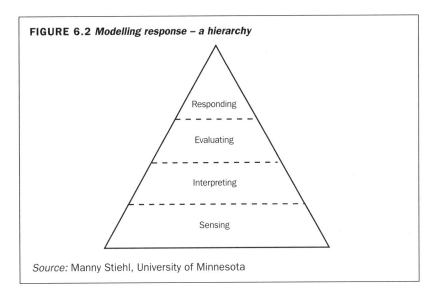

FIGURE 6.2 *Modelling response – a hierarchy*

Responding

Evaluating

Interpreting

Sensing

Source: Manny Stiehl, University of Minnesota

2. Interpret the message

As a sender, make sure the message has been understood by getting 'play back' of what has been said, preferably by building discussion. As a receiver, develop that discussion through questions. Good interpretation requires making a distinction between 'meaning' and 'words'. Words only have any value in the context of meaning – '*Words are but stepping stones for thought*', to quote Arthur Koestler.

3. Evaluate the message

Only now begin the evaluation. Delaying the evaluation until there is understanding about the other person's position, and where they are coming from, will increase the chances of avoiding emotional responses – which have a tendency to create barriers – and instead build up a shared view.

4. Respond

Only now, at this point, allow the luxury of response.

Persistency is vital. To be effective, structuring response must be systematic, overt and focused. With practice, once the tendency to evaluate has been slowed, they will interweave as a pattern.

BOX 6.1 *The purpose of message*

Sensing the purpose of message (Figure 6.2 and the explanation on pp. 102–3) is the base of building dialogue – knowing or finding out where the other person or group is coming from. The tendency, however, is to rush at the end activity – action – when this should be the result of a careful build up.

The 'messages' we send and receive can be categorized under four headings. Each of these represents a 'purpose', which underlies the reason for its use or presence.

These four levels of message can be seen to build, one on the other, as in Figure 6.3. The lower orders form a base which helps with the effective delivery of the higher. Without this base, the higher levels of message are insecure. They have no foundation; we have no relationship. In practice, and in normal dialogue, they interweave to a great degree but it is difficult to move fully to a higher level until a rapport has been established at the lower levels.

Phatic (Social)
These messages establish social contact and express sociability rather than convey specific meaning – at least for most people, most of the time.

Examples are: 'Did you enjoy the theatre last night?'; 'How are your family?'; 'A funny thing happened to me on my way to the meeting today!'

Such messages are the 'mortar' which binds together the building bricks of communication. Without them we may lose nothing, apparently, in content but as a listener, we will feel distant from the other person in the dialogue, the sender. We will feel a target because no bond has been established. The 'powerful' may choose to disregard this but it will never create dialogue and, in time, the power will become eroded or increase distance. To create dialogue, social messages are needed to establish a bond of humanity.

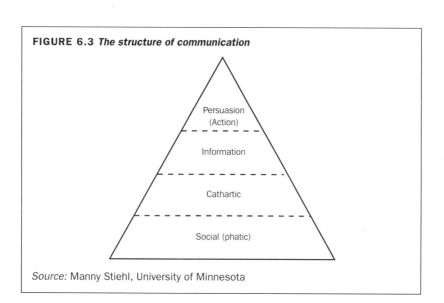

FIGURE 6.3 *The structure of communication*

Persuasion (Action)

Information

Cathartic

Social (phatic)

Source: Manny Stiehl, University of Minnesota

Cathartic
These messages are about bringing into the open our concerns and fears.
They may or may not be founded in fact, they may even be reflective of prejudice, but they will not only colour our perceptions of what we think but, more importantly, will colour our perceptions of what we hear. They can act as a block to hearing at all.

Examples are: 'But what about the problems we are having with the computers?'; 'How is this going to solve my problems with lack of staff?'; 'Will we finish in time for me to catch the last train home?'

Until someone has expressed such messages – and are sure they have been heard – it is often difficult if not impossible to get them to listen attentively and with a will. It is also difficult to consider concerns or prejudices, and establish a high level of joint thinking, unless you have both revealed and explored them.

Information
These messages are more obvious – getting across the content and the thinking behind it.
Information messages are much more complex – and neglected – than is generally realized. They are deeply interconnected with cathartic messages – 'my need' for particular information is going to be a reflection of my worries and concerns, a substantial variable which will make 'my hearing' different to the person next to me.

The importance is highlighted in the research into strategic cohesion (Chapter 4). A lack of confidence was more often an outcome of 'not being sure why something was being done' or 'not being sure it was the right thing', rather than any lack of knowledge in absolute terms. It was not quantitative; the facts. Rather it was qualitative, the chance to reconcile my understanding with change.

Persuasion (Action)
These are the messages of action – finally getting someone to do something.
The problem is that this is where many start the message; it is, or should be, the culmination. There are times when 'persuasion' will need to be up-front – in an emergency, for example. But generally, those giving 'push' messages of this type will be more successful where that event rests on the *previous* establishment of dialogue through building purpose in messages and communication consistently.

In a well-planned dialogue, it will often be very evident what the 'action' has to be – the building of the dialogue and the creation of understanding of the situation have all shown the way. Where such care has not been exercised, then failure at the phatic and cathartic levels can destroy any hope of true community of purpose.

In summary, there are seven points to watch for in structuring listening:

1 Deal with each level in turn.
2 Analyse the speaker.
3 Identify emotions, distractions.
4 Encourage release of information and knowledge.
5 Don't always rush to fill a vacuum!
6 Don't over record – keep notes simple/short.
7 Respond – but not always with an answer or question.

Internal communication

In a service, those involved are not simply colleagues but are the 'raw material' of the activity. To sustain individuality means recognizing the people within the organization as an 'audience' which needs to be given, at the very least, the same priority as the customer.

They are an integral part of the whole plan and their uncritical acceptance of what is planned for them cannot be assumed. Nor is it sufficient to think that they can simply put up with it or go elsewhere, because:

▶ unless they are both committed and convinced, they won't play their part to the full and the 'product' will not be what was planned – delivery will fall short;

▶ only consistent delivery, or recovery, on their part will deliver that extra quality of effort that makes superservice.

Southwest Airlines see 'marketing' as being as much support of the effort of employees as communicating with the market.

Lane Group (see Case Study 8.1) have seen the need for internal communication, getting everyone onside, as crucial to the achievement of their vision.

Accor Group, who own Novotel and a number of other restaurant and hotel chains, have invested heavily in internal communication.

Accor believe that such communications should be seen as relevant to the people who make Accor and, above all, should be read. One of the ways they have achieved this, is to use cartoons and have hired the 'Asterix' team to make specially-commissioned cartoon features. It is obviously not possible to show such a cartoon story in full, but Figure 6.4 gives some insight to a light-hearted story. Set many hundreds of years ago, the medieval king wanted to improve the environmental impact of his palace and the help he had from two innkeepers was crucial. It makes a number of valuable points in a way which both encourages the reader and is memorable.

Another organization which has placed great emphasis on internal communication is British Airways. They are taking a bold initiative with the use of television and are developing an internal 'British Airways TV' programme. This will be a daily news programme of high quality, objectively viewing current issues of immediate concern to British Airways and British Airways staff.

While the use of television may seem odd at first in the context, the circumstances of British Airways – worldwide, large numbers of influential and articulate staff working shifts – make it attractive.

FIGURE 6.4 *Accor Cartoon*

Source: 'Triera bien qui triera le dernier!', Accor internal communication ©

Television, unlike films, is a medium which because it comes into the home or workplace is seen more as dialogue, hence the reason people meeting television performers in the street are inclined to greet them as 'friends', rather than as performers.

Other ways of building dialogue are numerous – for example see the Hamburg Mannheimer story or the Accor cartoons, earlier in this chapter – but to be effective any internal communication needs not just to convey information but to:

▶ establish rapport, that is establish a phatic base (Box 6.3);

▶ identify and deal with concerns, that is clear any catharsis;

▶ get across not just the information but also the reasoning and purpose, and

▶ get the action which is proposed to be seen as a natural outcome of the message, not as merely a directive which may only achieve passive compliance.

The examples given share one other important characteristic – they take information directly to the end-user. 'Cascading' of messages is rarely as effective, because the messages get blocked or distorted in the process. Finding ways of conveying messages direct and linking this with the imaginative use of 'meetings' is more likely to achieve the cohesion needed. This is an important part of the learning process, outlined in Chapter 7, and also has deep implications for the role of middle management (p. 152).

The role of external communication

While advertising is the most immediately visible of external communication methods, it is often not the most important, even for services that advertise regularly. External communication is a two-way bridge between 'our world' and 'their world'. This includes the 'product' itself – the interaction, the personal sampling that is a part of this – for good or bad!

The ranking and importance of any particular method will vary widely. At one extreme, you have someone such as a retailer or hotel who may rely totally on location, sometimes cited as 'the three most important factors' in such businesses! Or it may be a mix, with word-of-mouth predominating – direct or via public relations – to the other extreme, a direct-mail operation, which may rely almost totally on advertising.

There are underlying reasons why advertising is not as crucial to a service as to a tangible product. Judie Lannon, former Director of European Research at J. Walter Thompson and now a freelance consultant on communication and research, makes the point that:

> *For the most part products have few distinctive values. This sounds a paradox but it is true; most products differ very little from competitors' in a given category and advantage can be quickly eroded. So, 'brand values' have to be created to magnify such differences*

as exist, so that it is not just a commodity, such as 'beer' or 'beans'. Nevertheless, a manufactured product is the same physical entity, time after time, whereas a service will vary from experience to experience. There is a constant validation and 'reality check'. As a result, consumers feel word of mouth is a more reliable source.

This puts considerable emphasis on speeding up the word-of-mouth process. Specifically, it may mean using public relations in some form so that others say what cannot easily be said direct. By definition, 'you' are prejudiced in your favour. You cannot, for example, make an easily accepted self-claim to be 'fair' or 'prompt' any more than you can self-claim modesty. What else might you be expected to say? Furthermore, the very claim itself may be seen as evidence of insincerity.

On the other hand, an editorial endorsement in the right journal (note the warning on 'wrong audiences' on p. 112) can be accepted as disinterested, as genuine. Public relations in this broader sense of developing relations is of enormous significance in helping to support the 'values' of the service brand, in adding to the core messages of advertising.

The creation of 'loyalty schemes' (see also 'Customer loyalty' on p. 166) has already started to go beyond just that and has led to organizations having the ability to 'talk' with their customers, as is the case with the British Airways Executive Club. The more focused the business, the more scope for either forming a 'club' of users or providing a service which fits neatly with that focus.

Mastercare (Case Study 2.1) is, in a very real way, another reflection of this approach, since the service centre in the shop is as much a symbol and focus of Dixons approach as it is a repair shop. It is creating an image which goes beyond selling and establishes Dixons as a particular type of store with particular values.

Advertising as a lever

The outcome of this is that advertising is most often to be viewed as a leverage device, a mechanism to capitalize upon people that the customer meets, the word-of-mouth message, the location.

So, for example, specific campaigns might:

▶ encourage satisfied customers to let others know;
▶ generate promotional material for customers to hand to non-customers;

▶ target messages at significant opinion formers;

▶ encourage prospective customers to seek out recommendations, and

▶ use testimonials.

Advertising, therefore, has a particularly important role in creating an 'umbrella' for activity, in giving a clear message to those involved – internally as well as externally – which helps to condition the interaction. A good example of this is Southwest Airlines. Joyce Rogge, Vice President says:

> *Our aim is to get across what is really different about Southwest and to educate the customer before they even reach us. We are a different kind of carrier and in the early days we had a particular need to get that across and explain what people had to expect – no closet for hanging bags, be there on time or we go and you don't, the slick embarkation and disembarkation procedures. But we also had to get across what you could expect – staff who will go out of their way to take care of you.*

Further, as a result of the deep changes in the market (Chapter 2), creating service values is also inextricably mixed with the move to function, not ownership, and the greater emphasis on creating a lifestyle. There is a shift to sociability/friendship themes (relationships), which are more responsive to dialogue. It is taking the brand to the customer, rather than sheltering behind the label. The line between what is advertising and what is other forms of communication, such as public relations, becomes blurred and maybe irrelevant.

For example, the French 'Relais' baby products have developed free nappy-changing rooms on autoroutes; 'Danone' have set up a 'Danone Food Institute', to teach healthy eating and take the message into schools; Sainsbury's magazine creates an interest in not just food but its preparation, its setting.

Communication and brand identity

Only 'strategic cohesion' (p. 53) can deliver the consistency of purpose needed for a 'service brand', but unless communication is also consistent such a consistency of purpose cannot exist. Since people increasingly seek dialogue rather than just being told, dialogue is, in turn, a key to brand identity in a service.

The importance of word of mouth whether person to person or through editorial matter, highlights the importance of consistency and the points made about brands in this respect:

- ▶ the brand in a service is essentially the culture of the organization;
- ▶ it is this which the customer is buying through the thousands, millions even, of interactions;
- ▶ the service organization is concerned about delivering consistency at this point, and
- ▶ the customer is concerned about receiving a level of response which is, at least, at the level of expectations.

A successful service brand will signal consistency, so that there are:

- ▶ clear messages about what to expect, on the part of the customer, and
- ▶ clear indications about what to do, on the part of the people in the organization.

Complete consistency can never be guaranteed. So the signals the brand must send, its communication, is primarily about the following.

1. Conditioning beliefs with the customer

The beliefs that the customer has about any particular service will be largely conditioned by experience.

A significant difference for a service, from a product, is that it does have lots of variances, one time from the other – that is what makes it individual. However, it is possible to create an expectation which helps the customer to both perceive a consistency and to recognize the factors that make that service what it is.

These are a critical part of the communication – it is not some separate activity with messages of its own through publicity and advertising, but an integral part of the service mix, playing a key role in establishing the brand as a reflection of the culture. It is no use creating expectations that cannot be met. Communication must be realistic.

Virgin Atlantic, for example, found at one time that the results of their research among Japanese passengers into reactions to the service they had received (Virgin always measure customer reactions in both absolute terms and in comparison with expectations), showed that there was a worrying discrepancy between perceptions of service and expectations among these passengers. Further investigation showed that in translating their advertising into Japanese, some unrealistic expectations were being created. The advertising was changed and the reactions of passengers to the service they received 'improved' – they now had realistic expectations, which could be reasonably met.

Virgin Atlantic have extremely sophisticated research to track customer experiences against expectations, so they were able to recognize this imbalance early on and correct it. Other organizations without such clear links between the 'service brand' and communication have not been so lucky.

Some years ago, Club Med allowed its advertising to get divorced from the reality of the brand – what people would experience from all of the elements of the Club Med service mix, including the other customers. As a result, they got a lot of wrong customers, people who did not fit with the Club. They found that those expensively won customers just never came back. Club Med have made great strides since then (see also pp. 130/226) but the potential for disaster in such situations goes beyond the 'dissatisfieds' because they can negatively influence other guests. Consistency includes customers!

Over the years, many service organizations have attempted to portray an unrealistic view of the service being offered. Financial organizations have been particularly bad in this respect. Customers are, therefore, cynical about claims and quick to recognize when an excessive claim has been made. The simple, believable claim will often work better, keeping expectations more in line with what the customer will actually experience. A good example is Motel 6, the Accor-owned chain of budget American motels. They make a very simple non-overstated claim, which still carries a sense of warmth and dialogue – 'A clean room, good location and we'll leave the light on for you'.

2. Conditioning the behaviour of staff

This is not a question of exhortation but of creating that cohesive culture so important in achieving service success. Again, it is a question of using all of the elements of communication to work in balance and harmony, not simply relying on any one element to work alone.

In particular, people will give a better and more consistent level of service where this is clearly the expectation not only of customers but of their colleagues too.

Failure as success

No organization is capable of total consistency. If it were, it would lose that vital element that service brings – individuality. There will be variations so there will be failures. The key is how failures are handled.

For Judie Lannon, '*Building relationships (with the customer) in a service is key. In fact, someone with a complaint has a better chance of building a relationship than an ordinary customer*'. Sue Moore at British Airways endorses this point very strongly: '*Like all service businesses, we do have lapses, but it is recovery that matters. In fact, our research shows that passengers who have complained have generally become more pro-BA as a result of the treatment they have received*'. (See p. 225 for more detail on this subject.)

Good recovery is key. The faster and more spontaneous it is, the better the chances of it being successful, of turning a failure into a success. Such recovery is a part of the brand and of the brand communication. Since 'my decision-making processes' are about 'my making a choice' in favour of 'those who understand' me (p. 33), it is at recovery that I can most clearly see this. At that point, either you are there to help me or you are not! So a successful recovery can create conviction in the brand – and a customer of a service is much more likely to talk about such a positive happening to others, than is the case with most manufactured products.

Good recovery means more than just putting right. It has to demonstrate that you are concerned, that you recognize the other point of view. The individual in the organization has to stand up at this point and act – but he or she can only act in a way which is a reflection of the culture, of the team.

Acknowledgements and further reading

page 93   Roger Smith, quoted by Wilton Woods in *Fortune*,
            13 February, 1989.
page 101   The work of Professor Manny Stiehl of the University
            of Minnesota, has been invaluable in developing the
            sections on dialogue and listening.
page 108   The input and advice of Judie Lannon, former European
            Research Director of J. Walter Thompson, has been
            invaluable in developing the sections on external
            communications, branding and advertising.
page 103   Koestler, A. (1964) *The Act of Creation*, MacMillan.
page 112   Club Med, from a retail study by Jacques Horowitz,
            quoted in *Management Today*, January, 1994.

Unfortunately there are no readily available writings by either Manny Stiehl or Judie Lannon. The subject is so wide that the interested reader would be advised to spend an hour or two at a good business bookshop selecting books from those specific areas of interest (and reading widely on the subject from books such as that of Arthur Koestler quoted above) but the following reading will provide some deeper insight into marketing and communication.

Bernstein, D. (1988) *Putting it Together: Put it Across – the craft of business presentation,* Cassell.

Irons, K. (1996) *The Marketing of Services,* McGraw-Hill.

McKenna, R. (1991) *Relationship Marketing,* Addison-Wesley.

Rogers, C.R. and Roethlisberger, F. J. (1991) 'Barriers and gateways to communication', *Harvard Business Review,* Nov/Dec.

Whelan, D.J. (1996) *I See What You Mean,* Sage Publications.

7 The learning organization

Many people dream of success. To me success can only be achieved through repeated failure and introspection. In fact, success represents the 1 per cent of work which results from the 99 per cent that is called failure.

Sochiro Honda, Founder of Honda

About this chapter

If strategic management is to be more than just another term for the old-style, dreary round of managing through plans and direction, an organization needs to be a learning organization. This is not simply problem solving or putting things right but learning, getting insight about oneself, the organization, the customer and the complex, interwoven relationship of these that goes to make a service. It requires being very clear and systematic about what to collect and how to use it – and avoiding using it as a source of punishment.

It also requires that development against the vision and the destination be monitored to provide real insight not merely evidence of immediate financial success. This will be covered in more depth in Chapter 12.

This chapter will look at what is involved in creating a learning organization.

▶ The principles involved in using strategy as a learning process.

▶ Management as the most frequent barrier to the process of learning.

▶ How everyday learning and meetings – yes, meetings – can play an important part.

▶ How to gather input and, in particular, how to use customer complaints.

▶ The pitfalls of measuring customer satisfaction.

From caribou bones to the exit society

It was common among certain American Indian tribes who had had a barren time hunting, to seek help from a medicine man. He would prepare the shoulder blade of a caribou in a fire so that the heat cracked the bone. He then used the cracks and lines to indicate where the hunters should hunt. While 'modern' man is inclined to scoff at this, it often worked because it was, in effect, a random number generator, deflecting the hunters away from an over-dependence on pre-learning and from experience bias and avoidance behaviour.

Given that, for many managers, management is about doing tomorrow what they did yesterday, but in the hope that it will somehow work better, the use of caribou bones could be a valuable method of 'learning'! The difficulties of breaking free from past experience are particularly strong in larger organizations and the inertia this engenders, linked to past success, can make the inclination towards avoidance behaviour almost insurmountable. Given the changes outlined in Chapter 2, such as the 'exit society', breaking from the past and the process of using learning to change, are critical.

Strategic management, that strategic process so suited to the service environment, is at heart a 'learning process'. Used properly, the organization will learn from that process by adaption to events – about those events and the changes that are needed to meet them effectively – and, above all, gain insights into the reasons for past success or failure. This is vital if the widely different conditions in the 'exit society' are to be understood and mastered.

The learning organization is one which is continually updating its understanding of its strategy, what it can achieve and its limitations. It is ready to modify the strategy in the light of experience but has sufficient self-knowledge – a sense of its own identity, with its customers, with its own people and within its owners – to know what it must not change.

The tangible part of this activity is the strategic guidelines, with the guiding light. It is possible to allow individuals to think for themselves about the best ways to achieve the ends within such guidelines. To encourage the behaviour that will help them act toward the same ends as their colleague, yet still act as individuals – to colour outside the lines.

It is this tangible guideline which gives a form and a coherency to both the strategic activity and the learning, and which prevents functional learning from becoming dominant, choking the chance to gain from real insight. Functional learning can be used to improve efficiency of finance, IT and marketing, but, on its own, it will rarely improve the effectiveness of the whole organization.

Management as a barrier

A significant barrier to learning is frequently the behaviour and reactions of management themselves. The more senior a manager, the less he or she is likely to find learning difficult and inclined to use experience as a filter. While this filter can be an invaluable way of bringing to bear experiences, it can also be a barrier to embracing new information, to dialogue. The more vivid that experience, the more the filter will act as a barrier.

Achieving such a new balance is not easy. Many managers find hierarchy and monologue comforting. Rather than create dialogue, they would rather leave the introduction of new initiatives to subordinates. As a result, when such ideas progress, they commonly become more and more imbued with the incidental features, while the great idea gets lost along the way.

A further problem is that top managers feel altogether too threatened if the process of change actually involves them. They prefer to champion change than change themselves – after all their style must be right or they wouldn't be there! Top managers will often adopt defensive routines and seek to control the situation by eliminating paradox or possible contradiction, since these make them feel vulnerable.

Figure 7.1 illustrates this. Taken from the book *Strategy, Change and Defensive Routines* by the American author Chris Argyris, James Bryant Conant Professor of Education and Organizational Behaviour at Harvard University, it represents his Model 1 Theory of Reaction, which he goes on to describe as, *'Self reinforcing and [so] not particularly good at self-correcting. [It] is so pervasive, it must be taught early in life'*.

Such behaviour is self-reinforcing and not particularly good at self-correction so it becomes self-perpetuating, a repetitive, historical process rather than a learning process. Since it is usually deep-seated in the behaviour and reactions of management, left untouched it will undermine any chance of dialogue. Managers may not mean to (though some will) but their reactions and behaviour will cause a block to development and feedback. Yet a key feature of a learning organization is its ability to create the climate in which the values of strategic management can be realized; where there is

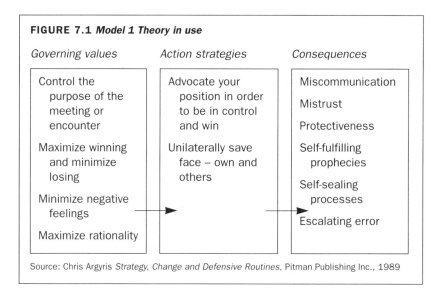

FIGURE 7.1 Model 1 Theory in use

Governing values	Action strategies	Consequences
Control the purpose of the meeting or encounter Maximize winning and minimize losing Minimize negative feelings Maximize rationality	Advocate your position in order to be in control and win Unilaterally save face – own and others	Miscommunication Mistrust Protectiveness Self-fulfilling prophecies Self-sealing processes Escalating error

Source: Chris Argyris *Strategy, Change and Defensive Routines*, Pitman Publishing Inc., 1989

an opportunity for the experiences of individuals and teams, of customers and staff, to give feedback in a manner which impacts on strategy, and modifies activity and behaviour.

Furthermore, the less failure a manager has experienced, the more difficult it is to understand failure in, or give support to, others – not least because it follows that, if I have never failed, then failure in others must be 'their fault'. As a result managers, especially top management, often lack:

▶ the scope to allow for insight from others;
▶ respect for others and humility concerning their own ability, and
▶ a willingness to shoulder blame and to encourage others.

Subordinates respond by avoiding putting forward the evidence that is needed for learning, not simply because they want to avoid being to blame – though that is a significant element – but because they may genuinely not want to be seen as negative.

Management as leaders

If management behaviour fails to support the needs of service, learning becomes a debased experience. Learning is about the things it is safe to rationalize – and so be put right by a tweak to the system or a further reorganization – when maybe what is required is a radically new approach. This is of great significance when change is not only within sectors of society and business, but is destroying or blurring the very boundaries that marked such sectors.

The role of the senior manager, or the parent company in a group, will be increasingly to act as a leader (Chapter 8) and encourage learning, about self and others. This requires that senior managers not only ask the right questions, they must also persuade others that they have to take on this responsibility – ask questions, create dialogue. The achievement of this takes time. Even in Svenska Handelsbanken, management still feel that they have a long way to go after 25 years of learning.

Novotel, too, have made learning from experience one of their key areas of gaining real competitive advantage, as Case Study 7.1 shows. It illustrates the need to share the passion, to treat learning as central to development – and the dangers of stopping the learning process – and how the free-form organization can enhance individual cooperation.

Everyday learning

Learning should not be about classroom activities, and conventional training. Instead, it should be part of everyday life. As the Novotel profile shows, the compartmentalization of learning has no place. The growth of strategic management thinking, the need to blur the edges between a strategy and its implementation are all leading to a pressure for 'everyday learning' where there are few distinctions between learning and daily activity.

As a result the boundaries between 'training' and 'work' become blurred, often disappear. Much of the formalized training that goes on in organizations – often more driven by a training department's need to justify its existence than any real need of the business – is dismantled and is replaced with more informal, on-the-job or close-to-the-job development.

Such a lessening of dependence on formal training – outside of purely technical skills – is an important part of the learning process. When management recognize a deficiency, the stock answer is to send someone on a course, whereas the probability is that we are witnessing a failure on the part of those who should have been teaching. This failure is often the managers themselves, but most likely the whole organization is simply not rewarded for learning – or teaching.

People are held at a distance, physically or metaphorically, or both. Time on communication, real communication (dialogue) is seen as wasted time. Yet such time is probably the most valuable investment an organization can make.

You could say that Novotel owed its start in life to being a learning organization. When it was originally conceived in 1967 the founders, Paul Dubrule and Gerard Pelisson, who are still co-presidents of Groupe Accor, of which Novotel is a part, had learnt much from the time they had spent working in the USA. They returned to Europe convinced that there was a great future for hotels that learnt from the American experience. Unlike many others who had attempted to import American ideas, Dubrule and Pelisson saw that the learning did not stop there – to succeed it had to be a blend. They saw that it was service that made the difference and that people made service. That they had to inspire others as much, maybe even more, than themselves. If it was to succeed it had to be within a culture that also drew on the traditional strengths of Europe, especially France, providing more structure and social support if it was to work.

Dubrele and Pelisson listened to customers, not simply in some conventional way, but to see through the contradictions and conflicts, and to ensure that they really understood their needs *relative* to their preparedness to pay. So Novotel was built around a (then) maximum of F300 a night, this being the most that the identified target market (middle-income business and leisure travellers) would happily pay. In the service mix were those things the customers really wanted (for example, large, well-appointed rooms) and out went those things they might like but did not care so much about (for example, porterage). It was to be the best balance – 'For this price we can provide this'.

They also listened to staff, creating a basis of involvement which was transparent and intellectually honest. The result was an unusual blend. Michael Flaxman, UK Managing Director, who joined from the Forte group, was:

> *Shocked on joining. It was not centralized, not hierarchical, quite unlike any other French organization I had ever known. There was a very high level of openness and honesty. Authority is much more by respect than power and jobs are built around using people to their best ability, not filling slots. We don't have organization charts or put people in boxes. When a new management job is advertised, it is usually not highly specific, as in its final form it will be built around who gets it – or more to the point, it will be up to the appointee to define the limits. The analogy I would draw is like a liquid on a non-absorbent surface, with a form but not fixed in space and with some fluidity. We believe that people work best and will learn more when we have a climate where we will tell them exactly what is happening. As a result we have a very high degree of cooperation.*

Maybe it was too big a success, maybe some of the learning stopped. By 1989 Novotel had slipped a little, had lost some of its original impact and no longer had a specific identity. Dominique Colliat, who is now the manager of the new Novotel at Waterloo in London, talks of the hotels, '*Beginning to look out-of-date and by today's standards, the decor was tired looking. We had lost that spark, that had made us a success in the hotel and with people. We had become hierarchical without noticing it – everyone was an "assistant manager" for this or that*'.

So in 1990, Novotel started the project that eventually became called 'Back to the Future', recapturing the original concepts that had made success possible, but taking them forward a further 25 years. Once again it was a listening process, involving all senior managers in both the basic research, inside and out, and in developing the concepts that would: '*Guide Novotel back to its pinnacle in the trade, as a reference point for three star hotels*', to quote Philippe Brizon, the President.

In 1992, 'Back to the Future' was launched as an integrated approach to changing Novotel and the customer experience. Out went hierarchy, in future there would be:

▶ A Manager of the hotel whose task would be summed up as 'Maître de Maison'. The Maître de Maison would be expected to work on creating an hotel which was unique to its particular circumstances and to meet with customers and staff – in short to be both a leader and 'mine host'.
▶ Under the Manager, a flat organization with heads of department and then staff – no assistant managers.

Dominique Colliat says:

> *The flat organization caused some concern, because many staff felt they had lost the chance to progress without intermediate steps. So we introduced 'Novotel Progress'. This was a new way to recognize and reward staff who wanted to commit themselves to progress. Within each of the six broad hotel and catering spheres of activity, there are four steps – bronze, silver, gold and platinum. Each employee can be assessed for progress to the next step at approximately six-month intervals. 'Bronze' is fairly basic, and confirms that the employee is able to practise all the necessary skills for a particular job. At the other end, 'platinum' is concerned only with management and marketing skills that are general, across the business. This way we are able to both develop and recognize staff without creating a hierarchy which interferes with our customer care and the day-to-day management.*

The major cultural change involved, and the intentions of Novotel management, are summed up in Figure 7.2, taken from the internal introductory literature for 'Back to the Future'. As Novotel recognize, only a constant learning process that involves everyone will allow it to succeed.

'*It is all part of a much wider approach to development, which we call 'The School of Life*'', says Philippe Brizon.

FIGURE 7.2 *The change in Novotel*

Novotel Yesterday	**Novotel Tomorrow**
Loyal to customers	Loyal to customers
Customer	Guest
Square	Round
Well-oiled	Côte Jardin*
Masculine	Feminine
Manager as administrator	Maître de Maison
Sacrosanct administration	Enterprising spirit
Pleasant/efficient	Warm
Cordial	Friendly
Parent-child	Adult-adult
Reception	Hospitality
Novotel idea	Multifaceted network
Standard	Family
Habit	Innovation
Stressed/office bound	Available/seeking contact
Prudent/resigned	Proud of my customers/my team

*Novotel's name for their new restaurant facilities
Source: Novotel internal literature

For many of our employees, this is the first chance they have in life to really show what they can do and we feel we have a responsibility to help them. We have an Assessment Centre which is assessing and then training all the managers, so that they can play the lead role in this in their role as 'Maître de Maison'. It is their task, together with the departmental heads, to implement this. It is not a static process but one we have to learn from all the time. We also have a 'university' to develop higher skills. It is a total professional life project.

We have what we call a 'spirit of open table' – everyone may have a view and voice it. We also have a slogan, 'Bienvenue à chez nous' – 'You are welcome' – and that applies as much to staff as to our guests.

At the same time, we have updated the image, introduced amenities that were a 'luxury' in a three-star hotel a few years ago but which customers have now come to expect, like air-conditioning, and made a major investment in upgrading the food side. We are also involving the manager, as 'Maître de Maison', in making each hotel much more individual, much more in touch with its surroundings, less uniform – though, of course, within a clearly-defined framework of what a Novotel is.

There is a considerable body of support for this concept. For example in 1984, Oslo University carried out research to identify those factors that promote or inhibit learning among management and staff. They discovered that well-being, that is, feelings of personal security and satisfaction, and learning do not always go hand in hand. For example, when people get new responsibilities, they often feel insecure but their 'learning curve' is steep. Two factors in particular stood out in this research.

1 With clearer, more structured, 'goal setting', there was more security but less learning.
2 Participation in 'many meetings' was not very satisfying at a personal level but increased learning.

This suggests that our views of delegation have got to change if those who are close to the customer are to take responsibility. There will be a need to accept that the long-term growth of an informed and responsible workforce is based not on detailed instruction but on clear guidelines and vigorous follow through by those who can give help and inspiration.

While such developments mirror the decisions taken by Novotel, Novotel are by no means alone:

▶ Swiss Re (the Swiss Reinsurance Company), one of the largest international reinsurers, have scrapped most of their non-technical training, and instead are concentrating on on-the-job development.
▶ Pret A Manger have a 'shooting star' scheme, whereby everyone who finishes a course or gets promoted is given some money, but is not allowed to keep it. Instead, they must give it to the people who helped train him or her.
▶ General Electric (page 21) have a strategic aim to move from being a manufacturing company to a service company. They have adapted a learning process to involve everyone, called 'Work-Out'. To quote Jack Welch from his 1995 *Letter to Shareholders,*

Work-Out is based on the simple belief that people closest to the work know, more than anyone, how it could be done better. People of disparate ranks and functions search for a better way, every day, gathering in a room for an hour, or eight, or three days .... producing real change instead of memos and promises of further study.

Welch goes on to credit the extraordinary continuing success of GE as being very much a product of Work-Out.

Meetings

Such experiences would suggest that we have to reappraise the value and purpose of 'meetings' – not just formal meetings, but all of those times when people get together to discuss the work in hand. Most managers are inclined to dismiss such events as a waste of time. The truth is that meetings typically provide the single biggest source of help, insight and development for people, especially those near the bottom or in a process of career development.

To do this effectively requires:

▶ meetings be seen and planned as developmental happenings, not just information relays;

▶ an increasing use of cross-functional project work for developmental tasks;

▶ managers – especially middle managers – becoming skilled at, and increasingly chosen for, their ability to coach, and

▶ trainers seeing their role as developing others to train and creating for them simple, easy-to-use material which allows personal development to blend directly with getting the job done.

Such a change in emphasis is already happening. SOL (p. 41) encourage informal meetings to settle issues quickly, providing not only conventional meeting spaces but tables where people can stand and talk briefly, without the necessity for a 'formal' meeting. General Electric have adopted Work-Out to a point where 'across GE today, holding a Work-Out session is as natural as coming to work'.

A similar approach which has been used extensively throughout Europe is outlined on p. 209, the 'Workshop' approach. It uses 'Five Key Questions' as a core for thinking through problems and issues and arriving at solutions. These are not only then good in quality but have the understanding and support of those involved in creating action. The Five Key Questions are as follows:

1 **What does it (the initiative, the change) mean to me?**
2 **What can I contribute?**
3 **What will be the benefit for me?**
4 **What will be the barriers that will prevent me/us from succeeding?**
5 **What help do I/we need?**

Whatever the specific approach adopted, the key point is that meetings should respond to the central needs of strategic management – become a focus for learning.

Gathering input

A further source of learning are the actual experiences, the events that colour the implementation of the plans. Every business has a vast amount of such information about itself but it is rarely collected in any systematic form. There will be patterns of behaviour, insights into the consistency of collective action and reaction which, properly understood, will reveal a great deal about what is successful and what is not.

Simply, there are two sources for this: internal and external. Most organizations, especially larger ones, appear to value the external more than the internal. According to the Henley Centre, organizations spend a staggering £7 billion on external information in the UK alone, most of which, Henley suggest from their research, is not used or isn't understood.

Few collect internal information – other than financial – on any planned and systematic basis, such that it can be used effectively to learn. When they do, as with the typical staff attitude survey, it fails to show how such attitudes, or their improvement, link 'our world' to 'their world'. Culture mapping (p. 54) is an example of bringing the worlds together. It is based on the belief that, at an everyday level, staff have an immense knowledge of customer reactions. These are often subconscious observations which, when properly collected and analysed, can reveal patterns of behaviour, previously undetected.

This is as true for business-to-business relationships as in the personal field. Business-to-business purchases are no more 'rational' – in the sense of being free of behavioural and other qualitative influences – than individual purchases. For example, one major reinsurance company who had never been able to define the profile of a profitable customer – except on an individual customer-to-customer basis – found that the 'behaviour' of their, generally very large, customers (insurance companies ceding risks) was a clear indication of profit or loss, regardless of geography, size and all the other 'hard' factors previously used.

It is also a systematic analysis of the actual dealings with and reactions of a group of small commercial customers of one insurance company which lies behind the illustration in Figure 7.3 (see also Chapter 9, for more detail on this type of structural analysis). This information was collected from staff and studies of existing customer information. It is based on the same 'Service dynamic profiling' techniques as those used for the compilation of Figure 3.3. It shows the buying and subsequent reaction patterns of two types of small commercial customer. Segment B projects a typical profile of a retailer/service organization, for example a hairdresser, whereas Segment A is reflective of a small manufacturer.

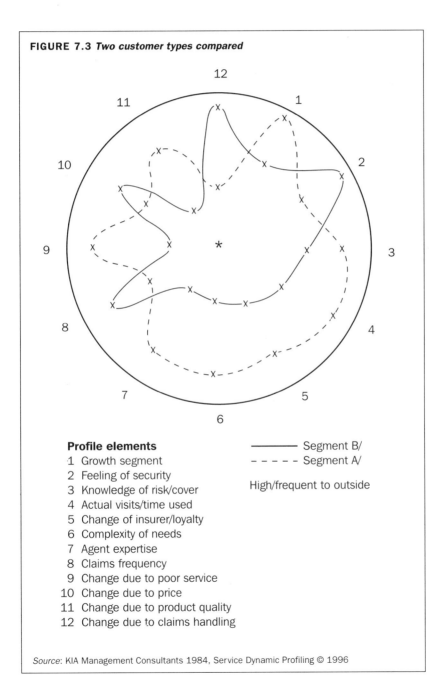

FIGURE 7.3 *Two customer types compared*

Profile elements
1 Growth segment
2 Feeling of security
3 Knowledge of risk/cover
4 Actual visits/time used
5 Change of insurer/loyalty
6 Complexity of needs
7 Agent expertise
8 Claims frequency
9 Change due to poor service
10 Change due to price
11 Change due to product quality
12 Change due to claims handling

——— Segment B/
– – – – Segment A/

High/frequent to outside

Source: KIA Management Consultants 1984, Service Dynamic Profiling © 1996

In general terms, A may be characterized as 'professional' in attitudes to and choice of insurer. The sense of security felt by A is well founded. It knows something about insurance. Segment A attaches great importance to the entire range of quality-related elements and less to price considerations.

In contrast, B may be characterized as 'amateur'. It is less dynamic than A; it knows less about insurance; it does not make heavy demands on the agent or on the qualities of the product; it is more sensitive to price. Segment B is loyal to the insurer it has chosen, except that in the claims situation it finds that its sense of security is unfounded. It has simply bought without going through any real process of comparison or consideration and feels let down when it comes to the crunch.

In this case, the knowledge that the company had was made to work, not left to lie unused in heads and on files. The implications for the company were enormous – that easy sales aren't always the best sales, among them. It simply would never have realized the significance unless it had 'ordered' the information which was there already into systematic form. Such an approach identifies:

▶ which customer groups should be targeted;
▶ what are their behaviour characteristics, and
▶ when and how resources should be applied.

These patterns are not going to be revealed by simple questionnaires since the patterns are most often primarily qualitative. 'Qualitative' does not mean 'unimportant', and, indeed, it is often more revealing than hard data, since it reveals concerns, fears, intentions. So, for example, the Lane Group believe that their drivers are one of their most important sources of information on the market and on problems and opportunities, one of the features which strongly influenced The Body Shop in awarding their distribution contract to them. Southwest Airlines consistently gather information from staff, through personal contact from management (Box 7.1).

BOX 7.1 *Listening in Southwest*

Extract from a paper on Southwest Airlines written by Janice Hunter

Embedded within Southwest's culture is the notion that effectiveness is highly dependent upon the ability to build strong and caring relationships. Regardless of position or title, employees at Southwest are expected to be available to one another. One Culture Committee member shared some interesting comments he had from a senior manager:

While I was out in the field visiting one of our stations, one of the managers mentioned to me that he wanted to put up a suggestion box. And I responded to that manager by saying, 'Sure, why don't you put up a suggestion box right here on the wall and admit you are a failure as a manager.' Our theory at Southwest is, if you have to put up a box so people can write down their ideas and toss them in, then it means that you are not doing what you are supposed to be doing. You are supposed to be setting your people up to be winners. To do that you should be there listening to them and available to them in person not via a suggestion box. And, for the most part, I think that most people employed here know that they can call anyone of our vice-presidents on the telephone and get heard, almost immediately.

The suggestion box gives managers an out. It relinquishes their responsibility to be accessible to their people and that's when we have gotten into trouble at Southwest, when we can no longer be responsive to our flight attendants or our ticket agents, when they can't gain accessibility to somebody who can give them resources and answers and so forth. Then what they invariably do, they turn to the next person who will respond to them in the manner that they want.

We need to spend at least a third of our time out of our office, walking around. And another thing we encourage and do is go out in the field. Load bags, sell tickets, serve drinks and peanuts, these jobs give us all valuable insight. They give us a better understanding of how our decisions here in the 'glass palace' affect people that are actually delivering the product or the service. When I do go out in the field, I am much more likely to find that some of the decisions I've made are stupid decisions, and I've seen how my decisions have terribly affected and inconvenienced some of our people.

And they definitely pay you with some kind of currency, and if you are incapable of changing things or fixing things or simply doing a self-audit, if you consistently try to sell your employees something they don't want, then what your employees are going to do is to fire you! And the problem is, some managers have been fired and don't even know it! But their people won't do business with them anymore. They go around them, they're not as committed, they don't have as much energy. When that happens our culture is in trouble.

Customers who complain

A further important source of learning is customers, but they rarely give insight spontaneously except when they complain. As a result, complaints are an important source of quality control, and maybe the only truly reliable source since customer defections or dissatisfactions are concrete and clear. Superservice organizations value customers who complain.

Club Med, for example, analyse every letter of complaint to understand the underlying concerns. They also have roundtable discussion groups with guests and staff while the guests are still with them.

However, in many organizations, complaints from customers are often actively suppressed because:

▶ first, they can be emotional in content and, even more, delivery;
▶ second, they are risky, with the potential to destabilize the lives of the staff involved.

Taking each of these in turn:

1. Emotion

▶ Few customers actually do complain. Typically, less than 1 in 10 will do anything after the event; 2 in 10 will comment verbally; 7 in 10 will just walk away, even saying they are satisfied (see also p. 134). Even when customers do complain, the unwillingness to engage in anything too 'emotional' leads to each side toning down the situation. The core of the complaint is often never clearly registered.
▶ When complaints do become 'emotional', it is either because the situation has been allowed to get beyond the early stages without being recognized and dealt with, or the complainant is someone who complains easily and aggressively. Either situation is difficult to handle and often results in a shut down of dialogue.
▶ Training staff to handle such situations requires more than simply getting them to act as if the 'customer is always right'. Sometimes they aren't! They can be opinionated, demanding and short of a full understanding as to what they have bought, but almost always they will have a legitimate point at the heart of their complaint – 'we have failed'.
▶ So although it is possibly an isolated incident – in which case it may say more about the complainant – the probability is the complainant is giving valuable clues. It is difficult to create a complaint out of absolutely nothing. *In virtually every case the complainant is telling*

the organization something about itself that other, quieter individuals, are failing to press home. Far from seeing such people as 'outrageous', they should be embraced, even rewarded, for taking the time and trouble to bring the problem to the fore.

2. Risk

Clearly, few are going to be objective in recording complaints if the outcome is going to be punishment. But as this is often the result, it is not surprising that many employees do their utmost to suppress them. This will also be true where complaints are used as a basis for 'reward' – for example, low numbers of complaints contributing to a bonus. Since more complaints equals no reward, they too will be suppressed, or at least under-recorded.

Learning from complaints

To learn from complaints, it is necessary to recognize that keeping the lid on solves nothing (p. 134 on customer satisfaction). Complaining has to be made easy and be seen as a valuable learning process.

Do all or at least some of the following and you will begin to learn.

▶ Give staff training in handling complaints and, in particular, show them the value of a complainant and how to recognize a complainant.
▶ Give staff the opportunity to feed back complaints in a way which is not threatening and which gives support to those who have difficulties – in other words, combine it with coaching.
▶ Give staff the means to settle complaints as far as possible on the spot – and record the costs of so doing because this is the real costs of the 'defect' (see Box 7.2).
▶ Make it easy for customers to complain by:
   – providing simple access by telephone to a dedicated number by using video booths in, for example, somewhere such as a baggage hall at an airport so that you collect immediate reactions;
   – providing simple, easy-to-complete forms that have at least one prominent, open-ended question. An interesting example is provided by Lexus in the USA who, on a research questionnaire sent to customers, put: 'If you are not happy with anything don't fill this in – just contact us so we can rectify it';
   – showing complainants you care and are interested, making sure that any expense on their part is compensated.

▶ Bring customers into a dialogue, as with Club Med.

▶ Set up a proper analysis system which avoids leagues of good or bad performers, since this will only serve to suppress discovery and to depress the real causes.

▶ See to it that such an analysis is followed rigorously.

▶ Have a proper 'defection' procedure.

▶ Keep trends, not just figures.

▶ Ensure that all management at every level talks to real customers, and not just others at their level – managing director to managing director, for example.

British Airways have recognized both the harm that complaints can do and the value that can be gained from treating them correctly. They have set up a Marketplace Performance Unit, who go way beyond the usual answering of letters to working right across the company, identifying causes, setting up systems and acting as a champion for the customer.

An example of an organization which has tackled these problems imaginatively is shown in Box 7.2.

External learning

Collecting and measuring the complaints of customers is a key part of external learning, but it is only a part. There is a need to know what could be done and to get early warning on problems – and learn about non-customers.

This is not just market research in the form of commissioned reports, but other forms of 'insight'. The systematic monitoring of press articles, omnibus reports and the studied gathering of customer views and comments – both yours and competitors.

Such learning needs to be systematic as with complaints. It will never have the same value if it is simply a loose set of data, with little or no way of relating either one piece of information to another or has no relationship over time. Learning must go beyond statistics to gain insights and be based on observing trends rather than on static results.

It is also necessary to be resolute in not looking for the silver lining just because there are storm clouds. A recent management report on a piece of external research for a large insurance company regularly referred throughout to the positive aspects: 'We met overall expectations of 63 per cent of our customers; 47 per cent have

BOX 7.2 *Understanding the true costs of failure*

Timothy Firnstahl, the owner of a chain of restaurants in and around Seattle, introduced a particularly interesting and constructive approach to using customer dissatisfaction. It is based on a customer guarantee and a 'system failure costs' analysis. The system accurately reflected failure costs by giving employees the authority to compensate customers, who were dissatisfied or had cause for dissatisfaction, without further reference. This ensured that not only were customers concerns seen to there and then, without hassle, but at the same time a 'cost' was created.

The 'system failure cost' worked because it concentrated on what is wrong with the system not the employee.

Further, Firnstahl said: '*By welcoming every guarantee pay-off – every system failure expense – as an otherwise lost insight you can make every problem pay a dividend. The trick is ... to insist on finding the ultimate cause of each problem and then demand and expect decisive change. In one case, our kitchens were turning out wrong orders at a rate that was costing thousands of dollars a month in wasted food. The cooks insisted that the food servers were punching incorrect orders into the kitchen printout computers. In times past, we might have ended the search right there, accused the food servers of sloppiness and asked everyone to be more careful. But now, adhering to the principle of system failure not people failure, we looked beyond the symptoms and found a flaw in our training. We had simply never taught food servers to double-check their orders on the computer screen and the system offered no reward for doing so. Mistakes plummeted (as soon as we rectified these points).*'

Firnstahl records that the system failure costs initially rose to $40,000 a month before falling over two years to $10,000 a month. Meanwhile sales rose by 25 per cent and profits doubled. He makes the critical point that, '*We used the same ultimate strategy to satisfy both customers and employees*'.

repurchased; 25 per cent would recommend us to a friend; 14 per cent felt valued as a customer' – while all the time downplaying or ignoring the negative aspects – '37 per cent were dissatisfied; 53 per cent had repurchased elsewhere; 39 per cent would never recommend us to anyone else [one in three of your customers had so little faith in you? – and it didn't even rate a mention in the accompanying text!]; 29 per cent were frustrated or annoyed'.

There is no point in doing research unless there is a preparedness to be honest about the answers. High percentages of failure may be unpleasant to contemplate but hiding behind the good figures – from people who generally don't complain or express their true feelings – is no use.

Customer satisfaction

Researching customer satisfaction is a key area of learning but it has some very special problems. Ninety-six per cent of unhappy customers don't complain and, typically, one in three of these will express 'satisfaction' but have no intention of either:

▶ **making a repeat purchase, if they have a choice;**
  or
▶ **recommending you to anyone else.**

These are the true tests of 'satisfaction'. Will you be the supplier of choice on some future occasion? Will the customer 'risk' a friendship by recommending you?

Few people are able to answer questions about 'satisfaction' in terms which are meaningful. There are a number of reasons for this.

▶ 'Being satisfied' has no absolute meaning. Maybe expectations were low so the outcome was, against those expectations, a welcome surprise. Perhaps the events in question were not that important to customers, either because they accord them a low priority or because there are plenty of alternatives.
▶ The general performance is so low that a particular event or happening may be simply of no consequence, it is merely a matter of waiting for an alternative to show up (see comments on the 'exit society' on p. 18).
▶ The general performance is so good that an event is not seen as being worth elevating to a criticism, although it may be of critical importance to you or the relationship with the customer in the longer run (see p. 44 on 'discontinuity').

To get at 'why?', and not simply 'what?', it is necessary to understand the true drivers of the customer's choice, preference and reaction. If you have a model of the 'process' which the customer is buying, and the discontinuities along this, this task will be a lot easier. For example:

▶ a passenger on a 'plane will be more likely to be 'driven' by issues such as the meals or other aspects of service on board than by issues of safety;
▶ a patient will be more likely to be 'driven' in their judgement of the value of hospital treatment as good or otherwise by the reception and care from nursing staff and the general facilities than from the consultant.

In the one case 'I can judge' and make comparisons; in the other I find it difficult to judge and anyway I am inclined to think that it must be all right. The drivers may, therefore, be quite different to those which are seen from within the business as key.

Acknowledgements and further reading

page 118   Argyris, C. (1989) *Strategy, Change and Defensive Routines*, Pitman.

page 124   Oslo University/Sparebankforeningen (Norway), and see article in *Sparbanklederen*, Issue No. 1, 1985.

page 124   *Letter to Shareholders*, Jack Welch *et al.* (p. 26)

page 129   'The Wind Beneath My Wings', a paper prepared for Dr David Jermison of University of Texas at Austin, by Janice Hunter, 1991.

page 133   ©1989 by the President and Fellows of Harvard College, all rights reserved, Firmstahl, T. W. (1989) 'My employees are my service guarantee', *Harvard Business Review*', July/August.

page 134   The input and advice of Chris Purves, Managing Director of the BMRB subsidiary, CSM, a part of the CSM Worldwide © network, was invaluable in developing the section on customer satisfaction.

Unfortunately, many of the writings quoted above are not generally available, though the book by Chris Argyris is – and well worth reading. Other reading which will give the interested manager further insights into 'learning' are:

Argyris, C. (1996) *Organizational Learning: Theory, Method and Practice*, Addison-Wesley.

(1996) 'Fire and forget?', *The Economist*, 20 April.

Jones, T. O. and Sasser, W. E. (1995) 'Why satisfied customers defect', *Harvard Business Review*, Nov/Dec.

Reicheld, F. F. (1996) *The Loyalty Effect. The Hidden Force behind Growth, Profits and Lasting Value*, Cambridge, MA: Harvard Business Press.

Stata, R. (1989) 'Organizational learning – the key to management innovation', *Sloan Management Review*, Spring.

Service leadership

It is a terrible thing to look over your shoulder when you are trying to lead – and find no one there.

Franklin D. Roosevelt

About this chapter

In a service the final processes cannot be finalized in a controlled situation, but are exposed to direct influence on the part of the customer at the interaction. To be successful, the strategic guideline must be open to the experiences of implementation. As a result, the role of management must change. What is needed are leaders, as a part of and not aloof from the everyday, inspiring coaching, creating that consistency needed to give staff – who 'manage' the interaction – the confidence to create distinction with the customer.

For those managers brought up on a belief that the 'correct' role model was a 'pirate', such as James Hanson (for many the archetype of the successful modern capitalist), this can be difficult to contemplate. Such chief executives as Rebecca Jenkins, Herb Kelleher, Arne Mårtensson or Julian Metcalfe, to name but four who have appeared so far in this book, are much closer to a role of 'building the ego' of the organization than that of swashbuckling pirate or predator pursuing mergers.

This chapter will look at what is involved in leadership.

▶ Why management cannot afford to have, or to be themselves, spectators.

▶ The recognition that there is nothing soft about being a leader – there is a need to demand performance, from oneself as well as others.

▶ The new compact that is emerging between managers and the managed.

▶ What is different about a leader and what makes for leadership.

▶ Why such change is more difficult than it seems.

▶ Why it needs a revolution to achieve.

When Rebecca Jenkins, the newly-appointed Managing Director of the distribution company, Lane Group, held her first open communication meeting for drivers and depot staff, she knew just what Roosevelt meant (see quote at the start of this chapter).

> *Looking back on it, I was naive, but I was shocked when I had my first open communication meeting and only one person attended! Drivers are independent minded but I knew we had to get all that energy and use it better. It sounds pompous but I believe it to be true, since I had seen at first hand the difference drivers can make. At first, it was difficult, but I persevered because they have a serious impact, as we can see when we get a bad report.*

The problem highlighted in Roosevelt's quote at the start of this chapter is faced by many managers in service businesses. It is less likely to be the proverbial 'going over the top of the trench', and finding yourself alone, than of finding that everyone appears to be standing back. They are there but simply watching and waiting for you to succeed or fail. Spectators to the events rather than participants or accomplices in achievement.

In *Zen and the Art of Motorcycle Maintenance*, Robert Pirsig makes exactly this point. The people he meets in the shop and who write the manuals, that never quite gave the insight needed, are all 'spectators': *'It (they) have no relationship to you, you have no relationship to it (them),'* and goes on to say, *'There was no manual that deals with the real business of motorcycle maintenance ... caring about what you are doing'.*

For service to become more than just good, a superservice, management have to have a vision and a passion, and they need to share that passion. They must be as concerned with the financial outcome as those managers who focus on the figures and budgets, but they must equally care – with a passion – that what they are doing has a value to, and creates a good experience for the customer. This has already been seen with Paul Dubrule and Gerard Pelisson, co-founders of Novotel, and Julian Metcalfe and Robin Sinclair, co-founders of Pret A Manger. In some form it is repeated in every long-term service success story.

The mutual purpose, the concern has to be so worthwhile, so compelling, that no one wants to be a spectator any longer – or simply cannot remain as a spectator – on the sidelines.

The destruction of the spectator syndrome is a core task for the leader in a service organization, linking effort to:

▶ a clear vision as to where the organization is going, and

▶ a collective belief and will on the part of the management team to go in that direction, achieve those specific aims and see that everyone shares the credit – not just in some empty phrase in the Report and Accounts, but as the 'heroes' who have made it all possible.

It means giving people the freedom to interpret within the guidelines, to make decisions: '*The right to be wrong*', to quote Michael Flaxman at Novotel, '*To be cherished for having made the decision rather than simply criticized for the mistake*'.

It's down to me!

With such empowerment goes responsibility. While superservice will provide great scope for the individual to exercise his or her abilities, it equally requires a need to accept the responsibility – to give more than the minimum, to colour outside the lines.

To quote Peter Drucker:

> '... *You have to focus on a person's performance. The individual must shoulder the burden of what his or her own contribution will be ... take more responsibility for himself or herself, rather than depend on the company*' and '*We have to demand – and demand is the word, nothing permissive – that people think through what constitutes the greatest contribution that they can make to the company in the next 18 months or 2 years*'.

It is why recruitment is so key (p. 62). Recognize, though, that if you want good staff you have to accept that they, too, will be demanding – of you! Recruitment of the best will achieve nothing if, when the recruits arrive, they are indulged rather than stretched. The best will leave; the others will quickly slip into avoidance of discomfort and the learning experiences – of the job and of self.

An advanced example of what is needed is provided by SOL Cleaning in Helsinki (Case Study 3.1). They have developed a culture which epitomizes the mix of passion, mutual purpose and involvement on the one hand and, on the other, a refusal to accept spectators.

It is highly egalitarian. Everyone has the chance – and the right – to be involved, to be heard. People are trusted to balance their lives and to adjust their work schedules to fit with this balance. The work has to be done, it does not always have to be done precisely then. Mothers and fathers will work odd hours so they can look after a family, or bring them into work with them where this a practical possibility. But there are no excuses for non-delivery: A failure to meet a deadline, for whatever reason, is a failure – 'it's down to me'.

Managing in the round

Since there is a need for people to give something of themselves, there is also a need to recognize that they have to be seen 'in the round': As people who are not just assets to manipulate, such as through performance-related pay, but as people who are valued for themselves and their contribution.

They can no longer have the security of job they took for granted a few years ago, but they can expect an understanding of what this (insecurity) means and look for support in meeting this insecurity. This is no trivial matter. Insecurity about their future ability to work is the key concern for most people, exceeded only in those with children, who have a similar concern for their children's ability to find work in the future.

People can't bring all their private problems into work but equally they cannot be expected to work as if their lives in work and out of it had no connection. Staff are not hidden on the factory floor. They are visibly there, with customers and with colleagues, whose promises to the customer includes them.

Such management in the round is a critical part of strategic management in a service. Recognizing that requires an approach to leadership which accepts service achievement and individual responsibility as central and not peripheral to the objectives of the organization. For example Southwest Airlines have achieved a ratio of passengers carried to staff of 2,318 against an industry average of 843, by 'inspiring' staff to give a level of service which, despite the low fares, surpasses their experiences elsewhere.

A new compact

Such developments reflect deep changes in people's aspirations and beliefs. Even more it is a reflection of the emergence of a new basis of cooperation between managers and the managed. They are illustrated in the case of SOL, in a form which many managers will find extreme, yet reflects what needs to be achieved if the aspirations of both customers and staff are to be met.

Bob Tyrrell at The Henley Centre sees *'Great hope for the future, because I see a new contract arising between the management and the staff in companies. There is a change in the terms of engagement. The Chief Executive has to earn respect and has to create that respect in others, of the "server" for him- or herself, for example. Success needs much more empathy with people than it needed before'.*

In future, the heroes will increasingly be those who:

▶ can understand the concepts of market and choice on the part of the customer and can harness all of the resources toward ensuring that the customer can put a value on the 'offer';

▶ can grasp concepts and are able to turn them to practical use;

▶ are effective at listening (p. 102) and able to listen to people down the line, not just their immediate peers;

▶ are good at challenging people in a way which creates encouragement, not discouragement;

▶ have the courage to share both the burden through delegation and the reward through recognition that their effort is but one among many;

▶ can reduce the vastness of the information flows to the essence of the matter, so that people may concentrate on what is truly important, and know that this is the imperative;

▶ are not only good at judging people but see the enhancement and protection of this as a critical part of their task, through development and recruitment, at all levels;

▶ can be effective in the much more transparent and open cultures that are a fact of life in a society which is less deferential and more exposed to external scrutiny, and

▶ are not so addictive to their work that they cannot see and share the ambitions and frustrations of those they seek to inspire.

What's different?

Many of the points listed above have already been made but it is bringing them together, in balance, which distinguishes leadership from management. Achieving this requires a different mind-set if the potential for releasing individual initiative and responsibility is to be realized.

This was illustrated by a further aspect of the Culture mapping research touched on in Chapter 4, and the questions used shed an interesting light on the demands placed on the service leader. These are set out in Box 8.1.

These questions are the distillation of a great deal of observation, research and experience. It is possible to see, from Questions 2, 5 and 6, that the role of leader is closely liked to communication and learning, the subjects of the last two chapters. However, while Question 4 under 'style' is essentially 'control orientated', in most superservice organizations this receives a high score from management. This can be attributed to the fact that such organizations achieve success by making it crystal clear what is expected – and the

BOX 8.1 *Service leadership questions*

Questions regarding 'confidence'
(These are shown on the horizontal axis in Figure 8.1)

These determine the level of confidence (horizontal axis) felt by people within the organization. This is a direct result of their feeling of identification with what is happening and, even more specifically, with what they are personally being asked to do.

1 I understand how my job helps us to be successful with our customers.
2 Any personal problems I have at work are always taken into consideration.
3 There is always someone for me to discuss any problems I have with the work I do.
4 I am always kept well-informed about events or changes happening within the company.

Questions regarding 'style'
(These are shown on the vertical axis in Figure 8.1)

These signify the balance between, on the one hand, control – what is necessary to keep the ship on course and correct this as necessary – and, on the other, leadership – what is necessary to give inspiration to others.
It is important to my success:

1 That we concentrate above all on achieving set targets (e.g. sales).
2 That I consider the views of those I work with or who work for me.
3 That we have set procedures which we stick to at all times.
4 That people are told precisely what they have to do.
5 That my immediate manager is someone that I can use to help achieve my goals.
6 That people are given a chance to try out their own ideas.

basis of judgement of success or failure – and then give people freedom to achieve within the guidelines. In fact, where management see themselves as more 'leaders' than do their staff, it has been an invariable sign of trouble.

For what is different about leadership as opposed to management is that the leader still has to exert control, but that control is:

▶ clear and consistent, not capricious;
▶ related to achievement externally, not self-promotion;
▶ free of interference in implementation, and
▶ oriented toward encouraging others to accept responsibility and achieve reward.

Some actual results, taking the same two airline examples used in Chapter 4, are shown in Figure 8.1.

It is possible to see once more that the airline with the superior performance, A, has a markedly more coherent pattern than the other, B. They are both similar in 'confidence' – airlines 'sexy' image

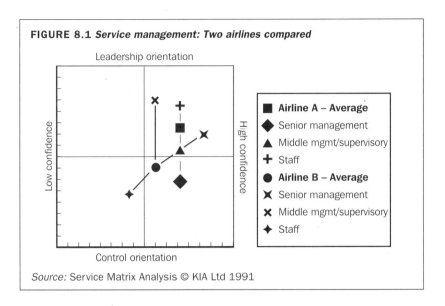

FIGURE 8.1 *Service management: Two airlines compared*

Source: Service Matrix Analysis © KIA Ltd 1991

means that they usually attract and keep good, self-confident staff, the difference being that they do not always use them well – but B:

▶ has results which are more widespread, and
▶ has a management result of greater significance, which inverts the control/leadership axis – their staff do not see them as the leaders they see themselves to be.

Overall, two key points emerge from such research.

1. It is an invariable danger sign when 'management' score more toward 'leadership' than their subordinates on the 'control/leadership orientation' dimension – the vertical.

Even slight variations in this direction are associated with lack of cohesion over objectives or values, or both. Often at a time of change, managers seem to disappear 'northwards', where they take refuge in being 'leaders'. They have often been encouraged in this by training courses on leadership which have filled them with a belief about what they should do but not the confidence to go with it! In extreme cases this can lead them into 'the aimless quarter' – top left quarter on the map – by which time there is little hope!

2. As importantly, it proved difficult for organizations that scored low on the 'confidence' dimension – the horizontal – to achieve consistent service.

In particular, note that the most common factor for 'lack of confidence' is not 'lack of knowledge' (of what was going on), but 'not understanding why' and 'not being able to reconcile personal concerns about developments'. In other words, people suffered from 'role conflict', between their personal understandings, or lack of them, and beliefs and what they were being asked to do.

What makes a leader?

Leading a service organization to produce superservice takes an approach to managing which relies heavily on giving inspirational direction rather than detailed operational control. It is about developing a collaborative culture throughout the organization, where:

▶ **everyone plays their role, regardless of rank or position, ensuring that the customers' expectations are known and met;**

▶ **everyday learning is commonplace, a part of the job;**

▶ **'soft', psychodynamic, factors are integrated with 'hard' market achievement and demands on individual and team contributions.**

The management task has to be seen as a service, provided so that the organization can work to achieve its ambitions. Yet for many, management is an end in itself. That this is no new phenomenon, is illustrated by the quote from William Shakespeare's *As You Like It* (written about 1600), when Orlando says:

> *Thou art not for the fashion of these times*
> *Where none will sweat but for promotion*
> *And having that do choke their service up.*

Nor is the need simply the result of the service revolution, but rather, as the service revolution itself, it is a result of dramatic shifts in the make up and ambitions of society, particularly the shifts toward individuality, femininity and economic independence. John Harvey-Jones, formerly Chief Executive for ICI, has written: '*I believe absolutely that in the future it will be the company that conforms to the individual that attracts and motivates the best people. Companies will have to be more flexible in their demands, to accommodate more and more the individual's different hopes, wishes and ambitions.*'

Jack Welch, at General Electric, also talks of the 'transformation' of management and the need for 'business leaders' rather than managers. He stresses that this is not primarily a system or organizational change but is a, '*Redefining [of] the relationship between boss and subordinate*'. He goes on to stress that this behavioural change is a crucial ingredient of GE's success and echoes the comments on recruitment (p. 62), by stressing that it will only work where management make sure that their management team reflect their values. Writing in the 1995 *Letter to Shareholders*, he says:

> It was at Work-Out sessions that it became clear that some of the rhetoric heard at the corporate level – about involvement and excitement and turning people loose – did not match the realities of life in the businesses. The problem was that some of our leaders were unwilling, or unable, to abandon big-company, big-shot autocracy and embrace the values we were trying to grow. So we redefined our management styles, or types, and how they furthered or blocked our values. And then we acted.
>
> Type I not only delivers on performance commitments, but believes in and furthers GE's 'small company' values. The trajectory of this group is 'onward and upward', and the men and women who comprise it will represent the core of our senior leadership in the next century.
>
> Type II does not meet commitments, nor share our values – nor last long at GE.
>
> Type III believes in the values but sometimes misses commitments. We encourage taking swings, and Type III is typically given another chance.
>
> Type IV. The 'calls' on the first two types are easy. Type III takes some judgement; but Type IV is the most difficult. One is always tempted to avoid taking action, because Type IV's deliver short-term results. But Type IV's do so without regard to values and, in fact, often diminish them by grinding people down, squeezing them, stifling them. Some of these learned to change; most couldn't. The decision to begin removing Type IV's was a watershed – the ultimate test of our ability to 'walk the talk', but it had to be done if we wanted GE people to be open, to speak up, to share, and to act boldly outside of traditional 'lines of authority' and 'functional boxes' in this new learning environment.

Handelsbanken management comment on this need to be firm about values and the difficulty some managers have. '*It was tough at first; some managers failed to adjust. It took some years. We still have to work at it*' (after 25 years), and '*We [still] have to be prepared to deal with people who cannot measure up to the values of responsibility – probably much more than most organizations have to elsewhere.*'

The challenge of such leadership is to ensure that the sum is greater than the parts. Like the conductor of an orchestra, it will be the ability to create something more than can be given by the individuals in the orchestra and by the soloists – many of whom may be individually more brilliant and gifted than the conductor. A conductor does not need to be charismatic, though some are, but he or she does need to convey a clear vision of what is to be achieved from the performance, to be clear and consistent in direction and unswerving in control.

This is difficult for many managers to accept, particularly if they have been brought up in an Anglo-Saxon world, where it was sufficient to say, '*A manager has to manage*' to forgive almost any action. Of course managers have to manage, but if they want to consistently deliver superservice in today's social climate, they have to manage differently – they have to give collective inspiration and gain collective support. Leadership involves some toleration of chaos because of the need to stress individual responsibility and the creation of involvement. It is a very different task from that of managers working in a conventional environment, who seek order and control.

What it means to be a leader in a service environment, and some of the trials and difficulties to be met, are well summarized by the experiences of Rebecca Jenkins and her colleagues at Lane Group, in Case Study 8.1. It shows that:

- ▶ leaders need to have a passion and need to share that passion;
- ▶ success requires a sufficient depth of belief as to make it possible to be persistent in adversity;
- ▶ everyone in the organization has something to contribute;
- ▶ you need to demonstrate that you really mean what you say, persevere and show that it has real meaning, it is not just words;
- ▶ an investment of this kind in the 'easy times' can pay-off handsomely in the 'hard times', and
- ▶ it is not a once-and-for-all task.

Change highlights need

Organizations which have built their success over many decades by growth from a strong national basis or from a local culture or family influence look to the future with some concern. They appreciate that the very strength of their past success has the potential to frustrate their need to create changes in the way people work. It is at a time of change that the need to adopt new approaches to management becomes most evident.

One Lufthansa manager said: '*In the past, we focused almost too much on just delivering reliable products. Now our customers not only expect reliability, they also expect excellent service, and we have to work harder than ever to respond to their needs*'.

CASE STUDY 8.1 – LANE GROUP

When Rebecca Jenkins became Managing Director of Lane Group in 1988, she was convinced that Lane had to adopt a strategy of building strong relationships with like-minded customers.

> We could see that for us to survive and prosper in competition with many, much bigger competitors, we would have to develop a strong competitive edge. From our experience and knowledge, we saw that that had to come from demonstrating that we understood their problems better than others and would go that little bit further to help them solve them. We could not just deliver goods. To do that effectively, we had to have the involved support of everyone in the company, and our suppliers, too.
>
> As I had started in this business as a driver, I knew that it was particularly important for us to get them onside. I knew the amount of information a driver had about what was happening, with our customers and our competitors, and the real difference they could make in getting across our interest and concern. I also knew how little they were asked to contribute in reality – anywhere! So, if we could mobilize that potential, we had an enormous advantage.

So Lane Group began a major change, centred around more open communication and demonstrated to everyone through actions that the culture was going to change. For example, meetings were organized for drivers, where they could talk with top management.

> At first, it was difficult [see quote at beginning of this chapter] but I persevered because they have a serious impact, as we can see when we get a bad report. So it was a question of not letting go, of posting up results of meetings, letting people see that we were creating dialogue on things that mattered to them. For example, which new vehicles we should be buying, or changes to the style of uniform. And, of course, we talked about the problems they were encountering and what changes were needed.
>
> It has worked. Now such meetings are well attended, despite the fact that many of them work long hours for many days, often away from home. We have also learnt that it is not enough to communicate. You have to explain 'why' you want to communicate; what you hope to achieve. People have to see that it is going to work both ways. The Unions have not been directly involved in this process but they are definitely more committed to responding now; less immediately rejecting of change.
>
> We have made a conscious effort to consolidate our thinking and two years ago the management team spent some time agreeing our

*key values. There was almost complete unanimity so we went for-
ward and said we would live by them. We still have a lot to do to
live by them fully, but making that decision has pushed a lot faster.*

*Of course, whilst things were going well we didn't realize how
relatively easy it was. But 1994 was a bad year. Then we learnt how
easy it had been to tell people things in the good times. But we
persevered and showed not only that we meant it but that we
needed their support. They could see this and we are a stronger
company for that bad year.*

Eight years on, and it is clear that people really do care, that the values
talked of in head office do inform the way that people work, out in the
depots and on the road. For Gary Hutchinson, the manager of the
Normanton distribution depot, *'The values are really important. I have
children and I am particularly impressed with the environmental
approach the company adopts'.* He goes on to talk about the difference
it makes working in an environment where people are really concerned.
*'I came from a family background in haulage, so I know the differ-
ences. We really do try to get the best out of people. Sometimes they
make mistakes but that is how they learn. We try and learn from it and
see if there couldn't have been a better way.'*

*'No one could say that the management don't take their values
seriously. They really are something they work by',* commented Simon
Mayo, who runs the Next contract.

'Yet, we are still learning,' says Rebecca Jenkins, *'I think getting
The Body Shop contract has been important to us, because it has
helped to support and encourage us in the direction we knew we
had to take. Now, creating a relationship with the customer is no
more than a way of doing business. It is difficult to quantify. We
have had success but might we have done anyway? We do know,
however, from research that lack of contact or individual attention
account for over two-thirds of contracts not being renewed and that
this far outweighs lower prices or better services as a cause.*

*Where to in the future? We already have a stable workforce by
industry standards but this has to be a high priority because we are
not nearly as good as someone like UPS in the States, for example.
We have a 4.5 per cent annual turnover against an industry average
of 13 per cent, but UPS have just 2 per cent! There is lots of room
for improvement here. It means we have to put more effort into
recruitment and given our philosophy, we really can't afford to lose
them. We need continuity.'*

Sainsburys' management echoes this: '*Our characteristic is a strong, hands-on management style. But as the company grows larger, we have to empower a greater number of management throughout the organization. We must help them take risks; accept the odd mistake, and help them learn from it. That means we [top management] have to give a little too. We cannot simply put in a new rule book. We have to enable managers more than in the past*'.

A merger will also highlight differences – and uncovering the real beliefs of those involved can reveal hidden synergy. For example, Falck – a Danish company which uniquely runs fire services for local authorities, as well as ambulance and breakdown services from a series of 'fire stations' across Denmark – bought an alarm company, Securitas. The commercial fit was obvious; the cultural fit less so. However, Culture mapping revealed that both organizations had deep-seated value systems, many of the components of which they held in common. It was possible to build a sound merger plan at grassroots level based on this commonality.

When the French Lyonnaise des Eaux, a water and other local services organization, bought the construction company Dumez, the contrast in values was even stronger. As Guy de Panafieu, the Managing Director of Lyonnaise des Eaux describes:

> *We take a very long-term view of service. If we see something needs doing [with the customer], we do it first and discuss who pays afterwards. We are in it for the long-term and this [attitude] is a sound investment. But such values are not shared by everyone. We always used to steer clear of becoming involved in construction work, because we saw the contractors as hunters who were interested in making a kill and then moving on. Essentially we are farmers, although maybe given the attitudes in construction and the long-term nature of our business, conquerors and foresters are better analogies; we know we will be here tomorrow and that we have to live with the results.*
>
> *However, more and more we realize that even when customers start a project, of say, building an office, they don't want to be hunted; they want to get the value of the investment over the lifetime of its use – a farming concept. So we have gone back into construction [with the merger with Dumez], but this time as part of the service, so that there is no break between building and the running of it afterwards. That's a big cultural problem we have to tackle. To integrate the values of service into the initial construction of a project – whether it's a new waterworks, or a new bridge – and create a unity out of both this [construction] and the service maintenance, once it has been built.*

This shift to seeing the provision of the 'hard goods' and subsequent service as indivisible is reflected, too, in the General Electric moves, quoted earlier, and is in turn a reflection of the shift in society from possession to usage. However, the change is not as easy as just wanting to do it, as Jack Welch acknowledged, saying, *'It's been hard for the old equipment businesses, where building the latest high-efficiency this and high-efficiency that was the route to epaulettes on your shoulder'*. Some service competitors doubt GE will make it, one of them commenting, rightly, *'Moving from being a product company to a service company is much more difficult than some of these folks think'*. 'Why?' is bound-up with the whole change in the value system that has to accompany such a move, if service is to be more than an add-on. What is involved is illustrated in the article reproduced in Box 8.2.

Middle management in a squeeze

For one group of managers, these changes create a particular problem which they cannot solve solely by themselves – middle management, who are in a squeeze between the new 'leaders' and the increasingly self-managed workforce. Their traditional source of power with the workforce – knowledge power – has gone, yet they are still expected by their superior management to 'be in control'.

The confusion is well illustrated when two such eminent writers as Peter Drucker and Tom Peters can be quoted in *The Economist*, in 1988, as saying that, *'Middle management are, or will be, a thing of the past'*, but by 1994 can be writing, *'That there is a gap and supervisors are a neglected species'*. Why the change? Because what has happened – is happening – is that the role of middle managers is changing from:

▶ the person who 'knows what management want, so do as I say';
▶ to the person who 'knows no more than you do, but I can give you a lead on how we might tackle that';
▶ and 'I have influence enough to bring about change – if that is what is needed'.

In this context, the 'middle manager' is any manager who is in the 'middle', that is, is carrying out the implementation, rather than being directional. Apart from a very few at the top, all managers are 'middle managers' in some way, at some time.

BOX 8.2 *Hunters and Farmers – a change parallel*

It seems to us in retrospect, and it seemed to the American Indians themselves at the time, an idyllic life. Land was plentiful, nature was bountiful and it was easy to move on across the vastness of the continent, living from the proceeds of hunting and gathering. And how exciting that hunting could be. There were certainties to life, too. These were essentially masculine certainties, agreed, but for everyone life had a structure which was clear and understandable. Of course, it was often harsh and brutal, usually unforgiving, but that's life!

It was a society that was about to die and nothing could save it, for another continent was exporting its surplus labour. Land was going to become too valuable for the wasteful methods of hunting and gathering; farming was going to be the key to future prosperity. But farming is not just different from hunting in its structure but in its whole culture. It requires stability, a consistent and persistent work input and greater interdependence between peoples to be effective.

Many American Indians could see the inevitability of change, and many wanted to change too, but their whole style of managing their affairs, the way they 'chose' heroes and won fame, was as alien to a farming culture as was the incomer's culture to them. It was sad, but many brave, and hitherto successful, men and women were to die in the transition.

The story of the American West is, of course, much more complex than that and the real story is only recently being looked at from all sides; but in simple terms it can be seen as an inevitable change, which could only have been dealt with more humanely and honestly, but probably not fundamentally altered.

Today as the world moves from a manufacturing culture to a service culture, as more and more competitors arrive on the scene to divert away our customers, we can see industry and commerce going through a change as far reaching as that facing the American Indians in the nineteenth century.

Managers everywhere are reacting to this. Indeed, already it seems as if every business has suddenly rediscovered that they have existing customers to 'farm', to build relationships with. But as with the American Indians, such attempts are most often doomed to failure, to flounder in a whirlpool of misunderstood signals and unimagined reactions. For it requires not just 'knowing' but rather a wholesale change in the way we work. The 'heroes' in such a culture are different; the ways to win fame and fortune less simple, less clear cut. Even the 'hunting' that is left is changed. Dead animals and scalps are no longer enough; the need is to hunt for stock that can be husbanded and developed.

Extracted from an article by the author which appeared in the 1995 Summer edition of *Baakbericht*, the Magazine of de Baak Centrum in Nordwijk, The Netherlands.

Middle managers are necessary because in today's organization, where technology provides information to all and employees are less deferential, it is the middle manager who holds the fabric together. He or she is the 'enabler', taking the guiding light and ensuring that its ideals reach the point of interaction, and that there is feedback and adjustment to the plans.

Good middle managers will move away from treating work as a series of transactions, meriting reward or punishment, to the encouragement of people to bend their own self-interest toward the interests of the group. He or she will be a key part of the process of lifelong learning and continuous change that will characterize most organizations in future and will be a key figure in everyday learning (p. 120) Novotel, for example, refer in their internal literature to the Maître de Maison (p. 121) as being, 'More like the coach of a sports team than a conventional manager'.

Revolution not evolution

The changes that management have to face are far reaching in their effect and in their impact on individuals. They are in fact, revolutionary and nothing short of a revolutionary change will bring them about. Attempts to evolve are almost always doomed to failure, with people agreeing on the rightness of change but their vested interests, or fear of learning new tricks, keeping their feet firmly on the old path.

Achieving service leadership cannot be partial. You are either going to be a butterfly or stay a caterpillar. You are either going to have service leadership or you are not. The management style is either supportive of learning from experience, gaining insight from mistakes as well as success, or it is not.

With evolution, reforms become modified to meet the resistance of those who see little benefit from change – and a great deal of risk and loss of simple 'do as I say' power – and are then deflected from the main purpose, to break down the old control and command, essentially hierarchical, approach to management. Partial reform too often moves from 'telling' to 'stop telling and make them guess' – or so it appears to those at the receiving end. It is also responsible for the 'drift' to aimlessness, seen in the culture mapping research (p. 54).

What needs to happen – what is happening in successful service organizations – is nothing short of a revolution in management of which the key constituents are as follows:

► Staff close to the customer are becoming their own managers, more able to control the content and pace of their work relative to the demands of the customers.

► Managers are, in turn, increasingly taking up tasks previously left to subordinates – we are all telephonists now and, increasingly,

FIGURE 8.2 *Change cannot be partial!*

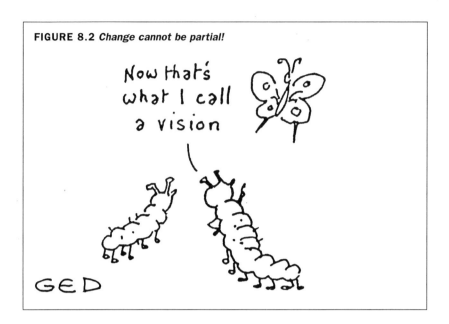

secretaries, too! – and it is less and less acceptable that 'the boss' stands aloof.

▶ Middle managers are losing their traditional power – 'Do as I say because I know and because I say so' – and instead are acquiring a new power based on influence, an influence to get things changed because the strategy and its implementation are no longer sequential but are interwoven, with the capacity to feed back the reality of that implementation and get modifications in the light of experience.

▶ Traditional top managers' roles, of command and control, are having to give way to a less 'heroic' role, in which it is encouraging the performance of others which is key, humility not self-glorification.

Like all revolutions, it will fall short of its original ideals, at least at the beginning. Not everything will be achieved at once, nor will some things ever be achieved, not least because the process itself will open up new and previously unimagined opportunities and reveal new problems. Yet the attempt at revolution has to be made or the impetus to overcome inertia will never be sufficiently strong.

page 139   Pirsig, A. (1974) *Zen and the Art of Motorcycle Maintenance,* Bodley Head.

page 140   Peter Drucker (1993) quoted in the *Harvard Business Review,* May/June.

page 141   The Henley Centre for Forecasting.

page 142   Ken Irons (1990) 'Managing Service Companies – strategies for success', *Economist Intelligence Unit Management Guides,* No P651.

page 145   Harvey-Jones, J. (1988) *Making it Happen,* Collins.

page 145   Jack Welch, quoted by N. Tichy and R. Chavan (1989) in *Harvard Business Review,* Sept/Oct.

page 146   'Letter to Shareholders', Jack Welch *et al.* (p. 26).

page 151   Interview with Guy de Panafieu, Managing Director of Lyonnaise des Eaux, quoted from 'Managing Service Companies: strategies for success' (p. 14).

page 151   Jack Welch quoted in *Business Week,* 28 October (1996).

In addition to the published works quoted from above, and the already recommended works of Charles Handy and Chris Argyris (see pages 27, 70 and 135), further reading on management and leadership includes:

Badaracco, J. and Ellsworth, R. (1996) 'Leadership and the quest for integrity', *Harvard Business Review,* Nov/Dec.

Farkas, C. M. and DeBacker, P. (1996) *The World's Leading CEOs Share their Five Strategies,* Henry Holt.

Handy, C. (1991) *Gods of Management – the changing world of organizations,* Business Books.

Syer, J. (1996) *How Teamwork Works,* McGraw-Hill.

Teal, T. (1996) *Tales of Management – Courage and Tenacity,* Harvard Business School Press.

Waldrop, J. and Butler, T. (1996) 'The executive as coach', *Harvard Business Review,* Nov/Dec.

Value to the customer

There is a huge difference between 'the best money can buy' and 'the best value for the dollar'. Knowing which is more important for the customer is crucial.

Henry Ford

About this chapter

'Value' is about providing value to the customer, not just about internal notions of 'quality' or setting standards. Pricing and costs need to be seen in relationship to this view of value because, despite the apparent emphasis placed on price by the customer, other factors can, and do, play a highly significant role. Quality also needs to be viewed as part of the overall culture or it may simply absolve people of the responsibility of responding to the customer.

This chapter will look at what is involved in providing value to the customer.

▶ Looking at what value means to the customer.

▶ Why it is important to design around the customer.

▶ Looking at the impact of this thinking on price.

▶ Why a value of thrift is more important than cost cutting.

▶ Why stability of customers and staff is an important factor in productivity.

▶ The importance of viewing value – and quality – holistically.

▶ Reviewing the introduction of structured approaches to quality and standards.

The Texan paradox

Roy Jespersen (not his real name) is a successful attorney with a practice based in Albuquerque, New Mexico. Catching Southwest Airlines Flight 1439 to Dallas of a morning has become something of a routine because, for reasons he can't quite remember now, he has built up a number of clients in Texas.

Roy used to fly American Airlines, but one of his clients made him feel a bit uncomfortable one day by questioning why he spent all that money when Southwest was so much cheaper – and then laughed when he replied that he 'wanted service'.

He has since found out why, because he actually got service on Southwest. They treated him as a human being, something he had rarely experienced on any airline before – and it was a third of the price, which wasn't unimportant given the pressures on fees these days. Gone were the days when clients just accepted the invoice; now they would expect an estimate or even ask for a fixed fee.

Business was good, and Roy had often thought he should open an office in Dallas, but he spent enough time away from the family as it was. When he needed to stop over, the Four Seasons hotel at Irving, nearby, had become something of a home-away-from-home. There were much cheaper hotels, of course, but the service was great and it impressed his clients. Besides, he could get all the services he needed from the hotel to make an effective office – and they would bring him a meal at 2 o'clock in the morning if he wanted it, so why bother?

Each and every day we see this paradox repeated, as customers and companies chase down costs and prices, yet customers still spend, sometimes lavishly, on items – or services – they want. The existence, side by side of a Four Seasons hotel and a Novotel may reasonably be seen as a reflection of different customers and different expectations – though some people stay in both at different times, even when they have the choice.

'Why?' is a key question in any consideration of what is value in a service.

What is the value to me?

In fact, Roy Jespersen is demonstrating very clearly 'why'. He has made decisions which reflect his belief in what is important for him.

He has decided that:

▶ He loses nothing by flying Southwest, indeed he looks smarter and, as Herb Kelleher at Southwest says, *'People are willing to give up perfection in a service, for some kind of human recognition'*;

▶ By staying at the Four Seasons he gains the social recognition he feels he needs for his work and stays in surroundings he finds are convenient and congenial, again with human recognition.

Roy is also demonstrating two deeper truths.

▶ Value to the customer lies in the utilization of a purchase – the functionality related to purpose – not the intrinsic values of the purchase itself.

▶ Being yourself, demonstrating smartness in your choice, even if subconsciously, it is a vitally important part of the process of choosing and buying.

Research shows that customers will often choose a low price service – or product – because they don't want to appear stupid by having paid too much. They know, if not from themselves then from the media and colleagues and friends, that they have a choice and they feel obliged to exercise this, to look smart. Unless they have a convincing justification, or are given one, why pay more?

Designing around the customer

Customers may see in an item or a service a value which has merit in terms of the status, the pride of possession, contact with like-minded people, rubbing shoulders with the great or in being healthy – all heavily subjective. Such considerations are also more important when 'I have a choice' – which people increasingly do. The belief that price is the only factor in this choice is a false interpretation of the trends in the market today. What customers are doing is showing that they have choice – and they intend to exercise it.

In organizations which aspire to be service leaders:

▶ it is customer's expectations which are the basis of design of the service;

▶ customer experiences which will be the judge of success or failure.

Novotel and Southwest, have designed their whole business around such a clear definition of customer needs, relative to the price they are prepared to pay. For both companies it has been a question of rigorous analysis of what the customer wanted and was prepared to pay for, and eliminating those things that were perhaps of interest – 'and I'll have them if you give them to me' – but which were not really important.

How many organizations can truly measure up to this? How many organizations have cut really deeply into the organization and said of every cost, 'What value does this bring to the customer'?

What is almost always missing in most service initiatives – total quality, cost cutting and the rest – is any identifiable, sustained attempt at creating a more stable base through added value for the customer, or improving productivity by gaining new or retaining existing customers. As functionality eats into strategy, odd services are added here, a new core product variant there. Novotel call this 'amenity creep', the constant, marginal accretions, each one on its own of small cost – and usually small consequence, in terms of effect – creates cost structures out of line with customers willingness to pay, and then creates a 'cost-cutting' backlash.

Nor is much done to 'educate' the customer. Frequently, those staff who could do the explaining are the very staff who have been eliminated in the cost reduction drive. Any that are left are far too busy coping with the imperatives of the business, such as budgets or compliance with unchanged procedures, to have the time.

It needs to be more. If the operation is to be driven by the customer it needs to be designed around the customer. In this design, quality of service and cost are companions, not opposite ends of a continuum. The right balance needs to be made at the interaction.

Price platforms

Of course, price is a key factor – and in some cases possibly the decisive factor. The increasingly 'discriminating aware customer' we first met in Chapter 1, is often acutely aware of a lack of substantiation of price provided by many, if not most, service organizations. This can be of special significance when the 'high-risk' nature of buying a service (p. 96) is taken into account; the need for reassurance that a price is justified is even greater.

In the design of the offer to the customer, price cannot be seen in purely economic terms. Pricing is grounded in economic theory, but it is not economics. It is equally important to consider the price platform which you occupy, and to recognize that, depending on the answer to this, the part that price plays may be significantly different.

In service markets, indeed in most markets today, the classical views of the relationship between supply and demand and of a single market for price, are of questionable value in arriving at pricing decisions. Such relationships are more likely to be over a number of separate bands of price/value relationships, which progressively degenerate at either end. This effect is shown in Figure 9.1, where there are three bands representing three different markets, from a 'commodity supplier', through a 'standard supplier', to a 'premium supplier'.

With the 'commodity supplier' and the 'standard supplier' price/demand relationships are both close to the classical view, though they have considerable differences, one from the other. For the most part, with a 'standard' product or service, large changes in price may result in only small changes in demand. Whereas, for a 'commodity', changes in price can have a significant effect on demand. However, with a 'premium supplier', the 'classical' effect is unlikely and the incentive to reduce price is small.

Obviously, such general representations are just indications and what is important in viewing price/demand relationships in this way, is to recognize that shifts in price can only be sure of their effect in a situation where there is a clear view of both the 'platform' you are on and 'where' on this platform. In particular, note:

▶ A small variation in price may have a direct relationship, as in the classical 'supply/demand' model. Even then, the impact of inflation and more volatile price conditions may equally make small adjustments less sensitive.

▶ However, a large change in price may break such a relationship entirely, as illustrated in Figure 9.1.

What is 'small' and what is 'large' must be a matter for specific judgement in a particular case. A Four Seasons hotel, for example, will be on the higher of the price platforms. By contrast, the low price Formule 1 hotels of the Accor Group will be on the lower platform. A slight variation of price in the, say, $250 (approximately £110) charge for a room at a Four Seasons will probably have little effect; a slight variation in price with Formule 1 (approximately £19), even in slight percentage terms, will probably have a big effect. A big variation in the price of a Four Seasons room price

Value to the customer

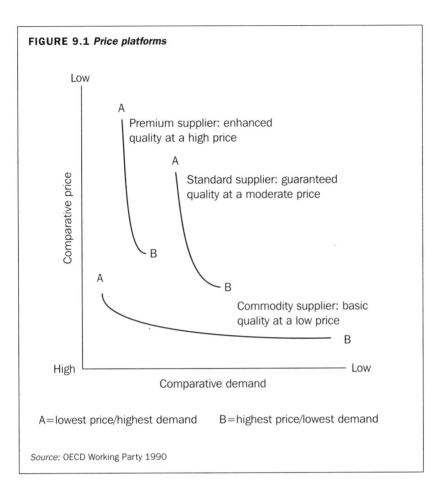

FIGURE 9.1 Price platforms

Low

A

Premium supplier: enhanced
quality at a high price

A

Standard supplier: guaranteed
quality at a moderate price

B

A

B

Commodity supplier: basic
quality at a low price

B

Comparative price

High

Low

Comparative demand

A=lowest price/highest demand   B=highest price/lowest demand

Source: OECD Working Party 1990

downwards would most likely not so much stimulate demand as raise conflicts in customers minds about the 'value'. It would shift Four Seasons onto another price platform, and put price out of line with the other elements of the service mix. Since Formule 1 could only experience a big shift upwards, it would completely alter the balance of market perceptions and reactions to experience.

Airlines typically operate across a number of price platforms. This has a tendency to make them inflexible, and achieve a cost base which is satisfactory to one 'platform' but not the others, even, sometimes, none of them. Regulation and other barriers to entry have made it possible for airlines to continue with this but, as Southwest Airlines shows, an airline concentrating on just one clear platform, with no confusions, can succeed like no other.

All the same, British Airways cannot adopt the simplicity of Southwest across their intercontinental network. Starting from the premise that they 'sell not a seat but an experience orchestrated across the whole airline', BA seek to add value in a number of small ways which allow them to compete within the various price platforms at a marginal premium rate, typically 5 per cent or so. However, the cost base of the two airlines is in no way comparable, because Southwest are able to be rigorous in the application of costs to a single, and very specific, target.

Costs and customer value

When a service is designed around the customer, and as a result the customer perceives service beyond the ordinary, it is noticeable how often this results in that organization being among the lowest-cost operators for their sector of the market. This is because costs are directed against those things that matter to the customer; other costs are eliminated. For them, thrift is a part of the culture, not the result of destructive cost-cutting campaigns.

Many cost-cutting exercises fail to achieve their objectives in other than the short term, because the links between usage of internal resources and revenue generating activity is not established. The analysis is of the cost structure itself not of the cost benefits. One way of overcoming this lack of a link is outlined in 'Action planning' (Chapter 11).

Even with the delivery of superservice, few top managers have followed cost saving with the vigorousness of SOL Cleaning (Case Study 3.1), where even the Chairman's office has been chased out of existence as unnecessary for the customer. Most, though, have not shrunk from linking effective cost expenditure to their success, or in involving people in the organization in the pursuit of keeping costs down. They make cost effectiveness a key value as in, '*We only spend money that creates value for our customer*' (SOL), or, '*It is good to be thrifty. We are lean and hungry. That is an important part of our image*' (Handelsbanken). Others find imaginative ways of talking about costs, so that people can see the links between expenditure and result, as illustrated in Box 9.1, an extract from the Southwest in-house magazine. (Incidentally, Love Field Airport, Dallas, is the home of Southwest – hence 'LUV Lines'!)

Few companies would launch a new market initiative without at least some research or insight into customer needs, yet cost reduction is frequently carried out in this way. Sometimes the analysis is so badly carried out, that the model selected is one that, in reality, performs badly. Management in that branch or sector are simply working the 'system' to get good results, without reference to the customer.

BOX 9.1 *Being low cost and proud of it!*

'How important is *every* customer to our future? Our Finance Department reports that our break-even customers per flight in 1994 was 74.5, which means that, on average, only when Customer Number 75 came on board did a flight become profitable! That statistic confirms the necessity of *every* customer to a high-volume business like ours.

Aside from that statistical data, let me share with you a down-to-earth formula devised by our Dallas Chief Pilot, Ken Gile. It utilizes our annual profit and total flights flown to clearly illustrate how vital each customer is to our profitability and our very existence.

When you divide our 1994 annual profit by total flights flown, you get profit per flight:

$$\frac{\$179,331,000 \text{ (annual profit)}}{624,476 \text{ (total flights flown)}} = \$287 \text{ (profit } \textit{per flight)}$$

Then, divide profit per flight by our systemwide average one-way fare of $58:

$$\frac{\$287 \text{ (profit per flight)}}{\$58 \text{ (average one-way fare)}} = 5 \text{ (one-way fares [}\textit{customers!}\text{])}$$

The bottom line, only *five* customers per flight accounted for our total 1994 profit! In other words, just five customers per flight – only three million of our total 40 million customers – meant the difference between profit and loss for our airline in 1994. To take it a step further, to have lost the business of only *one* of those customers would have meant a 20 per cent loss on that flight. That's how valuable each customer is to Southwest and you!'

Extract from *LUV Lines*, November 1995

To take an example, one insurance company created Customer Service teams in branches, to deal with routine incoming enquiries from the public. Brokers could use the service, but were encouraged to go direct to their specific customer handling team. One branch had particularly good results in 'training' brokers to do this, with consequent cost savings in staff time. They were held up as a model – but later, research showed that the reason for this 'success' was due to the unhelpfulness of the staff involved. Brokers quickly got the message, but success was not what it seemed. They had gone elsewhere because of poor service – not the intended, or measured, result.

Productivity from stability

Consistency in the containment of costs will come from making thrift core to the philosophy; recognizing it as a value, not a purely financial concern. Such a longer-term approach will be enhanced where there is

stability – stability of staff and stability of customers. The productivity of a service – that is, the result of optimizing the balance between inputs (costs) and outputs (revenue) – will be more affected by this than other single factor.

There are a great number of examples where, by stabilizing the workforce or customer base, or both, the result has been to dramatically increase productivity, and so profit. Among these are the following.

▶ American Express Cards, who have introduced 'relationship billing' – sending details of special offers or events, carefully tailored to the lifestyles of the specific cardholder and deduced from analysis of spending patterns. They have been able to extend the life of the card by five years and treble profits per customer.

▶ Coca Cola – not an obvious service but in distribution engaged in service issues – who have spent considerable time and money on customer retention. They have seen an increase of 10 per cent retailer retention flow through to a 20 per cent increase in sales.

▶ Taco Bell, who have found that the 20 per cent of their stores which have the lowest rate of staff turnover have a profitability which is 55 per cent higher than the 20 per cent of branches with the highest rate of staff turnover.

▶ Canadian Pacific Hotels, who have found that staff recruited under their new scheme of ensuring suitability for the job (Case Study 12.1) are not only less likely to be absent or have lower workers compensation claims but are also more likely to get higher ratings for the quality of their work.

These two critical aspects are discussed in more depth on the following pages.

Customer retention

Securing customers is critical. The individuality that the delivery of good service confers has another important aspect – it creates the potential for a closer bond between the parties involved and for reducing costs by building on acquisition expenditure, not constantly repeating it.

Services are at the heart of relationships even though they may not be overtly recognized or even desired by the parties involved. Indeed, customers are by nature promiscuous, and will often be negative about the very idea, preferring to retain the freedom to change as they will – a reference back to the exit society referred to in Chapter 2. But they are relationships, all the same, though transient.

It is important to recognize that building *deeper* relationships – creating a more stable customer base – is only going to be really effective when it is done in the true interests of both parties. The creation of 'negative' barriers – and most discount schemes and loyalty schemes or cards fall into this category, because they only offer negative restraint, as in 'I don't feel I can afford to break away' – is not deep relationship building, though both can play a role in such development.

For example, as outlined previously, American Express are using their database of knowledge about a customer's spending not simply to increase revenue, though this is a prime aim, but to build the relationship through understanding and responding to his or her preferences and developing specific offers – dining, sports, travel – which they will find attractive.

British Airways have interlinked Air Miles, a 'bribe', with their Executive Club, so that they build up a long-term relationship through specific benefits for frequent flyers, such as dedicated airport lounges, and the capturing of detailed information on travel preferences.

Saga, who have built their whole business around relationships, demonstrating to older people that 'they understand them and their problems' have done so by making sure it is two way. As we saw (page 12), when they received a number of complaints about one particular hotel in their brochure, they decided it must have affected many others, who had not complained, and sent a cheque in compensation to everyone who had stayed there that year.

All of these examples build a stable customer base, but not by simply giving bribes. They promote what is, in effect, a value exchange, with each party benefiting in some way from the process, though with the customer still in control.

Such considerations are not only for personal services. The same rules and strictures apply in business-to-business transactions too. This is an explicit part of Lane Group's philosophy and success. Another example is O.I.L., who have found that building relationships with their customers has distinct benefits (Case Study 9.1).

Like attempts in the personal field, it is vital to remember that a relationship has to have value to both parties. Some organizations are simply not interested in long-term relationships, even though they may never publicly say so. For them, exploiting the immediate opportunity is all – they are the 'hunters' and they cannot adjust easily to a 'farming' concept. They may well be successful, maybe even more so in the short term – especially if they have a monopoly or near-monopoly situation or the alternatives are not easy for the customer to access – but that success is most unlikely to be built on extraordinary service.

CASE STUDY 9.1 O.I.L. AND RELATIONSHIPS

O.I.L. has a worldwide fleet of offshore supply ships, mainly working with the major oil companies. Jamie Buchan, the Marketing Director of O.I.L., has no illusions about relationships, and does not see them as an automatic ticket to success. But he does see them as a crucial part of the success of their business.

> *To me, building customer relationships is an integral part of doing business effectively in a service industry like ours. However, there is a lot of talk in this area but much less real action.*
>
> *It should not necessarily be seen as a way of getting a better price but, when other things are equal, of providing a secure cost and service structure to both parties. There should be no surprises and you can plan more effectively, giving more chance for both the business and the people to grow. It is more about 'quality of earnings' than price. It is also far more fun, for those involved, to be able to add value and not just fight over price alone.*
>
> *It also gives us an entrée to the future. If we have done a consistently good job, we may progressively expect to achieve supplier-of-choice status when it comes to future tender opportunities. It also allows us to build up a structure which can move on to turn-key operations and to be the first to hear about new initiatives. Knowing where and when to add value for the customer is where I believe relationships are critical.*
>
> *As an example, our recent very effective progress in this respect in the North Sea has strengthened our image generally. We are seen as more serious, more knowledgeable and more forward looking. We have become a supplier of choice and progressively a 'safe bet'. We can also utilize assets more effectively because we achieve a higher success rate in charters, but we still have to accept the prevalence of the market rate.*
>
> *There are three other values I see to building relationships:*
>
> ▶ *We get to learn about our customers' problems and therefore have the opportunity to identify solutions.*
> ▶ *We are much more likely to be aware of bad service and so both be able to put it right and learn for the future.*
> ▶ *We can raise the confidence level of our people and of our customers in those people.*
>
> *We have to do it; we have to get better at it or, not least, we will be simply picking up the dregs.*

To take an example. Another company which has built its success on long-term relationships is the Danish-owned, but worldwide, industrial cleaning company, ISS. For them, as David Openshaw the Managing Director of the ISS cleaning operations in the UK says, *'It's a way of life, we simply would not dream of working any other way'*, and they held to this despite a well-publicized, and hurtful, loss of a 'relationship contract' with BAA at Heathrow's Terminal 1.

For David Openshaw,

> *That contract was near and dear to my heart and we put in six months of preparation, working closely with BAA to build a specification of a contract which would radically improve the quality of cleaning at Terminal 1 and enhance the job for the cleaners. It would also give an added benefit to the passengers, by providing staff who, because they could speak English and had been given basic orientation training on the terminal and on giving help, would be able to respond to their problems on the spot. The hurt was not that we lost it at the end of the initial two-year contract, that was a straight commercial risk we took, but that it went in a way, and to a firm, which signalled to us that the quality we had mutually established didn't really matter. However, such a setback does not change the way we work because we have used the experience to learn more and to get similar contracts in airports elsewhere.*

Building productivity through relationships is not for the unwary. As with the Lane Group and ISS, there is a need for it to be 'the way we work', not be an add-on. It needs to be expressed within the value system, not be a tactical afterthought.

Employee retention

The building of relationships with customers can have a clear benefit. To realize these to the full, however, it is necessary to match this internally. This follows from the points made in Chapter 4. It is unrealistic to expect relationships with customers unless there are relationships internally. The need for the involvement that a relationship brings, requires a style of management that permits this. The retention of employees is a crucial part.

For example, O.I.L. did not really succeed in developing relationships with their partners until they brought their employees into the dialogue and showed them that they could afford to take the risks associated with helping the customer. Holding on to staff is not important simply because of the costs of recruitment, though these are much higher than the direct costs would suggest, but because:

▶ effective service comes from cohesion and team familiarity – frequent changes of personnel disrupt this;

▶ high turnover means management focus and time becomes directed to maintaining the workforce, not giving it leadership;

▶ training costs are not only higher but are directed against a constant theme of low-level skill, rather than against enhancing the higher-level skills, and

▶ customer perceptions of service often come from an 'unofficial' network of contacts within the organization, which are disrupted by frequent changes – and may even be carried to the next job by a well-thought of member of staff.

The researches quoted in Chapter 4, show that staff who work in surroundings where the culture supports their beliefs in customer service not only give better service to the customer but are more likely to stay and to have, both as individuals and as a part of the 'team', a positive effect on others.

While securing staff, keeping employees loyal, is critical to service success, this must not be 'negative' securing. Historically, many service organizations have had 'loyal' staff but have not necessarily achieved a high level of service, at least in the customers' eyes – banks and insurance companies are an obvious example. Staff must stay because they are stretched and fulfilled, because they have demands placed upon them yet their response is recognized and rewarded.

Such concern with the *reasons* for loyalty is of great importance. In an 'exit society', attempts to hold people through negative restraint are likely to misfire. Like customers, staff will simply resent that restraint and, as a result, not give a contribution from the heart, the very essence of good service.

Tending the orchard

To achieve real quality in the context of customers' expectations, 'superservice quality', it is necessary to take an holistic approach. There is the old story of the apple producer who consistently produced the best apples. Asked how one day by a pleased but inquisitive customer, he replied, 'Well, there are three ways of producing good apples. Sort the good from the bad; sort the bad from the good, or tend the orchard. I tend the orchard'.

In a service, tending the orchard is creating that culture which:

▶ reflects the customer understanding – meeting, even exceeding, expectations;
▶ is cohesive, has clear, close values, which everyone believes in – as theirs, and
▶ as a result has low levels of role ambiguity and role conflict, among staff – and management.

One of the problems with most structured approaches to quality is that they have a tendency to become internalized and to develop a bureaucracy in support. The much-applauded Florida Light & Power Company, birthplace of the work of Crosby and the first non-Japanese winner of the Deming Award, were quoted in *The Economist* as having had to cut back their 85-strong quality department to just six people and their 1,900 'quality teams' to just a handful because 'the customer had been lost sight of in the system'.

They can also lead to:

▶ Setting 'minimums', because that is all anyone is prepared to guarantee, but which provide no 'stretch' to the individuals.
▶ Seeing a standard as an 'absolute' – that is all you need to do to fulfil your duty – a pleasing outcome for some because as John Harvey-Jones, the former Chief Executive of ICI, has observed, *'In all companies there is a lot of comfort to be derived from administrative systems that purport to be "fair" but in reality remove from individual managers their responsibility'.*
▶ The creation of a new vocabulary which can reflect favourably on the inventors – give 'power' even – but may only result in it being seen as just one of a series of unrelated initiatives, a 'flavour of the month'.

If the aim is to achieve something beyond the ordinary – superservice – then it is necessary to first develop the culture which sees quality as a natural part of what everyone is doing. There are clearly times when standards are appropriate (p. 173), but they will only work effectively when 'the orchard is tended', when the overall climate encourages people to support others, to 'take risks' in keeping the customer, to be open about problems and failures, and recognizes and applauds these things when they are done. Some interesting observations on this are made by Herb Kelleher of Southwest Airlines in Box 9.2.

If the base work of developing a strategic guideline has been done well, then much of the basis for a quality system has already

BOX 9.2 *An interview with Herb Kelleher*

Most efficiency experts . . . totally overlook [the fact] that, essentially, every service business comes down to the contact that you have with the customer, and what the reaction is to that individual contact. It's much more of an interpersonal thing than it is something you can quantify like you could a General Motors or a Motorola [product], because ultimately, when you get down to it, even though you have performed imperfectly in getting from A to B, if your people have treated the passenger right, the passenger goes away saying, 'I forgive them; they're terrific people. I like their style, I like their form, I like everything about them, and I'm going to go back'.

It goes way beyond what you can quantify. That's why reading customer letters is important. It wouldn't do you any good to keep statistics on how many customer letters we get on this or that, because in lots of cases, it's not the number but the passion in the letters that you get [that's important].

When you get into this systemic approach to your company, the quantitative aspect of it, you lose an awful lot of what should be true about an excellent service company, which is not quantitative, it's qualitative. It's not objective, it's subjective. There's a chemistry and magic to a service business. You can't measure charisma.

Having 14 [accountants] in the back room churning out bits of information probably is not very productive for a service business. In fact it may be distracting from what should be your primary preoccupation. I think American

business is being submerged in irrelevant information, and you tend to lose sight of your goals and objectives because you get so much information that you can't digest it, nor can you ever come to a conclusion about it. You're just frantically reading things all the time.

How do you measure the amount of customer satisfaction that's derived from dealing with people who are warm and hospitable? You can't. That's the product of the culture of an organization; if you try to quantify it, you destroy it.

I would hate to impair what we have by trying to get an award. We were solicited to apply for [the Malcolm Baldrige Award]. When I took a look at it, I said 'We'd probably have to take 100 people spending six months trying to wind this thing. And you know what those people wouldn't be doing during that time? Paying attention to our customers'.

. . . the process, after all, is not the end; the process is simply a means. You don't want to make the mistake of thinking the means is the be-all-end-all and forget what the end is supposed to be.

My suggestion to [the Malcolm Baldrige committee] would be that it's a spiritual thing, it's an attitudinal thing, it's a cultural thing, and to the extent that you subject it to processes, the processes in and of themselves many times become the important thing. What's important is not doing things right, because you can do the wrong things right; its doing the right thing.

(Extracts from an interview with Herb Kelleher, 20 March 1991, conducted by Janice Hunter.)

been established. There may be no need to introduce yet another set of terminology. Rather, the task should be to concentrate single-mindedly on getting the vision, the objectives and the values across to everyone through communication, learning and leadership.

In fact, quality is in effect a part of the 'destination', the immediate achievement of the vision, which is outlined in Chapter 11, 'Getting started'. Such a destination should turn the broad generalizations of the guideline into concrete and linked factors and help individuals to focus on those things that have to be done to make it happen. In such an environment, 'tending the orchard' is about making sure that the overall culture is naturally conscious about quality – that is 'value' – for the customer, using 'rules' – that is standards – only as necessary.

Quality and standards

Unfortunately, many service companies still believe they can achieve improved service, better relationships and more profit, solely from setting standards. As a result, issues such as quality improvement, are seen simply as a question of defect correction rather than as a management tool to achieve cohesion toward adding value for the customer. Like costs, it is viewed in isolation from the effects. But unlike cost, quality is ephemeral, difficult to define and highly subjective.

It is difficult to see how true service quality can be effectively standardized, as, for example, with the accepted British and International Standards (BS 5750/ISO 9000). Dixons, for example (see also Case Study 2.1) have purposely avoided this and, interestingly, most 'superservice' organizations have never had an overt quality improvement programme.

Despite this, some cultures are such that working to entirely qualitative concepts is an impossibility. McDonalds, for example, is an entirely standards-driven company. Its success is that of a bureaucracy, in the sense in which it is used in the research in Chapter 4. It is successful because it is true to its values throughout but it is doubtful if it will enjoy such high success in the future, at least in advanced markets where there is increasing pressure from less bureaucratic competitors, such as Taco Bell. This is not simply customers' desire for greater flexibility and individuality, but staff, too. It will become increasingly difficult to hold good people in bureaucratic style organizations (see also p. 53).

In a number of instances in a large number of organizations, standards will be necessary, safety being a graphic example, though Pret's rules about the quality of their sandwiches is a more common and prosaic example. Such a drive for standards should be the fulfilment of one simple concept – how to fulfil customers' expectations? For this question to be answered satisfactorily, it is first necessary to know:

▶ What are those expectations – of such a purchase, generally, and of us, specifically?

▶ What is driving those views – in other words, what is the customer trying to achieve?

▶ How can we give a consistent delivery against such a demand?

▶ What would be the measure of the success of this, in the eyes of the customer?

This may be seen as an echo of 'Taking a position' (p. 87) and until that exercise has been completed, it will be virtually impossible to set any form of standards. Indeed, as with quality, it is better to see such initiatives as simply the more concrete expression of these earlier exercises, than allow them to be new exercises, in their own right, spawning a new bureaucracy and vocabulary.

It is also important to recognize the following:

▶ Most standards are about 'threshold' values, the basic value of a product or service. These are merely the values a customer expects as a basic right of purchase, such as safety in an airline or accurate handling of an account in a bank. They are usually only noticed when they are missing and they confer no competitive distinction – unless everyone else is so bad that even that is welcome! So in achieving a threshold standard all that is usually happening is that the customer is getting what they thought they should get. This is clearly of value, but not a basis for superior service.

▶ 'Incremental' values, on the other hand, are the values that give distinction. Sometimes they are highly subjective, a feeling the customer has, but most often they are related directly to the way the customer has perceived the service they have received (see page 33 for more detail on this). It is important that any standards take note of these reactions – 'how' you are dealt with may be more important than 'how quickly'.

▶ It is a natural tendency to 'beat the system' and standards encourage this. So make sure that the system has checks and balances and as few opportunities to be 'beaten' as possible. So, for example, a standard of '90 per cent of mail will be answered within 24 hours' is, on its own, an invitation to beat the system. In answering the 90 per cent, it is highly likely that the difficult cases may have to wait for a very long time. Better to have either 'all mail will be answered within 48 hours' or '90 per cent of mail . . . within 24 hours and all mail within three days'.

▶ The objectives and values enshrined in the guidelines (Chapter 5) contain the basic steer for any necessary standards. It is important that the links between them, and the rest of business development planning (Chapter 11) are clear and clearly made – don't invent a new vocabulary.

▶ Equally, standards should be integrated into the 'learning' process (Chapter 7) and performance against them should be part of how the organization, as a whole, learns from experience.

▶ In particular, 'inputs' should be related to 'outputs' – has that performance made any difference where it matters, with the customer or in improving staff morale and ability or confidence to meet with the customer – or to profit?

Acknowledgements and further reading

page 166   Taco Bell, quoted in 'The Service-Driven Service Company', Schlesinger, L. and Heskett, J. (1991) *Harvard Business Review*, Sept/Oct.

page 171   Florida Light and Power Company, quoted in *The Economist*, 17 September 1994.

page 171   John Harvey-Jones, *Making it Happen* (p. 155).

page 172   Interview with Herb Kelleher by Janice Hunter (p. 135)

The following companies all gave generously of their time and material in providing insights for the background to this and other chapters:

O.I.L Ltd, Woking, Surrey.
ISS London Ltd, London.

The article, 'The Service-Driven Service Company' (see above) is especially relevant, as is the reading listed under 'The Learning Organization' (Chapter 7). Other recommended reading on the subject of quality and value in context includes:

Binney, G. *Making Quality Work* (p. 26).
Egan, G. (1994) *Re-engineering the Company Culture*, Egan/Hall Partnership.
Irons, K. *The Marketing of Services* (p. 48).
Zeithamel, V.A., Parasuraman, A. and Berry, L.I. (1990) *Delivering Quality Service – Balancing customer perceptions and expectations*, The Free Press.

Delivering the promise

In great enterprises, the very 'I will' is enough.

Sextus Propertius, Roman author, c. 20BC

About this chapter

Delivery is a key area of strategy. It is the customer experience which determines if the promise has been met. In such a situation, delivery must add value, not just be a cost. These points highlight the need for operations to be both central to any service and to be part of the strategic management process – not with delivery merely following strategy.

This chapter will look at what is involved in the delivery of a service.

▶ Why delivery is strategic.

▶ The importance of delivery adding value, not being just a cost.

▶ What segmentation, defining precise markets, means in the context of service.

▶ Behaviour as a key element of market definitions.

▶ The balance to be achieved between the system and enthusiasm for the customer.

▶ The issues which govern channel-of-sale decisions.

▶ A particular look at structure and franchising.

The age-old show biz cliché has been, and still is, uttered by many in the business as they hope, against all the evidence to the contrary, that somehow when the moment of truth comes that it will all be made to work. It makes it all seem a matter of luck as to whether the ideas will be delivered. Yet the truth is that the great majority of professional entertainment succeeds because those, whose job it is to make it possible, have tirelessly worked to make it happen.

The Royal Albert Hall has always been a prestigious venue. Many world-famous classical musicians, pop stars and other entertainers have wanted to make at least one appearance there in their career. But promoters hated it! The building, with its distinctive and elegant round shape has been a London landmark since 1871. It was difficult to use and, worse, management seemed to delight in that difficulty, in stressing the problems and the need for security. Staff were notorious for rudeness. Shows often started late. Financially it was a disaster. It had a dismal reputation with customers, too. Even the Queen had been known to be kept waiting outside of closed doors because everything was not all right on the night!

The problem was that the management was product fixated and the product, the Hall, was elegant and prestigious, but intrinsically difficult to use. Over the years this has become an excuse for difficulties and failures and, as Patrick Deuchar who took over as Chief Executive relates,

> *There was an arcane mystery about the Hall which got in the way of objectivity about its purpose. Today, we no longer see ourselves in terms of our being an historical venue but as an entertainment centre, who happen to have a magnificent historical building. We have clarified our mission to be 'the premier entertainment venue to the promoter, the performer and the public', what we call the 'three Ps'. This shift may seem small but it has been crucial to getting people to see that enjoying the experience at the Hall was the critical issue.*

Today, the Royal Albert Hall is acclaimed for its successes and has a reputation of being one of the best-run entertainment venues in the world. The building is still elegant and it is not only prestigious but actively sought after as a venue by artists and promoters alike, winning a number of international awards. David Elliott, Deputy Chief Executive, makes the point that,

We have to work with the product we have, but through being more effective and focused on our customers and their experiences, not just putting shows on, we can improve the quality of the events we have. This not only adds to our prestige even further but boosts our 'secondary take', catering and the like. Although we are non-profit making, it allows us to run very healthy financial surpluses and, in turn, this allows us to make the Hall a much better place to use.

The differences show visibly, not just physically but in the attitudes and behaviours of the people you meet, from the stage doorman through the stewards to the management. For the Albert Hall, success has been a matter of seeing that the core product can even be a barrier to achievement. It is the delivery of the idea that counts.

The customer experience

Crucially, it is the customer experience which makes for success or failure in service. To deliver good experiences time and again, with consistency and integrity, there is a need for the right:

▶ abilities – largely a matter of having the right people, but also an outcome of the development of their talents;

▶ beliefs – clear goals everyone believes in linked to a clear value system, and

▶ context – with operational procedures and processes, environment, rewards and recognition, all in balance.

All of these points must apply internally as well as externally. Internal culture and external culture will balance out over time, so to maintain a consistent delivery of successful service needs a consistent back up. That is why it is important to see 'customer relations' skills as being skills for everyone. Too often, a finger is pointed at the hapless telephonist or cashier with the admonition, 'You have to become better at dealing with the customer', when that person may feel they are already doing all they can – and see clearly they could do a far better job with the right systems or back-up from management.

Customer relation skills are key to implementation and care should be exercised to ensure it is not just seen in terms of training. Nor should it be left to outsiders to take the sole responsibility for this. Management themselves are the primary source of learning the right behaviours. Before they 'point fingers' they would be well-advised to look carefully at the ideas contained in Chapters 6 and 7 on communication and learning, and seek to ensure that there is a firm basis of dialogue internally.

Such 'company care' should precede 'customer care' and, where courses are being developed for customer-relations skills, it would be valuable for management to undertake this first, themselves. This is especially true if an outside agency is involved.

Questions to ask of such training are:

▶ Has it helped *me* to be more effective in handling people and situations?
▶ Has it helped us to be more effective as a management team in communicating with each other and with other colleagues?
▶ Does the vocabulary used fit with our strategic guideline documents?
▶ Do the values it promotes reflect our value system?
▶ Can I see how I can support the thinking in my everyday contacts?

If the answers are not positive, then it is unlikely to achieve much effect.

Delivery is strategic

Customer relations are not a discrete activity; everything needs to be centred on creating success at delivery. Anything else should be subordinate to it, designed to give support. If any aspect cannot, or does not, then it should be dropped. This is the basis of the Service Star (Figure 3.2), and there are some 'live' examples of this model later in this chapter (Figures 10.2 and 10.3). Delivery decisions are not, therefore, simply an afterthought to the core product decisions – an outcome of strategy – but an integral part of strategy.

For delivery to achieve this, there is a need for it to be:

▶ a part of the process of adding value to the 'offer' in the eyes of the customer, and
▶ anchored securely within the feedback process of strategic management.

SOL Cleaning, the highly-successful Finnish cleaning company, have made this the centre of their whole business (Case Study 3.1). Not many organizations would be prepared to take their strong stand, and not every type of service business would respond to the approach they have adopted, but the basics of what they have done are true for any service:

▶ There is a vision of the business and a feeling which is shared by everyone that they are there to do something worthwhile, not just for themselves but for others, too.

▶ The customer is not perceived as a passive target in this but as a part of the value creation in a dialogue.

▶ This process, and in particular the interaction with the customer, is the focus of the business.

▶ The distinction between sales and delivery is deliberately narrowed, so what is sold is what is delivered.

▶ Those who are closest to the customer are the heroes of the business.

▶ Staff roles are there to support this main function.

▶ There are only managers where there is a clear need for leadership.

▶ Such management as does exist, is there more as a support to the front-line operatives, not just control them.

▶ There is no hierarchy in any accepted sense nor any symbols of hierarchy, because they are unnecessary for the effective running of the business.

The 'SOL approach' is right for SOL and the underlying principles universal, but the extent to which this particular approach or any other is applicable will vary, depending on the specific industry, the needs of the customers and the precise conditions at the time, not least the competitive situation.

The need for delivery to be viewed as strategic is heightened by the development of technology, which can result in a transfer of 'power' to the customer. For example, Federal Express allows customers to track packages through the FedEx system via the Internet. This meant they had to have staff that were equally able to respond to the customer power – exercise power themselves. As Bertil Thorngren, Strategic Planning Director at Telia, the Swedish telecom organization, comments, *'Giving power to the customer is no use unless you give authority to those near him or her'*. In the case of FedEx, they have the power already, otherwise the development would have simply created problems. The more knowledgeable the customer, the more the staff have to be able to react without reference.

Delivery as added value

Because delivery is an integral part of the value-added process, it is important that the decisions on structure be driven by the events at delivery and not the other way round. Where customers get value from delivery is where it is designed with their needs as central.

This should have been an outcome of 'Taking a position' (p. 87), but rarely do those carrying out such an exercise go on to use the knowledge they have gained in designing structure, so that it, too, is part of the process. To take an example, most organizations tend to simplistically classify 'small business customers' as a segment. This is because the analysis of customer need – and of where the customer gets value – has been product focused. The 'technical' requirements of products and product skills may well be broadly similar for most small business customers but such a focus ignores:

▶ the interaction, which is not playing any part at all in the definition, even though it is the crucial factor, and

▶ the responsiveness which a service needs to display in creating distinctiveness with its chosen market at this point – a distinctiveness which comes through the delivery, more than the product.

The differences that occur when the interaction is taken as the focus were shown in Figures 3.3 and 7.3. In both cases, two customer types, small commercial enterprises, are compared. It is shown even more graphically in Figure 10.1, where the comparison of the profile for artisans, from Figure 3.3, is matched to one for the 'over 65s'. Despite the differences on product criteria, 5 and 6, the overall patterns of the relationship are strikingly similar. In fact, these two, together with some other customer types, would form part of one service segment, with similar demands for service against which customers will judge satisfaction – and gain value.

In the product-driven linkage inherent in the profile in Figure 3.3, delivery would not be adding value – it would be merely a cost. In the linkage inherent in Figure 10.1, delivery would be an integral part of the value-added process.

Following through the implications of the maps in Figures 3.3 and 10.1, it is possible to see that there are very real differences in the way in which the two small commercial customer types should be dealt with. 'What', is shown in the two Service Star models in Figures 10.2 and 10.3, built around the two 'segments' identified.

Defining markets in terms of customer usage/perceptions, rather than product is becoming increasingly important. Saga (p. 11) is a notable example. Another is Lyonnaise des Eaux. Originally a water company, they now define themselves as meeting the needs of local (and similar) authorities, because they see this skill as adding more value to the customer .

Telecom organizations, too, are having to come to terms with the fact that the distinction between traditional telephony and mobile telephones is largely a technical one and that the customer will increasingly seek to see these as one. Again to quote Bertil

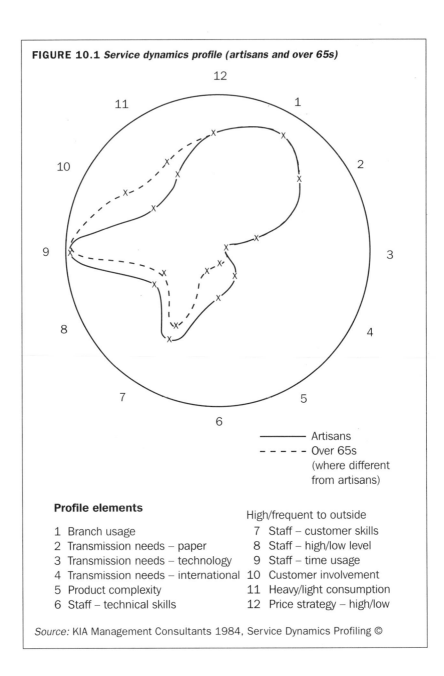

FIGURE 10.1 *Service dynamics profile (artisans and over 65s)*

——— Artisans
- - - - Over 65s
(where different
from artisans)

Profile elements

High/frequent to outside

1 Branch usage
2 Transmission needs – paper
3 Transmission needs – technology
4 Transmission needs – international
5 Product complexity
6 Staff – technical skills
7 Staff – customer skills
8 Staff – high/low level
9 Staff – time usage
10 Customer involvement
11 Heavy/light consumption
12 Price strategy – high/low

Source: KIA Management Consultants 1984, Service Dynamics Profiling ©

Thorngren, from Telia, '*For the customers it is just a phone and they
don't care about the technology. They ask why they should have two
invoice systems, why they can't combine the benefits? It is only the
phone companies who see a difference. That cannot go on*'.

Service segmentation

Such segmentation, is not the conventional segmentation of most marketing – frequently just those elements which describe the top axis of the service triangle (Figure 3.1). It is service segmentation – the alignment of the whole organization around the delivery of its promise.

The elements that have to be considered in structuring a service around a specific market are those in the Service Star. They all have to be in balance at the point of interaction with the customer, the focus of the 'star' and it is this focus which defines the segment. That is to say, the segment should be built around the experiences the customer is seeking, not a product or a broad, generalized customer description.

Woolworths, for example, have a clear view that the experience the customer has is key to their 'brand', what it is that Woolworths bring to the customer, consistently. They don't want the stores to be intimidating. They do want, though, that mothers with children, for example, should feel at ease. It is a clear focus. It does appeal to the Woolworths' customer. It does not appeal to everyone, but that is often the case for, and strength of, good strategy – it ensures that the offer is distinctive to the specific market that is best suited to its unique qualities.

On the other hand, many organizations have found to their cost that the crude importation of marketing techniques from fields such as consumer goods does not work effectively in the service situation. The most notable example was probably the Midland Bank, which bundled together a series of products, such as a specific account with a particular credit card, and gave this inflexible package an unrelated brand name. It was not a success.

At another level, London suffers more than other major cities because it has no integrated transport. The focus is on the 'product', the bus or the train as an operating unit, when the passenger's focus is on the effectiveness of the process, of which the products are but a part.

The purpose of adapting the techniques of segmentation to designing service structures must be to:

▶ allow an organization to market to groupings of customers or potential customers, with like characteristics in terms of what are their expectations;
▶ be distinctive by developing a clear positioning, like Woolworths, against the chosen segment or segments, such that 'your personality' – your culture and what it offers across all the factors

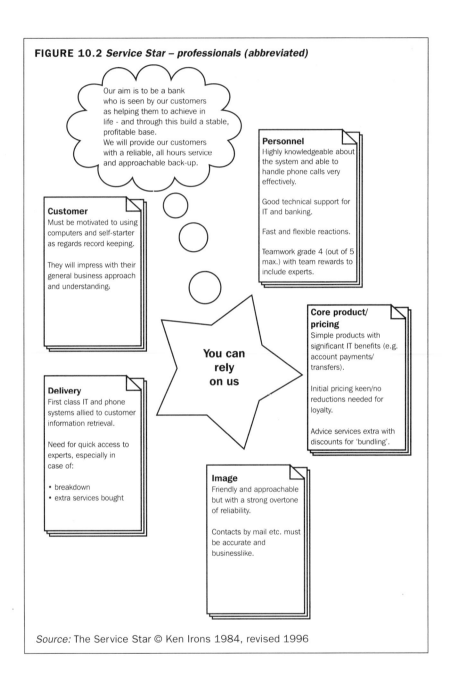

FIGURE 10.2 *Service Star – professionals (abbreviated)*

Our aim is to be a bank who is seen by our customers as helping them to achieve in life - and through this build a stable, profitable base.
We will provide our customers with a reliable, all hours service and approachable back-up.

Customer
Must be motivated to using computers and self-starter as regards record keeping.

They will impress with their general business approach and understanding.

Personnel
Highly knowledgeable about the system and able to handle phone calls very effectively.

Good technical support for IT and banking.

Fast and flexible reactions.

Teamwork grade 4 (out of 5 max.) with team rewards to include experts.

Delivery
First class IT and phone systems allied to customer information retrieval.

Need for quick access to experts, especially in case of:

• breakdown
• extra services bought

You can rely on us

Core product/ pricing
Simple products with significant IT benefits (e.g. account payments/ transfers).

Initial pricing keen/no reductions needed for loyalty.

Advice services extra with discounts for 'bundling'.

Image
Friendly and approachable but with a strong overtone of reliability.

Contacts by mail etc. must be accurate and businesslike.

Source: The Service Star © Ken Irons 1984, revised 1996

involved in the service mix – is recognized and valued by the customer, as compared with substitutes they could make, and

▶ allow a concentration of resources against the fulfilment of these specific customer expectations, rather than dissipate them across too many different and undifferentiated sectors of the market.

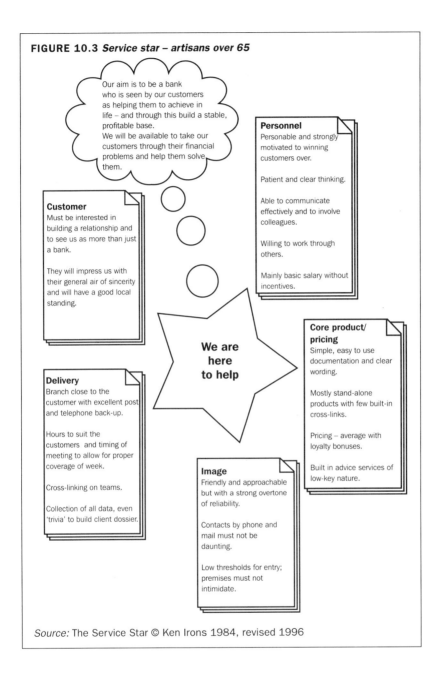

FIGURE 10.3 *Service star – artisans over 65*

Our aim is to be a bank who is seen by our customers as helping them to achieve in life – and through this build a stable, profitable base.
We will be available to take our customers through their financial problems and help them solve them.

Customer
Must be interested in building a relationship and to see us as more than just a bank.

They will impress us with their general air of sincerity and will have a good local standing.

Personnel
Personable and strongly motivated to winning customers over.

Patient and clear thinking.

Able to communicate effectively and to involve colleagues.

Willing to work through others.

Mainly basic salary without incentives.

We are here to help

Delivery
Branch close to the customer with excellent post and telephone back-up.

Hours to suit the customers and timing of meeting to allow for proper coverage of week.

Cross-linking on teams.

Collection of all data, even 'trivia' to build client dossier.

Core product/ pricing
Simple, easy to use documentation and clear wording.

Mostly stand-alone products with few built-in cross-links.

Pricing – average with loyalty bonuses.

Built in advice services of low-key nature.

Image
Friendly and approachable but with a strong overtone of reliability.

Contacts by phone and mail must not be daunting.

Low thresholds for entry; premises must not intimidate.

Source: The Service Star © Ken Irons 1984, revised 1996

Behaviour as value

Since delivery is central to the strategy, to the value-adding process, it can also be seen that behaviour at this point is also central. This is clear in the case of the bank in Figures 10.2 and 10.3. The people involved will have to create a different culture for dealing with a market

which is driven by the need for help and advice – the artisans and older people – than one which is largely transaction driven – professionals.

It reinforces the need for cost containment (Chapter 9) to be linked to outcomes. The invasive surgery of most cost-cutting campaigns cuts deeply into the delivery relationships, frequently taking out the seasoned staff and middle management who were the customers' access to the organization. With the right behaviours born of knowledge and experience, they could cut through the intricacies. Now there are black holes instead. The customer has become disconnected.

The question of behaviours as an integral part of the added value does not rest solely between the customers and the staff they meet. Because of the triangular nature of a service situation, the behaviours internally also form a part.

The old-style mind-set which saw personal behaviour and action as divorced from what the organization had said it was trying to do is highlighted by the debacle at British Gas in 1995. As a privatized utility, the organization claimed to be working toward providing better service to the customer, but without competition to provide a check on this, it was reduced to levels that were clearly achieving the opposite. To show comprehensively that this was not understood, it culminated in a massive redundancy of service-to-the-customer staff coinciding with a massive hike in the remuneration of the managing director. It has not only had a major impact on British Gas but on the whole perception of, and attitudes toward, the privatized utilities in the UK.

The industrial-age behaviour demonstrated by British Gas will rarely lead to sustained good service for the customer. The consistency of effort against the customer requires those who are close to the customer to respond because they want to; because they see this as the values of the organization around them, including their leaders.

Many of the issues involved in developing delivery as an integrated element are highlighted in the experiences of Four Seasons in Case Study 10.1, where:

▶ management recognize that their behaviour is an integral part of what they offer to their customers;
▶ people are seen as key, despite having a superb physical product;
▶ 'inputs' to staff are seen as the necessary preliminary to outputs to customers, and
▶ learning is seen as crucial and learning from others as more important than training or manuals.

Bureaucracy or enthusiasm?

There is a need to release an entrepreneurial drive at the interface with the customer but, at the same time, to create a structure which supports this, ensuring that the drive is not lost – that the necessary level of 'anarchy' to be effective in responding to customers does not turn into chaos. That is the need to respond to the customer, in the customer's own terms – enthusiasm – and on the other hand the need to work within clear and defined routines – bureaucracy (p. 52).

SOL Cleaning and Southwest Airlines are both fairly free-wheeling organizations and both depend for success on the release of a lot of both energy and responsibility on the part of their people. But the precise approach that has worked for SOL would not work for Southwest. Southwest have schedules to keep and highly-sensitive pieces of equipment to maintain in absolute safety, so, like all airlines, they have to work within some very defined routines. The similarity is, that both seek to respond to the customer in a way which makes the routine, the bureaucracy, the least possible inconvenience to the customer.

To take a different example, British Airways is a totally different type of business to either SOL or Southwest, one in which historically bureaucracy ran rife, but which has been equally successful, releasing an immense amount of energy where it matters, with the customer.

The unintended – and for the most part unaccepted by BA – secret of their success has been that that they have done this despite the retention of a rather bureaucratic central organization. Bringing in top-flight marketing and human resource people skilled in working in bureaucracies has probably been an inspired move, even if for reasons other than that originally intended. For example, most big company consumer-goods marketing is itself bureaucratic and entails a great deal of working within the system to minimize the impact of internal bureaucracy on the customer. BA is, and will probably remain, two worlds and its success lies in releasing the one that deals directly with the customer and taming the other, the central bureaucracy, to be the helpful, if not always obedient, servant to all that anarchy, enabling it to function.

Rightly widely admired, British Airways is no more a total model than, say, SOL or Southwest though each stands as an inspiration to anyone who seeks to achieve superservice. But whatever the balance, it is people who have to be central and it needs people who feel deeply about what they are doing to make that delivery 'super' and not just ordinary. People who will spontaneously remark, for example:

'Although I recognize we have to use computers on reception, to me they are a block to giving good service. You can see how people lose eye contact; they have another focus, no matter how good they are'.

Dominique Colliat, Maître de Maison, Novotel Waterloo.

It's a great job. I'd not want to do anything else. I just like people and this company lets you do that. All companies have rules but some are more flexible than others and they (Southwest) say 'if it worries you (about a customer's concern or request) then go ahead and do what you think is right'. I used to have my own firm and I guess this is the nearest you can find to that.'

Janee Gallozzi, Customer Service Agent,
Southwest Airlines, Love Field, Dallas.

CASE STUDY 10.1 FOUR SEASONS

Unusually among world-class five-star hotels, Four Seasons has been able to develop their reputation under one name. Few other hotel organizations have attempted this above three/four star level. Even Forte were decidedly cautious in using their name in connection with their range of 'exclusive' luxury hotels. So what is it that Four Seasons have done right to be able to 'deliver' their ideas across the world, so successfully?

John Sharpe, President, puts it down to the fact that,

More of what starts here ends up there because the people we employ at that point of contact are self-motivated people waiting to hear the right messages. They want to do a good job. Also, we do not see ourselves as exclusive hotels, indeed we try consciously to be 'inclusive'. Although we will often be the most expensive hotel in town, we aim to provide a feeling of comfort and luxury in an environment that is hospitable. We are not aloof, condescending or formal but are there for the convenience of guests – not as many 'exclusive' hotels seem to see themselves.

We try to get our message across clearly – to our guests and our staff – in the way we do things. So, for example, 25 years ago, when we opened the Inn on the Park in London (now the Four Seasons) we had women receptionists – warm, hospitable and caring people. This is commonplace now but revolutionary in such an hotel in London then, when employees at all levels could, and sometimes did, treat customers in a superior way. We believe that hotel is now, and has been for some years, the most profitable hotel in Europe, largely built on its reputation for service and hospitality.

The thing about any hotel is that you cannot control and measure quality in the way you can a manufactured product. You can't

This dichotomy, therefore lies at the very heart of the decisions about service delivery.

▶ What is the right balance for our market, for our particular customers?
▶ What can we deliver, given:
  – the competition;
  – the type of 'raw material' we start with, and
  – our own abilities to develop or supplement this?

These demands are increasingly leading to a direct challenge to the notions of hierarchy in structures. Future structures are more likely to resemble a web than the conventional, hierarchy reinforcing, structures traditionally used in organizations. The ability to transfer

control the outputs directly, just the inputs – have you given that member of staff enthusiasm, hospitality, shown them a welcome? Customers being comfortable in their environment can only come from staff being comfortable in theirs.

What is more in our case, it is a luxury product but it is being directly produced by relatively low-paid staff. We can't make cleaning out garbage bins or toilets fun. We can't make it well paid. But we can show the people who do it that we respect them and treat them with dignity so that they feel better than they would elsewhere, doing this job.

As managers we have to show we are part of the team. When we stay at our hotels we don't have the biggest suite or finest amenities. We don't block phone calls, here in head office or in the hotels, whether by machines or secretaries, and no one is allowed to use an answering machine during the day.

You have to think about people and give consistent messages over a long period, whether it is the busy season or the quiet. It is not so much a glamorous job as tedious; not so much constantly doing new things as doing the same basic things, again and again – and correctly.

We believe in learning from the culture around you. Take our new hotel in Los Angeles. Typically, a hotel would move 15 or so of its most senior management into a new hotel, to set it up. We moved 50 people, including many staff doing jobs such as room service, so they could act as role models. This is much more effective than training.

As I said, to get more of your thinking through to where it matters you have got to have the right people, at every step, down the line.

messages accurately from top to bottom in an organization, conferred by technology, accentuates this even further. In some service sectors, technology is allowing customer-facing units to act directly, where previously it was thought impossible. In insurance, for example, it is possible to use expert systems to allow local staff to make underwriting decisions that would have had to be referred to a head office function just a few years ago.

Channel-of-sale decisions

Channel-of-sale decisions should be an outcome of strategy, not a controlling element. They are but a part of the overall set of decisions about delivering the promise. Yet, many organizations would typically see the choice of channel-of-sale, that is the choice about where to 'meet' the customer, as the central, maybe only, decision, in this area.

Delivery is one of the five elements of the service mix and the choices need to be an integral part of the balancing of that mix. Channel-of-sale should flow from this, part of an integrated decision overall, not be the first choice, with other considerations trailing in its wake. The Dixons/Mastercare decision (Case Study 2.1) is a good example. Previously, the choice of 'channel' – home service in working hours, supported by a centralized factory – was the 'strategy'. All else flowed *from* this. Now the choice of channel is subordinate to the strategy. Delivery is an integrated part of what the Group are seeking to achieve with the customer. It is an integrated part of adding value for the customer, not just a cost which has, somehow, to be recovered.

Such a choice should always add value. It is possible to immediately recognize the 'added value' that a retailer like Aspreys or Harrods confers on a product or service, but how often is this given proper consideration? For example:

▶ Does a bank add value to insurance core products?
▶ Is this added value the same whether or not it is a life policy or, say, a household policy?
▶ Is it the same if the customer motivation is 'investment' or 'security'?
▶ What is the 'added value' in commercial business? Is it the same as for personal business?
▶ In the case of a third-party channel-to-market, is a franchising arrangement likely to add value more effectively than another form of agreement, an agency or even retention of outright control?

Such channel-of-sale decisions are not one-offs, but a continuous design and redesign activity where, in the long run, there is total freedom, but in the short run, may be constrained by existing arrangements, such as a franchise or the usage of agents or brokers. Such short-term constraints can be of real significance and may, for example, cause a package-holiday company dependent on agents or an insurer dependent on brokers to subordinate the long term for immediate delivery decisions.

But the development of channel-of-sale decisions as part of a delivery strategy means asking fundamental questions about the role of delivery within the total service mix and, specifically, the role in building relationships.

Intermediaries pose some particularly important questions in respect of relationships, since, whether for sales or service or both, they can enhance the relationship or take it away, at least as far as the end-user is concerned. Intermediaries must either add value to a relationship directly (because they reach people you could not, at a reasonable cost) or indirectly (because, although they could be reached, they – the intermediary – add a value to the business purpose). In other words, the 'focus' at the interaction, with the ultimate customer, works more effectively with an intermediary involved, than it would directly.

Reverting to the Service Triangle (Figure 3.1), this can be illustrated in two ways: as one integrated triangle, as in Figure 10.4, or as two triangles, one in series with the other, as in Figure 10.5.

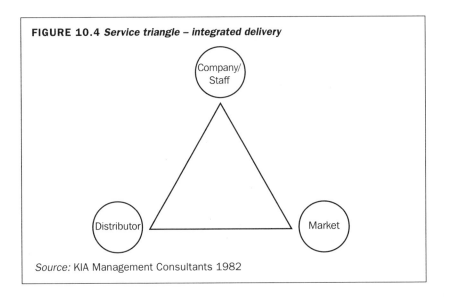

FIGURE 10.4 *Service triangle – integrated delivery*

Source: KIA Management Consultants 1982

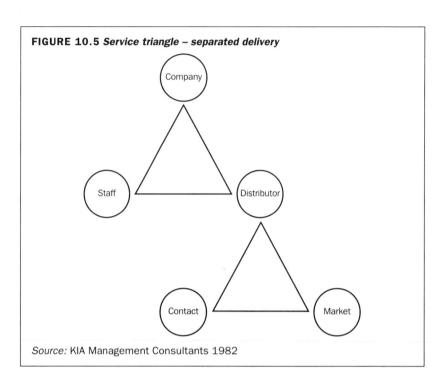

FIGURE 10.5 *Service triangle – separated delivery*

Source: KIA Management Consultants 1982

In both cases, it is necessary to understand what is required by the ultimate customer from the interaction, but in Figure 10.4 the interaction is integral – we are all part of one family, e.g. a franchisee, say – while in Figure 10.5 the intermediary is an independent unit – e.g. an agent.

In either case, the intermediary assumes the role of a part of the value creation and must be involved in the same way as customers or staff. Caterpillar, for example, who have always prided themselves on their service, believe that the tight working relationships they have forged with their independent dealers 'to meet our customers' needs' is the 'biggest reason for Caterpillar's success'.

Decisions on the best channel-of-sale to adopt will have to be made by reference to the particular type of business. The checklist in Box 10.1 will help.

The whole concept of channel-of-sale selection raises more issues than can be covered in a general book, but three are worthy of a brief examination because of their importance.

► What is the balance of centralization vs. decentralization?
► What is the resulting demand on structure?
► What is the value of franchising?

BOX 10.1 *Selecting the channel-of-sale*

1. What type of distribution is needed:
   - for sales?
   - for developing the relationship?
   - for specific areas of servicing?
     (e.g. claims/complaints).

(Consider the business purpose and the demands at the focus; how effective would each of the above be in meeting these?)

2. What demands of relationship building/loyalty does the business purpose/focus impose, in each of the above? In other words, how important is continuity?

3. What are the likely requirements for fast-moving change?

4. What characteristics of culture/skills/rewards are required?

5. (a) What about current distribution? How does this relate to each of the answers given?
   (b) Can any shortfall be overcome by:

   - modifying the plans without fundamental loss?
   - training, development or special selection?

6. Is enough understood about the chosen distribution(s) to answer:
   (a) What are the distributors' own problems? For example, what are their motivations, their difficulties in achieving adequate financial controls or in marketing plans?
   (b) How do the distributors perceive 'you' in relation to these needs?
   (c) What can you bring/what is involved, in the plans to help distributors find solutions to their own problems?

7. (a) What are the:
   - training needs?
   - communication needs?
   - monitoring needs?
   (b) Is it possible to meet them?

8. What are the cost implications?

Centralization or decentralization?

Whatever decisions are made, getting the delivery close to the customer is critical. With modern technology this does not necessarily mean physically close in the geographical sense. It does mean, though, that the customer has to be able to feel that he or she is able to influence the course of events and to feel part of a relationship, however transient.

In viewing their organization, Svenska Handelsbanken are clear that, *'Our branches are not a form of distribution. They are the bank and every decision regarding a customer is taken there, however big and important that customer is. Regions and head office are there to provide support and advice but the decision will be that of the branch manager'*. One branch manager recalls the first time he was faced with a major decision as, *'You certainly realized you were on your*

own – you were able to get lots of advice but no one was going to take the decision for you. You knew that was the situation but it was frightening first time'.

However, the real test is whether in any particular market that is what the customer sees as the way they want to do business. So, Dixons recognized that in their business being close to the customer meant that literally – being geographically close and on view! The best location for insurance may be much more to do with whether the customer is seeking 'security', when local may need to mean just that, or is simply concerned to 'get cover' or comply legally, in which case being physically local is less important.

Where centralised, the use of the telephone as the primary contact point can be extremely advantageous, not only in cost terms but in allowing for a greater certainty of a consistent delivery. Saga Group, for example, have achieved a very high level of customer belief in them as an organization which understands older people – their target market is the over-50s – but this has been done from one central location. The sense of a relationship has been developed by a combination of selection of staff, specialized training and the intelligent collection, and usage of, information on the customer – every enquiry, every interest shown, is recorded. First Direct in the financial field, have similarly built up a strong customer base by using the telephone from a central point.

The structure of delivery

Service organizations have traditionally been operations driven. Given the nature of the interaction relative to the rest of the business, this is likely to remain so for the future. However, the ability of operations to deliver will be very dependent on a delivery architecture which allows a free flow, between the customer and the organization and within the organization, from the customer interface to, if necessary, the very top.

The key points of this will be:

▶ The operative dealing with the customer is able to take decisions of a routine nature without reference, even if this may create immediate costs (see also Box 7.2).

▶ A clear, concise and quick chain of authority to deal with queries and complaints that cannot be settled immediately. Ideally, this should never involve more than one other person, that is, the customer is never more than two steps away from the ultimate decision maker.

▶ All other roles to be outside of the 'operational chain', either as staff or support roles.

▶ Technology integrated as an element of communication, shortening the distance between the customer and the organization.

The conventional organization chart is an abstraction which confuses notions of customer supremacy and focus – as indeed do most titles. In fact, many of the organizations quoted here simply do not have an organization chart as such. For example:

▶ SOL where it does not exist at all;

▶ Svenska Handelsbanken where 'It is the telephone directory', and

▶ most roles in Novotel are too fluid (p. 121) to fit in with a chart.

They all have managers, though fewer than average; they all have some structure. But they are flat organizations, with open networks for informal dialogue and quick, simple decision making on operational issues.

Although not specific to any one organization, the schematic layout in Figure 10.6 gives a representation of what this means. Top management have direct access to the mass of the organization and vice versa. 'Customer-action' decisions are not forced through a hierarchical decision maze. The tasks of administration are separate to operations. Intermediate management – regional managers, for example – will become 'support', rather than 'control'.

Precisely what architecture is 'right' must, again, depend on the exact situation. There can be no one solution and it is more important to learn from the underlying thinking that has brought success

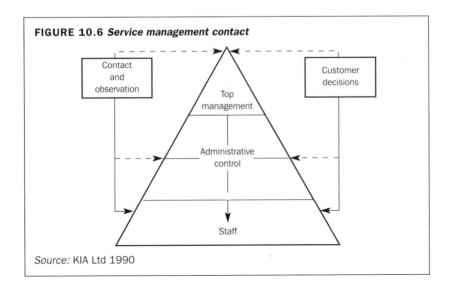

FIGURE 10.6 *Service management contact*

Contact and observation

Customer decisions

Top management

Administrative control

Staff

Source: KIA Ltd 1990

to others than to simply import ideas because they seem good. Some valuable comments on this are made by an experienced manager in Box 10.2.

Franchising

There is no standard legal structure for a franchise, in the sense that there are automatic definitions of this relative to other third party channels-to-market. The significant value of a franchise should be that it seeks to harness the energies of an entrepreneur with particular skills or opportunities that are lacking. It can also shorten time-scales.

BOX 10.2 *Improving customer contact*

Thorstein Øverland, Executive Group President of Kreditkassen, Norway's second largest bank, has spent the last 20 years in the financial services field, having worked initially in the field of fast moving consumer goods. He has come to a number of conclusions about successful delivery, based on his working experiences:

'I have several times witnessed managers trying to pool customer action decisions with administrative decisions – there is a belief that there must be a symmetry between responsibility and authority. We would see this as odd in, say, a hospital, if an administration manager interfered in an individual case but we seem often to accept it in financial services. I can quote from my own experience, in this respect.

In the first financial services company I joined in the seventies, an insurance company, there were only two levels of insurance decision making – the local office and head office. The local staff had wide authorities and when they needed help, they went direct to the relevant expert in head office.

We kept to that number of decision levels throughout two reorganizations after a merger in 1983, but in 1987 there was another reorganization

recommended by a firm of Norwegian consultants, which to assist decentralization brought in a new level of command, area managers. The idea was to move more specialists from head office out to these areas, but in fact it never happened because not enough of the good specialists were prepared to move. So, local offices continued to go direct to head office and Area Managers tried to force decentralization by "banning" direct contact!

It didn't improve our income, just the level of activity. Traffic on the electronic mail system, for example, went up by 40 per cent and the number of employees by 76 in the first year. With decreasing income and increasing costs, we went from being the most cost-effective insurance company to being the second most ineffective in just one year!

All of this had to be undone, and in 1989 we eliminated all area manage-ment and concentrated everyone at either head office or local offices. In nine months we reduced the overall number of employees by 120, out of a total of 1500, and the number of managers by 30, whilst increasing the number dealing direct with customers by 50'.

Because of this 'value', a franchise needs to build up a realizable equity stake for the franchisee and it is this which will, above all, set a franchise apart from, say, licensing. In principle you have brought in a partner who has a right to run the business and has realizable rights which go beyond the simple execution of centrally driven thinking. You harness the energy, the knowledge, the speed but you do sacrifice some control.

For The Body Shop this is not a problem, because they see their 'offer' to the customer as concrete enough to be sustained without any significant degree of degradation. They also need local translation of the core idea and local support.

For anyone considering the potential of a franchise there is a further critical factor. It needs the culture of a democratic dictatorship to work effectively, because any change will have to be 'sold' to the franchisees as of value to them – they will not be bought off by soft words or superficial statements – and they will expect to be involved, if not before at least in the final decision making. Of course, this is in line with the current changes in effective leadership generally but the situation with a franchise is significantly different.

For franchising to be a possibility this has to be based on the following:

▶ A well thought-out business proposition that acts as a simple, centrepiece to the relationship. The relative clarity of 'what is' The Body Shop is undoubtedly a key factor in their success in this respect.
▶ The business proposition and how it is to be fulfilled, with a legal framework in support, and not the other way round.
▶ A pre-identified set of key performance indicators which will make the business proposition work *and* retain its integrity.
▶ Short and clear lines of communication between the principles at both ends, not through 'staffers'.
▶ Clear systems with sufficiently detailed manuals as to ensure influence of day-to-day operations.
▶ Good training and follow through at all levels.
▶ A clear agreement on sale or change or ownership with a route out for the franchisee which realizes any capital gain, and to the franchiser when changed conditions make the original thinking untenable.

Acknowledgements and further reading

page 194   'Make your dealers your partners', Donald V. Fites, Chairman of Caterpillar, in the *Harvard Business Review*, Mar/Apr, 1996.

page 198   The input and advice of Max McHardy, an independent consultant and expert on franchising, was invaluable in developing the section on franchising.

The following companies both gave generously of their time and material in providing insights for the background to this and other chapters:

Royal Albert Hall, London.
Telia AB, Stockholm.

Much of the reading already recommended is appropriate for the subject of 'delivering the promise'. In particular, refer to the lists for Chapters 3, 4, 6, 7, 8 and 9, as well as the article above. One further book worthy of mention is:

Schneider, B. and Bowen, D.E. (1995) *Winning the Service Game*, Harvard Business Press.

Getting started

The distance is nothing; it is only the first step that is difficult.

Marquise du Deffand, *remark on the legend that St Denis,
carrying his head in his hands, walked two leagues*

About this chapter

Making it happen requires more than simply unveiling the plans. The best implementation will most often result from going back to the starting point, ensuring that the thinking behind the plans – the often agonizing but valuable processes of getting understanding and coming to terms with the implications – is shared.

Many key factors involved in implementation have already been covered, from Chapter 6, on communication, through to Chapter 10, on delivering the promise. To make it happen, though, requires a framework and a method. This chapter will look at what is involved in getting started and some further key issues central to taking the strategy through to implementation.

This chapter will cover:

▶ Why launching initiatives in a service is different.

▶ The value of creating a destination.

▶ The value of using a workshop style approach.

▶ Assessing culture relative to the task ahead.

▶ The process of turning guidelines into action plans.

▶ Linking inputs to outputs.

The burning platform

When the Piper Alpha oil rig exploded and caught fire, a number of people survived through jumping 50m (150 feet) into a stormy sea. They did it because the certain dangers of staying put outweighed the merely probable dangers of leaping into the unknown. That is the ultimate cost of change. Staying put, where you are, is an impossibility. Changing has dangers but carries with it the chance of success.

Such a scenario can be a useful way of developing a recognition that change just has to take place, however uncomfortable it may be, because trying to stay where you are is like trying to stay on a 'burning platform'. One way lies a certain end, the other some chance of salvation.

American Express Europe used it successfully in 1993–4, to bring about radical change in the way in which they ran the American Express card. Historically the card had been sold on a basis of prestige – the very ownership of an American Express card was felt to be smart. But times had changed.

The 1990s ushered in a new age. Customers were more discriminating and aware and interested in what the card could do for them, rather than in simply owning the card. Prestige was still important but this had to come through using the card and its utility – not the simple fact of owning the card. It also meant that the card had to be more cost effective. Only those things that gave value to the customer could be tolerated as expense in the future. It also had to be 'sold' more strongly to the merchants, whose support was so vital to the continuing usage of the card.

All of this might have been simply good thinking but have become lost along the way because to make it happen – to achieve the cost savings and refocusing that was required – meant a lot of people were going to have their lives and their routines disrupted. It was to be a painful change. So, American Express developed a 'burning platform' analogy, showing both how the current decline in profitability and of customer appreciation and usage of the card was leading to a situation which would be a lot more uncomfortable than that required to achieve the necessary change now.

It worked, and over a period of a year, American Express made dramatic changes in the way in which it handled its business, withdrawing the servicing to a single point in Europe and allowing the local management to concentrate on the task of marketing the card more effectively.

Such an approach can be effective. Few change situations are as dramatic or dangerous as the 'burning platform' illustration, but many organizations face a future in which change is going to be an important part of making it happen. Sometimes, however dangerous and painful, it is the only alternative to staying put, and dying!

The overuse of such dramatic scenarios can debase the coinage, so there is a need to exercise caution. Most often, it is a subtler situation – change, while desirable, can be put off or slowed down to suit the passive demands of those who find it uncomfortable. However, the wider point remains true, and demonstrates that to achieve change usually requires those involved to see an urgency – and achieving extraordinary service is almost always about change.

Do it differently!

Service gives the opportunity to create individuality through change. To break away from the sameness of so much that is on offer to the customer and to be truly distinctive. Even in the same field – even the same organization – a new venture, a new plan, a new idea, all present the opportunity to use change to create the individual. The best organizations build on this, use the potential it offers, and have the courage to be different.

That is the value, and it is also the cost. It is impossible to take advantage of this potential through simply recreating what was there before or following some pre-set series of steps. Every service launch, every service change, must be individual – planned around capturing a blend of past strengths and personality at the interaction, that moment of truth. Not through paper policies or bank accounts, seats on planes or rooms in hotels, ships on charter or trucks on the road, but the interaction.

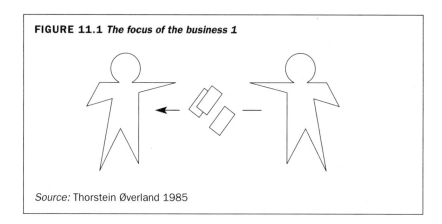

FIGURE 11.1 *The focus of the business 1*

Source: Thorstein Øverland 1985

Pushing product onto faceless customers (Figure 11.1) is the way of the industrial age. Creating value *with* the customer (Figure 11.2) is the way of the age of service, developing two-way communication, bringing people together.

For a manufacturer, the first production run of a new product or a variant is a rare moment of mixed apprehension and uncertainty; for those involved in a service it is a commonplace, to be repeated each day. In manufacturing, the product can be reasonably controlled and the results of production tested – to destruction, if need be. In a service you have little control. Only when it is all over can you determine success or failure. It is a constant ride on a switchback, sometimes exhilarating, sometimes scaring – even both at the same time.

Success in this will only be possible if those who are delivering service show a passion and urgency to achieve. It is this, rather than the perfect plan which will be the secret of success – which will deliver superservice. It is a fact of service life that:

▶ plans are in the hands of others at implementation – even if you are the manager directly responsible! – because events that make up the offer to the customer have yet to happen and are not predictable in their entirety;

▶ these events, then shape the strategy – implementation becomes intertwined and starts to change the strategy through its very happening.

Where implementation fails, by definition so has the planning. But the 'planning' failure will be as likely to do with the failure to capture everyone to the plan as the plan itself. For that reason, to make it happen there is a need to implement the following:

1 Develop an extremely clear view of where the organization is going.
2 Express this in terms which relate to those who must make it a reality.

FIGURE 11.2 *The focus of the business 2*

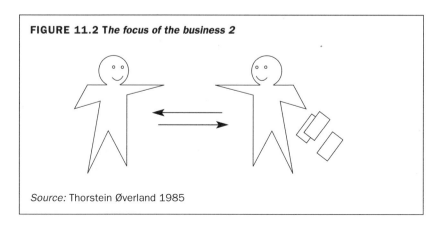

Source: Thorstein Øverland 1985

3 Create a dialogue around these points, such that the destination everyone is travelling to becomes 'ours', not just 'theirs'.

4 Maintain the momentum through continuing dialogue and through institutionalizing the aims in the fabric of everyday reward and recognition.

Points 1 and 2 have already been covered in Chapter 5. This chapter concentrates on the process involved in taking this forward, though the principles involved, such as creating dialogue through workshops, are totally applicable to the formulation process of the strategy itself.

Creating a destination

The best place to start is with the conversion of the guiding light into a more concrete form, so that those that must make it happen can look at and see what it will mean in reality – give them a 'destination'.

A destination is a graphic way of creating a focus on the road to the achievement of the vision. It is, however, more immediate, with a time scale which gives urgency to the tasks to be accomplished. Set within the strategic guidelines (Figure 5.2), it must demonstrate not only 'what' but 'how'. A destination should be:

▶ consistent with the guiding light;
▶ aspirational;
▶ sufficiently detailed to be credible and recognizable to those who must make it happen;
▶ a milestone on the way to achieving the objectives, and
▶ harmonious with the values.

Thorstein Øverland, the Group Executive President of the Norwegian bank, Kreditkassen, achieved this soon after he joined the bank, in 1996, by writing the narrative of the Report and Accounts for the year 2000. This device gave an expression of intent in a form which was not directive and yet allowed and encouraged dialogue.

A simpler example is given in Box 11.1 for 'European Airlines' (not its real name). Although simpler, it has the same purpose, to translate the guiding light into a picture of reality, to make the future live for those involved.

One important difference is that the 'Kreditkassen 2000' paper was written by one person, after substantial discussion, as a focus for detailed discussion. It is, in a sense, a combined guiding light and destination, though more the latter. 'European Airlines' destination was crafted through workshops (p. 209), from an existing 'guiding light' type of document. Both are legitimate approaches. There is no one route which is right.

BOX 11.1 *A destination*

European Airlines – Destination 1998
This document sets out how we intend to fulfil our vision over the immediate period of the next two years. Specifically, our vision says:

'To be an effective, stable point-to-point operator, gaining passengers not only through low fares but through a personal attention that is superior to competition and providing a stimulating and dynamic environment for the workforce at all levels and a fair return for our shareholders.'

To achieve this, by 1998 we will have:
▶ a route network of 12–15 intensively used routes
▶ fares which on average are 40 per cent of existing economy fares
▶ a dedicated fleet of Boeing 737 aircraft
▶ a cost base which allows us to break-even at a 60 per cent average load factor.

What will be different?
We will have:
▶ eliminated all routes which cannot sustain an intensive schedule (minimum three flights a day)
▶ condensed management levels from five to three
▶ sub-contracted all engineering services
▶ eliminated all 'optional' services, that is those which are not considered essential by the passengers we seek.

How will it feel different?
▶ There will be fewer people to turn to for decision making – you will more often have to decide for yourself.

▶ We will more often bring about changes needed through the usage of informal groups.
▶ Work patterns will more clearly respond to work demands – days will be less rigid and payments will be more geared to productive time worked than elapsed hours.
▶ There will be less training courses available for non-technical subjects – more on-the-job development.
▶ Planning will be dramatically simplified.

What we have to do to get there
▶ Concentrate costs on those things that matter to the passenger and eliminate waste on unnecessary items – this will be helped by route concentration.
▶ Develop a recruitment profile which will ensure that we reinforce a culture of 'can-do'.
▶ Carry-out an intensive development programme for managing the new culture.
▶ Set up a series of 'learning groups' which will concentrate on clearing key areas of need or barriers to achievement, as for example 'Core route network identification and allied marketing coordination'.
(The Appendix, not included in this extract, had a full list of the initial six projects).

Making plans live

A destination should be simple. It should also allow for contributions from others and flexibility in the face of events. If it is over-detailed, it will very likely result in implementation which is wooden, without heart, with no passion. Better, by far, to have the plan that is 80 per cent right with 100 per cent support than the plan that is 100 per cent right but has only 80 per cent support!

A major barrier to achieving this is the natural tendency of management to seek to avoid being 'caught out', to 'lose face' by appearing not to have thought of every angle (see page 118). Changing this is not an easy option. There is still the need to have thought through all of the consequences of a course of action, or as many as possible. But the aim must not be to then demonstrate a mastery of detail, but to use this understanding to create dialogue in which those who must implement the thinking can both own it and add their experience to 'how' – which may even lead to modifications of the core thinking. To requote a key passage in Chapter 5:

This is strategic management, in which the creation of strategy and the daily management of the business are acts of constant recreation in response to events and experience.

Plans are more likely to live when those who have to make them a reality understand 'why' – not just 'what' – and have had the chance to reconcile their own thinking; when they can act through understanding, not simply from instruction. A participative workshop approach can be of great benefit in this (Box 11.2). Most organizations that have tackled implementation successfully have found that approaches of this kind, which allows participation on a generally equal level, to be of particular value. It is, for example, a reflection of the highly successful 'Work-Out' sessions, used in General Electric. Not only does this develop better ideas but it creates commitment, avoids purely functional interpretation and stops people staying as spectators.

Assessing the raw material

However good the thinking behind the destination, and the quality of debate that brought it to life, it will be of no use if its achievement is beyond those whose task it is to make it happen. The raw material of a service is its people – without the right raw materials for the job that has to be done, no amount of planning will work effectively.

BOX 11.2 *The workshop approach*

The purpose of a participative workshop is to provide an opportunity to re-examine the thinking processes, question old values and look for optimal solutions on implementation from a different perspective.

Such participative workshops might be over two days, with a few people (about 12–16 is maximum). The first part would be devoted to a thorough discussion of the factors involved and is, primarily, an opportunity for drawing out contributions from and gaining the involvement of participants. Drawing conclusions and coming to decisions should be banned. The idea is to get people to think about the issues, to accept them as possibilities and to consider them against previous knowledge. It is a good idea, therefore, to have an overnight break between the two halves.

The second part would then be devoted to developing action. A key component of this can be the five key questions of service implementation. If participants can be encouraged to think of developments in these terms, they have gone a long way towards achieving a high level of coordination and involvement.

It is also an excellent framework for constructing middle management's role since the activity required to answer these questions is precisely the sort of activity that should be at the core of their role as leaders and facilitators – and a key part of the learning organization.

Plans remain plans without people. The plans that work best are the plans which build on the people in the organization and are a reflection of the strength of them and their collective culture. The *Harvard Business Review* of November/December 1996 carried an article, 'What holds the modern company together?' The answer was culture and the authors went on to describe a method of measuring culture.

Such research, and the Culture mapping research outlined in Chapters 4 and 8, can be of enormous value, providing insights into the degree of understanding and support for the strategy, throughout an organization. For example, with 'culture maps' available, it is possible to plan the way through to a sensible outcome, with the confidence that it is realizable. Such mapping will be more valuable than simple attitudinal research, as it provides direct links between the external aims of the organization and the raw material of those aims, the culture, the people and their beliefs.

However, such research can be both expensive and time consuming. In many circumstances this can be justified, where there is a need to explore deeply the current status or a chance to build a base for charting trends over time. But in many other cases, and especially in smaller organizations, this can be a luxury which neither money nor time allows.

BOX 11.3 *Service cultures – a simplified test*

This simplified test was developed originally as a classroom exercise to highlight cultural issues as an integral part of strategic management. It can, however, be used in more practical situations, always provided that it is recognized that it is a limited portrait. Treat the results with caution and use them to create debate. For example, how the culture can be used as a springboard for better implementation of plans and the cultural change that has to be achieved.

There are four simple steps.

1 Recording, which should be done by the individuals themselves without other discussion and on a basis of 'my view, as I see it from where I am'.
2 Scoring, which can be done centrally or individually, depending on the circumstances and numbers involved.
3 Plotting, transferring the results to a map which allows for comparisons and assessment, which again can be individual or collective.
4 Assessing, which should always be done as part of a workshop (Box 11.2) within the context of strategic planning and implementation as a whole.

Step 1 Your personal view
Below are a series of opposites, which describe typical components of a service culture. Consider each one quickly and circle the ranking which you feel best reflects your own organization. This is your personal view, so give it from the position you occupy and think about the business or division from that standpoint.

1. Considerate	7	6	5	4	3	2	1	Inconsiderate
2. Secretive	1	2	3	4	5	6	7	Informative
3. Rigid	1	2	3	4	5	6	7	Flexible
4. Listening	7	6	5	4	3	2	1	Telling
5. Relaxed	7	6	5	4	3	2	1	Tense
6. Innovative	7	6	5	4	3	2	1	Traditional
7. Impersonal	1	2	3	4	5	6	7	Individual
8. Quantitative	1	2	3	4	5	6	7	Qualitative
9. Supportive	7	6	5	4	3	2	1	Punishing
10. Rule-driven	1	2	3	4	5	6	7	Spontaneous
11. Critical	1	2	3	4	5	6	7	Indulgent
12. Sympathetic	7	6	5	4	3	2	1	Unsympathetic

Step 2 Scoring
Total the score against 1, 2, 4, 8, 9 and 12 and mark it on the vertical axis of the matrix.

Then total the score against 3, 5, 6, 7, 10 and 11 and mark it on the horizontal axis.

Then draw a line from the mark on the vertical line and another from the mark on the horizontal line. Mark the place where the two meet with a cross. This is the positioning of your service culture. An outline explanation is given in Step 4.

Step 3 – Charting

FIGURE 11.3 *Culture assessment chart*

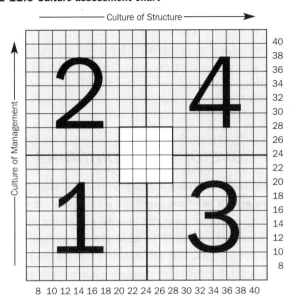

————— Culture of Structure —————→

Culture of Management

8 10 12 14 16 18 20 22 24 26 28 30 32 34 36 38 40

40 38 36 34 32 30 28 26 24 22 20 18 16 14 12 10 8

Step 4 Assessing

Quartile 1 Authoritarian
A hard-driving organization, geared to achieving strongly-defined goals. People are
largely a means to an end, and customers may be seen largely as targets, necessary
for the achievement of goals, but no more. The organization will expect a great deal of
people but give little leeway for failure. Some may find its simplicity congenial
especially if financial rewards are high.

Quartile 2 Mechanistic
Although people are seen as important, they are subordinate to the system. This
sets clear guidelines and minimizes the chances for individual failure – or maybe
even success. There will often be a strong sense of pride but the organization will
essentially be more conscious of achieving its own internal goals rather than of
external achievement. This may become fanatical.

Quartile 3 Aimless
Often undemanding, frequently capricious, such organizations will often be
inconsistent in their goals and in their ways of working. Although people will be
rated highly, many of the systems of review and judgement will be internal and even
indulgent. Such dysfunctional emphasis will often mean customer experiences are
uneven. Individuals will often seem to do their own thing!

Quartile 4 Relaxed
A demanding organization, built around people and with both structure and
management style in harmony. Leadership rather than management and it will be most
likely to be successful in situations where customers are highly discriminating and
need to feel they have had individual service. The organization will see people as the
key to creating this success and have a style which ensures they contribute diversity.
However, some people may find such organizations daunting and the tasks of day-to-
day direction difficult to live with.

© KIA Service Development 1992

Even so, it is vital to understand at least something of the current position even if the method is simple and merely indicative. How much are we all together? How much do we all share the same view of the culture and its implications for daily routine? A further method is outlined in Box 11.3. It is simple, so much so that it can only be viewed as a rough and ready guide. However, it will not only highlight some of the issues, but more importantly, focus attention on this often neglected area and stimulate discussion about 'us', 'who we are?' and 'what can we achieve?'.

Business development planning

The 'destination' is the first step in this process. Linked with an objective view of 'who we are', it will have produced a clear, and clearly felt, focus for the next stages. These must not only turn thinking into action but ensure that resources are used to best effect, forging a direct link between inputs and outputs. This will also then provide the basic data and input to the more detailed financial, marketing and other functional plans.

Clarity and simplicity are vital in the process of creating service plans. Services are particularly prone to degradation of thinking and fuzziness in implementation. The ideas have to travel through the organization and then be realized through a 'one-off' production process which is out of immediate control and involves the customer directly. It is not achieved by concentrating solely on fragmentary aspects. An abbreviated review of the entire process is given in Box 11.4.

Because business development plans have been seen as the core of the organizations planning process, the demands of finance, marketing, technology and other functions are seen as stemming from this process. In reality, there will be a more complex set of cross-links, depending on the business, and the strategic constraints – finance limits or needs, technological barriers, marketing restrictions and the like – should have been fed-in at the stage of preparing the guiding light, as Figure 5.2 shows.

A further point is that concerning 'divisions' or other breakdowns in the structure. It may be fruitful to develop a 'destination' for each 'business' or division, so that each part of the organization relates its particular destination – its future – to how it will achieve the overall vision. The precise way in which these will be constructed and cross-linked must be a variable, but in any situation an excellent final step at this stage is to prepare 'Service Star' models. These may have already been prepared as part of 'taking a position' (p. 87) and they can be reviewed and refined at this point. They will help to clarify the components of the plan and review the balance between them as well as providing a clearer focus for the next stage, action plans.

Action planning

The final point in the planning process is the crafting of action plans. The focus must now be on that point where the customer interacts with the organization. There is a need to build a clear set of links between the resources to be used and the results to be expected.

The earlier steps will have:

▶ provided a clear sense of direction;
▶ developed this into a firm definition of what it will mean to those involved, and
▶ created a firm view of the 'offer' to each specific market segment.

It is usually sensible to create a focus in action plans, based on an identified key resource, the 'Critical Unit of Measure' (CUM). For most service organizations, there is a key limiting factor, one resource which is not only usually the scarcest commodity but drags all other costs in its wake. This is especially true of costs in the short term. Once the CUM has been identified, it will usually be seen that time spent on measuring, recording and monitoring every single cost element is wasteful; all that is needed is to carefully control the 'critical unit of measure'.

Most often, the CUM is people-linked in some form, since it is usually people, and more particularly their time, which is the scarcest resource in any service organization. Citibank, for example, have identified that it is 'head count' which is the driver of their costs, and they use this as the key measure in their planning.

Choosing just one measure, even just a few, will simplify matters dramatically. Whatever is chosen as the CUM, it is vital that any action planning system allows for the following:

▶ The use of resources directly relative to the end results sought.
▶ The need for immediate income to be linked to the need to build for the long term.
▶ The need to establish a dialogue, both so as to gain ownership and to create a feedback loop of information from the meetings with the marketplace.
▶ The need to provide both a 'top-down' and 'bottom-up' influence.

BOX 11.4 *The planning process*

The following step-by-step approach is typical of the approach which is required. There can be no one model which can be applied to this. Every organization is different and the approach needs to reflect this. Nevertheless, the following five-stage outline will act as a guide.

The three middle stages are shown as subsets of one stage in order to emphasis the interrelated nature. Some of the content – such as a guiding light – has already been described. The rest is outlined in the ensuing pages.

Stage 1 Initial analysis

This would consist of gathering information to get a clear picture of the current situation. This would be needed for management to give proper consideration to the development of a guiding light in Stage 2, in particular, the task of 'taking a position'. The areas that need to be covered are:

▶ the dynamics of the market and the main trends at strategic level;
▶ the expectations of customers and the likely changes over the medium to long-term;
▶ the strategies of competitors and their strengths and weaknesses;
▶ relative performance in terms of key customer segments, resources allocated to those segments and profitability;
▶ the consistency and effectiveness of the operational activities within and across these segments;
▶ the profile of key skills within the organization;

▶ the degree or otherwise of strategic cohesion.

The output from this stage would be a set of position statements and potential future scenarios which would form the basis for management review and discussion.

Stage 2 Creating the plans

In a service business, strategy and implementation are interlinked. The second stage is therefore not truly sequential in nature but made up of a mix, back and forth, of the various elements described.

Stage 2(a) The guiding light

This has already been covered in Chapter 5. It is the creation of a longer-term strategic outline, the vision, the objectives that have to be achieved to make that vision a reality, and the values that will govern 'the way we work' in getting there. It would also include the task of 'taking a position', so that the information gathered is codified into a strongly externalized form and is rigorously analysed.

Stage 2(b) Business development plans

This stage provides the opportunity to take the guiding light forward with the people involved, to both use it as a guide and to hold it up to questioning and, if necessary, amendment in the light of that questioning. (Business development plans are described on p. 84). The core is the creation of a 'destination' (Box 11.1), a description of the vision in terms of everyday life, as it will be. This is not an incremental projection forward from today. It is a statement of intent about the future which allows those who must go into the future to 'stand' there and, by looking back, judge the actions and priorities that are needed. This is important in changing mind sets and is frequently a key factor in achieving success, especially in moving from a primarily 'push' environment to one of 'pull'. Service Stars can play a valuable role in finalizing the process.

Stage 2(c) Gearing up to deliver

This is about 'how to get to the destination'. The process of creating this would have highlighted this to a great extent but a checklist of issues would be:

Strategy/overall considerations
Financial considerations
Local destinations/business
    development plans
More detailed segmentation
Services/product development/
    technical and other asset
    development

Supporting processes
Action planning systems/budget
    links
Alignment of quality or other
    operational terminology/and
    processes

People/organization development
Top team development/leadership
    style
Structure related to segments
Ongoing development
Recruitment
Rewards and recognition

The chosen elements would form a change programme. Judgements would have to be made about the resource allocations, overall pace of change and the priorities of activities relative to these and to the 'mood' of the organization.

The actual task of carrying this through is one which lends itself to the creation of cross-functional project teams and the use of 'everyday learning'. In this way, personal and team development can be integrated into the project teams' task, which is considerably more effective than traditional management development.

Stage 3 Taking into action

The third (or fifth) stage would take the plans forward into action. The main distinction between Stage 2 and Stage 3 is that the activity moves from the future into the now. The plans need to become a part of the institutional framework, not an adjunct or veneer to it. Typically, there would be three strands:

1 A comprehensive communication programme to win and retain the support of those involved or whose commitment may be vital, such as shareholders. A key ingredient must be the usage of methods which will break down barriers, foster team achievement and reinforce early successes (see also Chapters 6 and 7).
2 Action plans – the development of the detailed local plans, linking resource usage to aims, to planned results, and providing input to budgets.
3 Continuity of the 'everyday learning' principles through the usage of cross-functional project groups, as in Stage 2(c).

These points are best balanced and reconciled locally, even if 'local' in this sense means a 'section' of head office. Local markets usually exhibit marked variations which can only be effectively identified and followed through at that level, so a 'bottom-up' input to planning is essential if the full potential of a local market is to be identified and realized. A view of the steps involved in developing action planning is given in Box 11.5.

BOX 11.5 *Action planning steps*

1 Identify the local market in terms of specific sectors or segments. Textbook definitions of segments are usually less useful here than the personal terminology of the planner; for example instead of 'skilled workers', a more accurate description might be 'miners, with wages paid weekly into a branch. This is specific, identifiable and creates a real feel for the market.

2 Clarify what the consumers want from you, that is, the problem to which they seek a solution. This may also be seen as defining the incremental values you have – what will make you distinctive. It will also be the focus in the service mix (Figure 3.2).

3 Identify the service products which will be the core solutions to these needs. These may be a hard product, for example bank accounts or 'plane seats, but may also be, or include, softer elements. The definition will stem from the work you have put in on the service mix.

4 Identify competition and decide on the best opportunities. Some segments may be less or more attractive, depending on these strengths.

5 Develop targets, segment by segment, and work out the activity levels you need to achieve these. At this point you are beginning to match resource usage to returns.

6 Assess the resources required and calculate the overall results. Do these fulfil company needs? Does the total activity give you the return you want? If not, you may need to make some revisions. It is possible to put such plans on a simple linear programme and so work out a number of alternative scenarios at this point.

7 Finalize and agree activity.

8 Integrate with company-wide plans and, if required, produce budgets.

An example of an action plan is given in Figure 11.4.

FIGURE 11.4 Action plan

Branch: Upville   Date: 6 months to 31.12.81   (Extracts)

Segment	Focus/Need	Solution/Product	Market size	Current share	Target	Average value	Estimated conversion	Estimated calls for success	Total calls/time	Personnel needs/training costs	Marketing needs/costs
Large professional connections		Both	146			(of connection)					Head Office mailing phone check £6K
(a) Existing	(a) No surprises	Standard mortgage and survey guarantee	(a) 32	32	32	£65K	100%	Monthly	192	–	
(b) New	(b) We are effective		(b) 114	–	6	£60K	1:3	4 sales then each fortnight	108	Training for new approach est. £5K	
Small professional connections		Both	151			(of connection)					Entertainment /sponsor-ship est. £10K
(a) Existing	(a) We can help build your practice	Standard mortgage and selective introductions	(a) 24	24	23*	£70K	100%	Monthly	138	–	
(b) New	(b) We have contacts		(b) 127	–	6	£60K	1:4	4 sales then each fortnight	132	Training for new approach est. £5K	
Houseowners +5 yrs 45 +		Both	1640								–
(a) Existing	(a) We can help to plan the future	New savings plan	(a) 95	95	90**	£3.5K	100%	No separate, counter discussion 5 minute discussion	37½ hrs	–	
(b) New (to us)	(b) We can help achieve your dream		(b) 1545	–	45	£3.5K	1:10	5 minute discussion		Training for new approach est. £5K	Leaflets etc. £2K
Houseowners New to market (and us)	We can guard against the unexpected	New savings plan	About 120	–	14	£0.2K	1:5	5 minute discussion	6 hrs	Training for new approach est. £5K	Included in above
					Total customers 216 of which new 71	Total Loans £4.4M Savings £0.5M Commission £88K			Totals 570 call = 1 man/year 43½ hrs = 1 clerk	Totals Personnel £17K estimates Training £10K***	Total marketing costs £18K Overall costs £45K

* Note, one merger
** Maturities, withdrawals, etc
*** Costs common to all sectors, so estimated total.

Source: KIA Management Consultants, 1981.

The key benefits of such decentralized decision making are as follows:

▶ **Effectiveness**, since it is easier to relate costs at local level to specific results.

▶ **Competitiveness**, since it helps to optimize the use of the most important resource, people, at the point of contact with the consumer.

▶ **(Often) better investment**, than in a new core product, since local plans cannot be easily copied, whereas products rarely remain unique for long.

A good action plan is most effective when there are a few, simple documents which allow those who originate the plans and those who monitor them, to see all of the information necessary on a few pieces of paper. The ideal is one side of A4, but this may not be practicable. An example of one type of action plan, based on a real situation, is shown in Figure 11.4.

The plan in Figure 11.4 has been much simplified. It can, anyway, only be an example. Each organization needs to build its own system, reflecting the specific situation it faces. Not infrequently, the best outlines come from local management and staff themselves. The points to note about this example which are critical to any local plan, are as follows:

▶ The plan is based on the segmentation arising from 'taking a position'.

▶ Though the segments have 'easy to identify' descriptions which help to clarify 'accessibility', more importantly they identify a segment by its needs. Notice that these may not be directly related to the core product. This is not uncommon, since the buyer may often obtain a supply of core products from a number of sources and what makes you distinctive is more likely to be your relevance in providing a solution to their problems – or the same core product can be a different solution for different segments (see Figure 5.4).

▶ It breaks the overall sales target down into manageable bits. It forces thinking about where to get the results; there is not just some loose, general sales figure.

▶ The core product is subordinated to (customer) 'need' but is clearly linked.

▶ Cost, time and revenue are all easily related. This result-oriented management of time can be very beneficial and illuminating. It is usually of more direct value than time management in isolation.

▶ The plan can be easily monitored and variances explained and corrected – it provides a basis for dialogue.

The more this type of planning is undertaken, the easier it becomes. Indeed, it is sensible to see the first attempt as purely development, since there is a need to both create confidence in its usage and a full understanding of the significance of the measures involved. Other key points are:

▶ it is best to select a short time period for review, say every three to six months, so that the direction of activity is not allowed to drift too far before review and any corrections;

▶ the action planning system is a basis for dialogue, since it allows for a genuine discussion about 'cause and effect' and not simply results, and

▶ the segmentation is in a form which has real meaning to those directly concerned. Note in Figure 11.4, the reference to 'existing' and 'new' connections. This a very real difference at action level, more so than that between the different types of professional connection.

Acknowledgements and further reading

page 209   Goff, R. and Jones, G. (1996) 'What holds the modern company together?', *Harvard Business Review*, Nov/Dec.

Most of the books to be recommended have already been mentioned in previous chapters but in addition there is:

Beckhard, R. and Pritchard, W. (1992) *Changing the Essence*, Jossey-Bass.
Hout, T.M. and Carter, J.C. (1995) 'Getting it done: New roles for senior executives', *Harvard Business Review*, Nov/Dec.

Keeping it going – 10 key areas

Business has to change to keep pace. I like to say that the definition of insanity is doing the same thing over and over and expecting different results.

Michael Quinlan, Chairman and Chief Executive, McDonalds

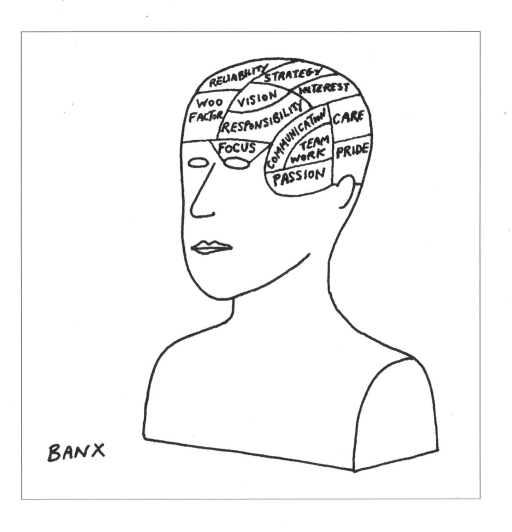

BANX

It's always changing

Covent Garden was established as a fruit, vegetable and flower market under a charter granted by Charles II in 1671 and was still in operation on its original site until a move to a less-congested site at Nine Elms, in 1975. The central square was designed in the Italianate style, together with the church of St Paul, nicknamed the 'handsomest barn in Christendom' for its severity, by Inigo Jones between 1630 and 1633. Rebuilt in the late eighteenth century after a fire, it remains, along with the Queen's House at Greenwich, his finest contribution to London's architecture. Now, saved by strong public protest from demolition, Covent Garden has become one of the most exciting areas of London with an enormous variety of shops, restaurants and entertainment, a great attraction for Londoners and visitors alike.

In this environment, Bureau, a large stationery shop on the western edge, still stands out, destroying any view that a stationery shop has to look dull. It is a place of simple lines and bright colours, 'The equivalent of pornography in stationery' (*The Guardian*, 24 April 1996). Yet for the manager, Alex Cross, who has worked there since it opened, it is less the stock and the surroundings but more the people who shop there that make the difference.

> *If I were to keep focusing on the sale each time, my approach would become stale and the routine of it would rapidly bring the whole team down. I am still fascinated by good design and the combination of practicality and colour you get with stationery, but what really adds spontaneity is the customer. They are always different, seeing new things, asking new questions. Evaluating their interests, tailoring suggestions to suit them, getting the right answers all keep me – and everyone else – fresh.*

This is the fascination and value of service and at times the frustration! It is always different, because for the customer it is an individual event, often of great importance or excitement. The best service organizations – the superservice organizations – relish this opportunity and build on it. For them, it is the customers and their expectations which are centre stage – the ever-changing input from the customers – not the static products, however interesting.

Yes, I'll be back again!

Maintaining the interest of those involved, not allowing routines to dominate spontaneity, constantly refining, even realigning, the strategy in the light of emerging experience, all call for a continuous effort and involve-

ment at implementation which has no real parallel in the world of manufacturing. Service has a relentless quality. Each and every day, working directly with the customer, usually at his or her choice of pace, you have 'to colour outside the lines'; climb that mountain again and again.

Given the nature of a service, with the product finally being 'manufactured' – and the customer's involvement at the point of sale – getting started is a big step, but only a part of the task. Without a clear focus and a passion to succeed with the customer, complacency or fatigue can quickly set in. There is a need for a considerable investment in time and effort (even money on occasions) if the original guiding idea is to remain a fact in the long haul, at the moment of truth.

This summary of 10 of the most important areas cannot be exhaustive (that would need another book), but it does set out the major issues that affect the ability of a service organization to maintain that freshness so essential to the delivery of superservice – time-after-time, day-after-day – so that customers regularly say, 'yes, I'll be back again'!

Key area 1 – keep the focus external

Make sure that it is the customers and their needs which are the driving force.

It seems so obvious yet it is perhaps the hardest thing of all, remembering that success comes from what you achieve on the outside. David Packard, co-founder of the immensely successful Hewlett Packard organization, once said the *'Companies should not see market share (and profit) as an object but as a reward'*. Such sentiment is not altruism but simple recognition that the purpose of business in a free-enterprise culture is to provide the customer with the goods and services they require in the most effective way possible.

Lacking a sufficiently clear focus, too many people in the organization remain unsure about the real priorities. Customer inconvenience is not usually intentional; they suffer simply as a consequence. But in the final analysis, it is the organization which is the real sufferer. Customers can go elsewhere or delay buying or spend their money on something else – if not now, then at some future date when there is competition.

Svenska Handelsbanken believe that the key to their success, and in particular their ability to be so consistently more profitable than their competitors is their involvement with the customer. As Arne Mårtensson describes it: *'Because we are extremely close to the customer, we are able to see quickly what is happening. We have a dialogue'*.

It is important to remember that the customers' focus is not 'product plus service' but service. To the customers, the product is only part of a process, whether they consciously recognize it or not. This process is what they are buying, in this service elements will typically account for some 70 per cent of the satisfaction or dissatisfaction generated. Small details make superservice. It is *'The many little experiences . . . that can turn a happy traveller into an unhappy one'* (Virgin Atlantic), which need to be the focus.

This is not just a matter for marketing but one for the whole organization. Conventional functional splits are likely to hamper a translation of a vision into reality, especially once the early energy has been expended.

Make the interactions between the customers and the people within the organization the focus of everything and everyone. Be clear about the organization's 'purpose' and how this will be realized through the interaction. Make these priorities clear and simple.

Key area 2 – create moral power

The gap between service and superservice is a belief in your own actions.

If people are to give of their best, not just some days but every day, they have to give of themselves. The 'moral power' of an organization is the belief that it is fulfilling some end beyond that of simply earning money. To achieve this, you need to have people who have lifted their eyes above the immediate job to see that they are fulfilling a valuable task.

Some organizations, The Body Shop is an obvious example, are built around the creation of a view of the organization as a force for good in the community. For most it is much more a recognition that by serving the interests of their customers and the world at large, they are creating something which has a deeper value in the eyes of their staff, as well as their customers. But this has to be an 'inner' and not just 'outer' conviction. The example of British Gas (p. 188) shows how real a barrier this is for many managers.

British Gas are not alone. Under pressure to perform, many managers take a short-term view about financial returns but, as example after example has shown, profit is equally to be made from taking the long-term view. What is more, if it is built around deep-seated beliefs that the actions are 'good', it has a greater stability of earnings.

Many 'long-term' organizations report how staff have rallied around when times became hard. Lane Group (Case Study 8.1) is one. Southwest Airlines is another, when during the Gulf War, staff set up a voluntary donation fund to defray the additional costs of fuel and keep the airline going – their airline, as they saw it. It was so successful that the fund was kept in being but converted to a fund to help colleagues experiencing unexpected financial problems.

Such moral power cannot be one way. There is a need to provide some security. Not necessarily the security of lifetime employment, but the security of knowing that you will be fairly treated, that the efforts you have made to create the right end to the service process, a satisfied customer, will be recognized and rewarded.

Creating value for all those involved in the transaction creates moral power. It is achieved by giving the person who has to complete the process, often a junior member of staff, the feeling that he or she is 'building the cathedral, not simply laying stones' (see page 49); that the pain of this, as well as the joy, is shared.

Key area 3 – don't allow spectators

Spectators are the cancer that gnaws away at any concept of superservice.

The battle for success is not won by dry statistics but by the efforts of everyone, including managers, to make the experience for the customers one they would like to repeat and would recommend to their friends.

Recovery situations are a particularly important part of this. Every organization makes mistakes – Southwest Airlines get 60,000 complaints a year, though unusually it gets five times that number of staff commendations from the customers, but it is *how* it deals with these mistakes, *not* the mistakes themselves, which counts. Southwest staff are expected to 'colour outside the lines', to do what they think is right at that moment for that customer. A great example of recovery is shown by the tale from Club Med in Case Study 12.1.

Opportunities for service recovery abound. Any problem that employees who are close to the customer can discover and resolve is a chance to go beyond the call of duty and win a customer for

CASE STUDY 12.1 THE PROFITABLE ART OF SERVICE RECOVERY

Mistakes are a critical part of every service. Hard as they try, even the best service companies cannot prevent the occasional late flight, burned steak, or missed delivery. The fact is, in services, often performed in the customer's presence, errors are inevitable.

But dissatisfied customers are not. While companies may not be able to prevent all problems, they can learn to recover from them. A good recovery can turn angry, frustrated customers into loyal ones. It can, in fact, create more goodwill than if things had gone smoothly in the first place.

Consider how Club Med-Cancun, in Mexico, part of Club Med, recovered from a service nightmare and won the loyalty of one group of vacationers.

The vacationers had nothing but trouble getting from New York to their Mexican destination. The flight took off six hours late, made two unexpected stops, and circled for 30 minutes before it could land. Because of all the delays and mishaps, the plane was en route for 10 hours more than planned and ran out of food and drinks. It finally arrived at two o'clock in the morning, with a landing so rough that oxygen masks and luggage dropped from overhead. By the time the plane pulled up to the gate, the passengers were faint with hunger and convinced that their vacation was ruined before it had even started. One lawyer on board was already collecting names and addresses for a class-action lawsuit.

Silvio de Bortoli, General Manager of the Cancun resort and a legend throughout the organization for his ability to satisfy customers, got word of the horrendous flight and immediately created an antidote. He took half the staff to the airport where they laid out a table of snacks and drinks and set up a stereo system to play lively music. As the guests filed through the gate, they received personal greetings, help with their bags, a sympathetic ear, and a chauffeured drive to the resort. Waiting for them at Club Med was a lavish banquet, complete with mariachi band and champagne. Moreover, the staff had rallied other guests to wait up and greet the newcomers, and the partying continued until sunrise. Many guests said it was the most fun they had had since college.

In the end, the vacationers had a better experience than if their flight from New York had gone like clockwork. Although the company probably couldn't measure it, Club Med won market share that night. After all, the battle for market share is won not by analysing demographic trends, ratings points, and other global measures, but rather by pleasing customers one at a time.

Source: *Harvard Business Review*, July/August 1990

life. We are not talking about chemical leaks in Bhopal or Tylenol poisonings, which threaten large-scale damage and clearly demand top management's attention. We are talking about wrong invoices and late deliveries, the seemingly small issues that can ignite a person's temper. The stuff angry letters to the chairman are made of.

Spectators cannot take the responsibility necessary to recover; they are waiting for someone else to make the decision, either because:

▶ they have never been given the confidence to take that decision in the first place, or the responsibility that goes with it,
▶ or, they have had the will taken away by a regime that 'punishes' error – there can be no admission of mistakes,
▶ or the procedure for recovery is a bureaucratic nightmare; so there is no recovery at all – just a worsening tale of woe!

Frequently, spectators exist because their management are spectators, too! Figure 12.1 shows a questionnaire which has been used to demonstrate the effect of the spectator syndrome in management teams. It is surprising how often issues are seen as being a team problem, which 'I, personally, don't have'. Such management teams breed the spectator syndrome.

Good recoveries from service problems happen because individuals are not spectators to events. They take the initiative – and responsibility – to solve a customer's problem. Organizations should take steps to ensure that everyone has the skill, motivation, and authority to make service recovery an integral part of operations. Management, in particular, should make sure that signs of the spectator syndrome are not simply a reflection of their own behaviour.

Key area 4 – recruit the right people

Having the right people is the only guarantee of the right attitudes.

The costs of poor recruitment in terms of management time and the benefits of recruiting the right people have already been outlined.

▶ Dixons/Mastercare have made it obligatory that engineers in their new Service Centres pass a customer-orientation test and are not just good technicians.
▶ Four Seasons invest very large amounts of management time in the task of recruitment of staff, whatever their job.
▶ Taco Bell have shown that emphasizing staff stability through recruiting and holding the right people is critical for productivity.

FIGURE 12.1 *The way we work*

The management team					Personal (Me)			
SD	D	A	SA		SD	D	A	SA
				Please mark your reaction to the following statements, on the four-point scale. Firstly, on a basis of your view of management as a whole; secondly your view of yourself. Where 'subsidiaries' is inappropriate substitute e.g. 'regional management'.				
				1. I/we tend to be over analytical and to feel most comfortable when I/we have researched the facts thoroughly.				
				2. I/we believe that others have more respect for us when we can clearly demonstrate that we have the answers.				
				3. Even when I/we have sorted out the detail, the subsidiaries still don't seem able to take the initiative on their own.				
				4. I/we sometimes find it difficult to express what we really think because it would sound negative.				
				5. I/we find it difficult to get ideas across because subsidiaries seem to see matters from too narrow a perspective.				
				6. I/we often find that areas are enthusiastically received but seem to have little staying power.				

SD = Strongly disagree; D = Disagree; A = Agree; SA = Strongly agree

© KIA Service Development 1994

▶ General Electric have emphasized how critically important it is to get the right management and get rid of the wrong – even when short-term performance is good.

▶ Canadian Pacific Hotels have put great emphasis on recruitment and in Case Study 12.2, Carolyn Clark, Vice President of Human Resources, describes the process they went through.

The emphasis on the recruitment of those who are a cultural fit, and in particular have the 'right' attitudes, is echoed in superservice organizations, time and again. Southwest Airlines will, 'Hire only employees who are "other" (as opposed to "me") directed, who are energetic, cooperative, friendly and who will contribute materially to the success and progress of Southwest Airlines'. At a more informal level, Café Rouge manager Virginé Bouquet makes the points,

> *We have to recruit the right people for the type of restaurant and, having got them, we have to use the best to tutor the new, help them to see the importance of observing and understanding customers – 'Why are they there?', 'What is it they seek by visiting us?', not just seeing them as diners – and then reacting to that understanding. You have to have people who will learn to love the job if it is to be done properly.*

It is vital to have the right people, the right raw material for the ambitions you have. This is not just a matter of technical proficiency, but of getting the people with the right motivation in the first place or slotting existing people into the job that is most likely to allow them to contribute. Getting the 'right stuff' is crucial.

Key area 5 – the role and purpose of rewards

Don't spoil the right stuff by creating the wrong reward system.

There is often a serious miscalculation in this connection. Monetary rewards are rarely sufficiently positive to the majority of those involved in implementation. Yet, such thinking lies behind many bonus and other such schemes, based on the assumption that the typical employee wants to be an entrepreneur or to take risks with his or her career. The majority don't, that is why they are employees. They do want to get satisfaction from their work and to feel that not only are they building a future for themselves but that they are in some way contributing to those around.

CASE STUDY 12.2 RECRUITING AT CANADIAN PACIFIC HOTELS

In 1987 Canadian Pacific Hotels carried out a major refocusing of their hotel business in Canada (see also Case Study 4.1). One of the key decisions was that the planned programme of refurbishment of their hotels had to be matched with the development of the staff. Clearly, there was little point in developing the wrong people, so recruitment – not just bringing the right new people in but helping existing people into the right job – was going to be key.

Carolyn Clark, who as Vice President, Human Resources, was a part of the team that brought about the changes, takes up the story.

> We initially spent six months investigating what made for successful employees in our business. A consultancy firm we retained had specialised in this area. They asked each manager to nominate a number of his 'best' employees and they then interviewed them, seeking to identify the characteristics that made for their success.
>
> As a result of this, they began to develop a series of profiles for each type of job we had and as part of a set of key themes. For example, for customer contact staff they found that the key themes were:
>
> ▶ a highly developed sense of responsibility;
> ▶ a great pride in their work;
> ▶ a genuine interest in creating satisfaction for guests;
> ▶ an ability to be good at teamwork;
> ▶ and finally, something they found difficult to describe but eventually called the 'WOO' factor – the ability to 'win others over'.
>
> With this type of understanding we were able to develop structured interviews for new employees which would give us a much, much higher chance of recruiting the right person for the right job. We have also used it to help people who were already with us to transfer to the right job.
>
> A number of management were sceptical at first. They felt that their experience was a much better basis of judgement but the results have convinced them. We not only get a much better performance level overall from employees who have been recruited or relocated using the new structured interviews but they have less absenteeism and less workers compensation claims. Management saw that the returns justified the investment and the sceptics have often become the champions. It has been a valuable investment.
>
> Now, we make it an absolute must for any new person joining Canadian Pacific Hotels – they must take the test. It takes about an hour – and they must demonstrate they meet our criteria before they can be offered a job, however good their technical qualifications.

The integrity of a service is heavily dependent on this. It is a part of the moral power. This is a recognition that 'all of us' are working to the same end and are sharing in the rewards and the pain, if not equally at least on some fair and equitable basis. Such morality needs to be transparent in its valuation of effort.

As with all of the aspects of the development of a service, it is vital to be sure exactly what are the objectives of a reward system. The following six questions are a starting point for discovering 'what?'.

1 What is the role and purpose of the reward system?
   ▶ Is it to get a short-term result to meet a crisis?
   ▶ Is it to achieve the objectives that stem from the vision and the destination?
2 Is it individual or collective gain which is crucial to the outcome?
3 Is the result going to be met by the effort of individuals or is it going to require the efforts of a group or groups? How interdependent are those groups, relative to the objectives?
4 How closely does the reward system reflect the values that have been set?
5 Will the reward system get long-term commitment or merely achieve short-term, and temporary, compliance?
6 Will the reward system obscure the real 'causes' of dissatisfaction or failure?
   For example, by rewarding low levels of customer complaint and so encouraging a suppression or, at the least a downplaying, of a vital quality control tool? (see also p. 130)

As a background to answering these questions, it will be useful to consider the pluses and minuses outlined in Box 12.1.

Monetary rewards, while the most obvious of rewards, are not always the most effective. They rarely create lasting commitment and while too little money can be a highly demotivating factor, it does not follow that simply paying more money will bring about a continuous improvement in performance. An analogy is food. A shortage of food can be very injurious to health but a continuous increase in the amount of food, especially of the wrong type of food, can be equally unsatisfactory.

BOX 12.1 Some pluses and minuses of reward systems

1 **Most reward systems, certainly most financial reward systems, are essentially manipulative.**
They can rebound to bad effect if they become perceived as such and, further, what was yesterday's reward can quickly become today's punishment.
Make sure the downside is not too great.

2 **That extra quality that sets superservice apart from simply good service comes more from inner motivation than external stimulus.**
True inner motivation will come as much from respect for the attitudes and mind sets that it reflects, as from 'gifts'. Children who have only gifts from their parents and no other recognition, rarely grow straight.
Is it money that will really make the difference?

3 **Gifts, that are in effect 'bribes', rarely work except to condition those who receive them to see bribes as their right.**
On the other hand, a reward that demonstrates that one has made a significant contribution to an outcome – and is being *fairly* rewarded for that – is not a bribe.
Ensure the system rewards the real contribution.

4 **Most successful service outcomes are the result of a collective effort.**
Even where there are 'heroes', maybe those who have made the immediate impact with the customer, success is still determined by those who provide support. It is the collective effort which should be the centre of the reward system, not just one individual's effort.
Don't create divisions; create unity.

5 **A clear aim, a guiding light, needs to be reflected in the system of reward.**
There is little point in talking of service, or anything else, being important if the rewards do not reflect this.
Line up rewards with the key objectives and values.

6 **Rewards are not just formal recognition.**
Often the informal rewards are the more important; the 'thank-you', the smile, the feeling not only of a job well done but of a well done job recognized as such.
What behaviours are key?

7 **Strongly financial rewards can make it difficult to bring about later change.**
In a situation in which people have become fat and satisfied simply doing what they are doing they will be averse to taking risks with change, indeed may personally find it financially impossible to do so. It may be necessary to set fire to the platform!
Don't create hostages to fortune, by making people too dependent on rewards.

Key area 6 – measure the right things

If what is measured is not a reflection of the reward system, it will not work.

The use of purely financial measures will drive forward the financial results in the short term but may – and in most cases, probably will – cut off the broader development of the business. If this was the purpose behind 'rewards and recognition', then it will be lost. The ability to have decided what are the drivers for the customer makes it immeasurably easier to decide what are the measures of success – and so what will be seen as the rewards.

Purely financial measures will provide a focus on the ultimate result, whether that is described as profit or contribution or whatever. Broader monitoring measures will concentrate on the 'where' and 'who' the income flow comes from and whether this is building the base for the continued development of the business.

Such a 'Multivariate measurement of performance' (MVMP) underpins a very large number of successful service companies performance. To be useful and used it needs to be based on a deep-seated belief that using such a broader spectrum of measurement has a significant value. It will only be worth the investment involved when it is used by management as a primary source of monitoring.

The MVMP should be based on the following points:

▶ A clearly expressed view of a vision and destination for the organization and so what must be the balance of the different measures over the time scale selected, short enough to keep up pressure yet long enough to secure change.

▶ What the customer is getting, not what is being provided. So, for example, Taco Bell measure their share of the customer's total 'stomach fill'; Citibank Financial Services Group their share of the customer's 'total wallet spend', both highly graphic descriptions which relate to usage, not supply.

▶ Time series, that is indicating the results in relationship over time, not grouped data, that is indicating salient features at a point in time.

▶ The commitment of all concerned to these as the relevant measures.

▶ A process of review which both allows and encourages debate and the development of response, not punishment.

▶ Links to 'rewards', not necessarily in strict financial terms, but in terms of how people see they are judged and their careers can develop.

A selection of typical measures is shown in Box 12.2.

Taking a broader set of measures need not lead to depression of short-term financial returns but will allow for a more refined control of both where and from whom an organization gets its business. In particular, this will discourage a dangerous build up of dependence on any one source or a constant churning of new customers, with no real stability.

Key area 7 – learn something, every day

Strategy is being reinterpreted every day – make sure the lessons are learned.

There are three broadly-defined sources of learning about how the strategy is being reinterpreted: the people doing the interpretation, first, customers and secondly, staff: and thirdly, what is happening elsewhere in the world, not just with competitors but in other service areas.

To take the last of these points first, there is no value in being pleased about improving your own service levels, if the views of the customer as to what is 'good' have moved on. Customer's

---

BOX 12.2 *Multivariate measurement of performance – criteria*

These are some typical criteria that might appear in an MVMP system. They are intended to stimulate thought, rather than be definitive.

Financial
Cash flow
Profit
Contribution (to profit and/or overhead)

Technical
Industry/sector dependent but could be 'on-time departures' (an airline) 'time-off station' (a boat charter)

Effectiveness
Hygiene
Security
Safety
'Cost' of rectification of errors
Costs relative to specific returns

People
Cohesion (common vision, shared beliefs etc.)
Headcount
Stability/persistency
'Improvement'

Market
Customer satisfaction, measured as:

▶ experience against expectations or
▶ preparedness to buy again/recommend

Persistency of relationships
Customer perceptions/beliefs
Progress against (defined) market position

experience is constantly being stretched and enriched, not least as they sample what is possible in other regions, other countries. How often does the travelling executive use this experience to question his or her own standards? How often do managers stop to consider how the different behaviour and expectations of people around them, their children for instance, are clues about the changes that customers and staff will expect?

While the clues to a future decline in performance may lie outside the organization, there are rich seams internally, too. Customers are constantly giving such clues through their behaviour and reactions. These are usable:

▶ at an immediate level, as with the comments of Virginé Bouquet at Café Rouge (p. 229) about observing customers to improve reactions to behaviour;

▶ at a longer-term level, to build models of what is happening or going to happen.

The 'Service dynamics profiling' research (p. 38) is an example of this, collecting information in a way which allows for its use on a structured basis. The 'Action planning' system (p. 213) is another. Yet another is British Airways' 'Marketplace Performance Unit'. They have created this not just to track customer experience but to learn – and do something about it. Christopher Swan, the Unit's head has been quoted as saying, *'Our unit is not supposed to fit comfortably with the rest of the organization. We're supposed to generate creative conflict. We're another reality check'*.

Finally, learn from the potential in internal dialogue, whether one-to-one situations or meetings. The best form of dialogue is where those involved see themselves as being enriched by the experience – learning from the process. Learning about themselves and about the ways they can improve themselves. Too often, learning is divorced from work, with stylized training courses seen as the place where you 'learn' and work the place where you 'implement'. More and more it is coming to be realized that the two are best when they exist in a symbiotic relationship, with learning seen as a natural part of the everyday activity.

As outlined in Chapter 7, although it is fashionable to deride meetings and their value, they play a significant role in learning. The problem is that there are too many meetings of the wrong sort – overstructured; no clearly thought-through purpose or reason; wrong people present; monologue not dialogue – and the approach to them is so laden with a desire to avoid any form of real involvement, that the result is never much in doubt – a waste of time.

However, if meetings are recognized for what they are, a source of development and learning without parallel, then they can be structured to have maximum impact as a source of everyday learning. This does not mean more meetings but constructing meetings with the purpose of creating dialogue and exchanging knowledge rather than simply for exchanging words.

Make learning a part of the everyday business. Learn from the world around, from customers and from the people in the organization. But make it structured, a positive attempt to learn and not the mere relating of anecdotal comment.

Key area 8 – be thrifty

Don't just cut costs – make thrift a key value of the organization.

For many organizations, cost saving has become an end in itself. It has also often (most often?) become an exercise divorced from the marketplace, and what needs to happen in that marketplace, to create value for the customer. 'Ten per cent off all costs', is a typical exhortation, regardless as to whether the costs that are being cut are adding vital value or are simply part of historic overhead. Even more importantly, cost saving often falls on service, rather than services.

Taking out costs because 'we can't afford them' or to meet some magical figure that fits with a pre-determined view of the cost base rarely works, at least beyond the short term. Often it fails to even come close to realizing the cost savings that could have been made, by seeing thrift as a value to be proud of.

When thrift is a value, people are more likely to think radically. For example, the decision by Southwest Airlines not to serve meals is more than a question of saving the cost of the meal. That is just a few dollars; but the saving in the fitting of galleys, the lifting of those galleys into the air many times a day and the space they take up, which is now being paid for by passengers, is significant. Eliminating tickets does not save just the cost of the ticket, but also the commission to sell that ticket and the costs of matching that ticket afterwards. The same applies to computer systems and the many other features of 'amenity creep' (to use the term from Novotel) which can gradually push up the costs in any service business.

Continuously designing the business from the customer back, and, as Novotel did, distinguishing between what the customer would 'like' and what the customer truly 'wants', is much more likely to produce a long-term stability of business. A key element of relating effort to result, the productivity of expenditure, is customer and staff retention (p. 169).

Costs should be related to ends. Costs that do not work directly for the customer should be rigorously chased out not just once but all the time, as an ongoing value of thrift.

Key area 9 – concentrate time on what matters

Too much time is unproductive. Concentrate time on the key issues.

It is unrealistic to expect managers and staff to take up the tasks of customer creation and satisfaction while at the same time reducing numbers and leaving in place all the baggage of systems and procedures from a past age.

Just as with costs, it is necessary to take a radical review of just what jobs need to be done and by whom. The costs of misdirected effort are often stunning in their magnitude. Domino's Pizza, for example, reckoned that they were able to save 20 hours a week of managers' time from routine administration, time which could now be used for customer and staff retention. When Roger Paffard joined C.E. Thornton, the chocolate manufacturer and retailer, he found that store managers spent $18\frac{1}{2}$ hours a week on administration.

Like 'amenity creep', 'time creep' is insidious; it grows slowly without being noticed.

The concerns about time are no more clearly evident than with the changing role of middle managers. As their task becomes increasingly one of coach and facilitator, it becomes even more essential that they are freed from the time spent on wasteful bureaucratic processes. Keeping administration separate from operational control (p. 196), will be of great benefit in achieving this. Even more, switching the core of the planning from budgets to action plans (Chapter 11) will concentrate the necessary planning time on outputs rather than just on inputs, and highlight the links.

In any service, time is a precious commodity (often the most precious commodity), since it reflects the availability and usage of the key resource, people. Treasure it and use it to effect.

Key area 10 – be caring, be consistent

'It is only the caring companies that will survive . . . [as] . . . it is only against the background of caring that continuous change can be combined with the maintenance of the company spirit and the ability to attract the best.'
Sir John Harvey-Jones, former Chief Executive of ICI

Caring is really a reflection of the points made in the previous section about continued involvement and interest. Failure in this results (as in BP where 'personal development plans' became cynically labelled as 'personal departure plans') in disillusionment and apathy. But it isn't just a passing whim or fad. Reference back to the deeper changes in society (Chapter 2) shows that what is seen here is firmly in line with these trends.

It is also about the very nature of a service – services are relationships, good services are good relationships. A relationship can only be a relationship if there is an element of care and concern. Since it is not possible to have an ambition for an external culture that is not at least empathetic to the internal culture, care and concern have to be a part of this. It is this relationship which is also the brand, and to be successful a brand has to be consistent. That is what sets it apart from a commodity. It has a clear set of properties which are what the customer relies on. To quote Leo McKee at Woolworths, *'Our brand and our culture are symbiotic, living one from the other.'*

'A puppy is not just for Christmas'. Developing a service approach is not a cuddly or shiny toy to be forgotten once the initial excitement has worn off but a long-term commitment to superior performance by building a sound relationship with your market. People 'colouring outside the lines' to create superservice can only do it if they do it every day.

Acknowledgements and further reading

page 223   David Packard, quoted in *Journal of Long Range Planning*, Volume 119, 1986.

page 226   ©1990 by the President and Fellows of Harvard College, all rights reserved, Hart, C., Heskett, J. and Sasser, W.E. (1990) 'The profitable art of service recovery', *Harvard Businss Review*, July/Aug.

page 235   ©1995 by the President and Fellows of Harvard College, all rights reserved, 'Competing on Customer Service – an interview with Sir Colin Marshall', Steven E. Prokesch. In *Harvard Business Review*, November/December.

page 237   Roger Paffard, quoted in *The Times*, 13 July, 1996.

page 238   Harvey-Jones, J, *Making it Happen*, (p. 155).

Most of the books to be recommended have already been mentioned in previous chapters but in addition there is:

Argyris, C. (1993) *Knowledge for Action: Guide to Overcoming Barriers to Organizational Change*, Jossey Bass.

Handy, C. (1991) *Inside Organisations: 21 Ideas for Managers*, BBC Books.

McCormack, M.H. (1984) *What They Don't Teach You at Harvard Business School*, Collins.

Pfaffer, J. (1993) *Competitive Advantage through People*, Harvard Business Press.

'They say miracles are past'

William Shakespeare, All's Well That Ends Well

Index

....

bold = key or main point   *italics = reference to figure*